Early Praise for *Modern Front-End Development for Rails*

This book sets an audacious goal—and delivers on it. It teaches up-to-date, comprehensive strategies on front-end development for your Rails app without straying too far from conventions familiar to Rails developers.

➤ **Kevin Murphy**
Software Developer

There's a night-and-day difference between how Stimulus/Hotwire and React think about client-side code. Noel's unique contribution in this book is that he deeply understands both tools—allowing him to accurately present the functionality, mindset, and use cases of each. This book will help you make an informed decision on your client-side approach, whether it's choosing one for the first time or assessing whether to make a change.

➤ **Josh Justice**
Web Platform Lead, Big Nerd Ranch

In my time working with Rails on the front end, I've never come across a single resource that covers as much ground with this level of detail. This is the book to get if you want to understand working with front-end Rails.

➤ **Emmanuel Hayford**
Senior Rails, WebRTC Engineer, DSIRF, Austria

The trouble with front-end development these days is the overwhelming number of things to learn just to get started. Frameworks, bundlers, flavors of JavaScript (just to name a few)—how is a person supposed to learn anything when it seems they need to know everything else first? This book walks you through not just how to use some popular front-end tools (and better than most other texts I've come across), but also gives you the context you need to decide for yourself which tool is best and when.

➤ **Jacob Stoebel**
    Software Engineer

Modern Front-End Development for Rails

Hotwire, Stimulus, Turbo, and React

Noel Rappin

The Pragmatic Bookshelf

Raleigh, North Carolina

Many of the designations used by manufacturers and sellers to distinguish their products are claimed as trademarks. Where those designations appear in this book, and The Pragmatic Programmers, LLC was aware of a trademark claim, the designations have been printed in initial capital letters or in all capitals. The Pragmatic Starter Kit, The Pragmatic Programmer, Pragmatic Programming, Pragmatic Bookshelf, PragProg and the linking *g* device are trademarks of The Pragmatic Programmers, LLC.

Every precaution was taken in the preparation of this book. However, the publisher assumes no responsibility for errors or omissions, or for damages that may result from the use of information (including program listings) contained herein.

For our complete catalog of hands-on, practical, and Pragmatic content for software developers, please visit *https://pragprog.com*.

The team that produced this book includes:

CEO: Dave Rankin
COO: Janet Furlow
Managing Editor: Tammy Coron
Development Editor: Katharine Dvorak
Copy Editor: Adaobi Obi Tulton
Indexing: Potomac Indexing, LLC
Layout: Gilson Graphics
Founders: Andy Hunt and Dave Thomas

For sales, volume licensing, and support, please contact *support@pragprog.com*.

For international rights, please contact *rights@pragprog.com*.

ISBN-13: 978-1-68050-721-8
Book version: P1.0—June 2021

Contents

Part II — Going Deeper

Part III — Managing Servers and State

Acknowledgments

As I write this, it's been nearly two and a half years since I had the idea for this book, which is a long time for a technical book.

First, I want to thank everybody at the Pragmatic Bookshelf. When I said that the book needed to be delayed indefinitely because the Rails team was going to release a big library some hand-wavy time in the future, they were completely in agreement.

Also, thanks to the people who bought this book in an early beta and have all been extremely patient waiting for the final version to come out.

My editor, Katharine Dvorak, is always great to work with. She helped immensely in structuring this book and making sure that all the book's topics followed clearly from one to the other.

This book depends on the work of many open source teams. Thanks to David Heinemeier Hansson and the Rails core team, Sam Stephenson, and Javan Makhmali and the Hotwire core teams. They were all very helpful and provided me with some information about Hotwire that enabled me to move quickly once Hotwire was released publicly. Thanks also to the React core team for all their work.

Betsy Haibel, Penelope Phippen, and Justin Searls are all people that I will occasionally message out of the blue asking them to verify something about how all these tools work. Thanks to all of them for thoughtful responses.

This book had a tremendous number of reviewers who helped find a number of errors and helped me clarify the text throughout. Thanks to Kevin Barnes, Dave Chmura, Nathan Dalo, Ashish Dixit, Betsy Haibel, Emmanuel Hayford, Koichi Hirano, Josh Justice, Aaron Kelton, Joel Lee, Gavin Montague, Kevin Murphy, Maricris Nonato, Adi Nugroho, Matt Polito, Americo Savinon, Jacob Stoebel, and Martin Streicher. Jeff Sutherland made a number of helpful errata posts on Devtalk. Matouš Borák wrote a series on Dev.to about Hey.com that was extremely helpful in understanding Hotwire.

As always, thanks to my family. It's always hard to find the words for how much you mean to me. To Amit and Elliot, who amaze me continually. And to Erin, for all the love and support, I love you so much.

So You Want to Write Some Client-Side Code

"I need a website," the client said.

"Great," you think. Ruby on Rails is a solid way to go. It's still the best way for a small team to be as productive as a big team. You are ready for this. You start thinking of estimates and modeling data structures...

"I want it to look cool, with lots of stuff moving around, and be extremely interactive," the client added.

"Ugh," you think. That brings in JavaScript. And with it, a whole lot of decisions. What language? There's not just JavaScript, but a host of languages that compile to JavaScript: TypeScript, Elm, ClojureScript. What framework? There are dozens: React, Vue, Ember, Hotwire, Svelte, Preact, and on and on. How to package the code and CSS? Should you use the Rails asset pipeline or Webpacker? What about that new Turbo thing the Rails team has been going on about?

Suddenly you are overwhelmed by the added complexity.

Although it's primarily a server-side tool, Ruby on Rails offers a lot of support for client-side code. Rails version 6.1 has tools that help you interact with the JavaScript ecosystem to build an exceptional front-end experience. In this book, you'll learn how you can enhance the user experience of a standard Rails application using front-end tools from the Rails ecosystem (Hotwire, Stimulus, Turbo, and Webpacker) and tools from the JavaScript ecosystem (webpack, TypeScript, and React) to create a great Rails-based app.

So that interactive website your client wants? No problem.

Basic Assumptions

Rails is an opinionated framework, and this is an opinionated book. Being opinionated means that Rails makes certain tasks easier if you are willing to structure your program the way the Rails core team thinks you should. For this book, being opinionated means not trying to show you every possible way Rails and JavaScript can combine, but instead focusing on the tools I think will be most useful. Perhaps the most important opinion is that we're going to use JavaScript to enhance a mostly server-side Rails application rather than use JavaScript to build a completely separate single-page application (SPA) that only uses Rails as an application programming interface (API).

My basic argument for not writing an SPA is that between Rails and a standard browser, a tremendous amount of complexity is already handled for you. Moving to an SPA structure requires you to build much of that functionality yourself. Over time, the front-end frameworks have gotten better at handling the complexity for you, but to me, it often feels like taking three right turns rather than just taking one left turn. For now and for my money, Rails is less complicated than an SPA for many applications.

That said, there are legitimate places where an SPA might make sense. If your user experience is so different from the normal web structure that the existing behavior of Rails and the browser isn't much help, then an SPA begins to look attractive. If your back end is already an API supporting a mobile app or external services, then an SPA can also act as a consumer of that API, saving you from duplicating view-layer logic (but you can use Rails and web views to go surprisingly far in a mobile app). However, my experience is that most of the time for most teams, starting by leveraging the Rails view and browser features is the best way to create a great application.

Within that assumption—Rails back end with some front-end interaction—there's still a wide range of tools, architectures, and techniques that might be appropriate for the application. We're going to navigate that space. And within that space, we are going to explore different ways of structuring a Rails/JavaScript collaboration.

The Tools We'll Use

Over the course of the book, we'll walk through the basics of getting Rails set up to use Webpacker to serve JavaScript and CSS to the browser. Then we will write code to get the browser to do things. We're going to talk about two different frameworks that have very different approaches.

- Hotwire is a framework that allows you to keep most of your logic on the server and communicate with the client by sending HTML.[1] Much of the Hotwire code uses Turbo, which is a library that allows you to do complex client-server interactions without writing custom JavaScript. Turbo itself consists of Turbo Drive, which is the successor to Turbolinks and allows you to speed up basic links through your site; Turbo Frames, which allows you to easily replace part of your page with new HTML from the server; and Turbo Streams, which allows you to do arbitrary DOM replacement without any custom JavaScript. Hotwire also includes Stimulus, a JavaScript library that manages client-side interactions more directly.

- React is a framework where most of the rendering logic is on the client.[2] In React, you describe your output using JSX, a language for specifying HTML in JavaScript. You also describe what variables make up the state of the system, and when that state changes, React automatically redraws the parts of the screen that reflect the new state. React typically communicates with the server as an API and frequently expects to receive JSON data in return, which is used to update the state.

We will use three more foundational tools—TypeScript, webpack, and Webpacker—to build the infrastructure of our application, no matter what JavaScript frameworks we use on top:

- TypeScript is an extension of JavaScript that provides type checking and type inference, which means TypeScript ensures that values in your code have the types you expect.[3] It's a superset of JavaScript, which means that any JavaScript program is valid TypeScript, but TypeScript also allows you to add some basic type checking to your code. More advanced usage of TypeScript allows you to use the type system to prevent invalid states at compile-time which can make runtime errors less likely.

- webpack (lowercase) calls itself a "static module bundler,"[4] which I think is pretty jargony, not that anybody asked me. webpack's purpose in life is to convert developer-friendly inputs to browser-friendly outputs. The inputs are the code you write—JavaScript, TypeScript, CSS, what have you—all arranged in a hopefully logical structure. webpack converts all the files to JavaScript and CSS that the browser can understand, which involves translating code and also resolving references to code in different

---

1. https://www.hotwire.dev
2. https://reactjs.org
3. https://www.typescriptlang.org
4. https://webpack.js.org

files. The converted HTML and CSS and JavaScript files can then be sent to a browser.

- Webpacker (uppercase) is a Rails-specific front-end wrapper around webpack.[5] The similarity in names might be confusing, so I'll try to make it as clear as possible when referring to one tool or the other. The most important thing Webpacker gives is some Rails-style convention over configuration structure to your webpack builds. It also builds in support for common tools and adds default setups for common frameworks like the ones we'll be using in this book.

How This Book Is Organized

This book is divided into four parts.

In the first part, we'll install and start using the tools we need to get Rails working with the JavaScript ecosystem. We'll start with a basic introduction to installing the front-end Rails tools. Then we'll add Hotwire and Turbo to the mix for richer interactions, sprinkle that with Stimulus, and then show how React can interact with Rails. Then we'll augment both tools by showing some great ways to use CSS tools in our applications. Finally, we'll take a closer look at our foundation, including the basics of TypeScript, webpack, and Webpacker.

The second part starts with a deeper look at TypeScript, webpack, and Webpacker, and takes a look at one important concern for front-end code: communicating with the server.

In the third part, we'll look at managing the state of the data in your client-side application. We'll look at a JavaScript pattern called a reducer and then talk about Redux, a library that implements the reducer pattern and is commonly used with React.

The fourth part is about validating your code. We go further into TypeScript and take a look at how we can use the type system to prevent error conditions. We then talk about debugging and testing our applications.

By the end of the book, you'll have options that will show you how to structure your code for different levels of client-side needs.

---

5.   https://github.com/rails/webpacker

Let's Build an App

Before we start talking about front-end structure, we need to have an app to attach all that front-end structure to. I've created a sample website for a fictional music festival called North By, where multiple bands will perform at various concerts during the event. This app contains a schedule of all the concerts and venues. There isn't much to this app. I used Rails scaffolding for a minimal amount of administration, but it's just a structure that lets us get at the two pages we'll be managing in this book: the schedule page and the concert display page.

The schedule page shows all the concerts, acts, and times for the entire festival. We'll be adding features to this for inline editing, date filters, and search. We'll let users list favorite concerts, and eventually we'll show up-to-date information on how many tickets have been purchased.

The concert page shows you a simplified theater diagram for each concert and lets you select seats for a simulated ticket purchase. On this page, users can select seats and see their subtotal increase or search for a block of seats and see which seats are available.

The data model for the app looks like this:

- The festival includes several concerts that take place at particular start times.

- Each concert has a venue, and each venue has a number of rows and a number of seats per row (which I realize is vastly simplified from real music venues, but we're just going to pretend for now, because that gets very complicated very quickly).

- Each concert has one or more gigs that make up the concert.

- Each gig matches a band to a concert, and has a start order and a duration.

- Each concert has a bunch of sold tickets, which link a concert to a particular row and seat in the venue.

- We've got users. A user can have tickets and a list of favorite concerts.

Here's a diagram of the data model:

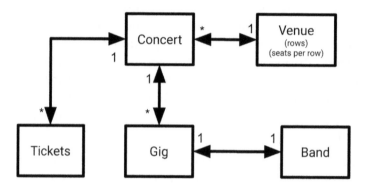

The app uses the Tailwind CSS framework,[6] though when we talk about cascading style sheets (CSS) later in the book, we will generally be writing our own CSS.

The Sample Code

If you'd like to follow along with the application throughout the course of the book, you can download the sample code files from the book page on the Pragmatic Bookshelf website.[7]

The version of the code in the main directory is the complete app setup with all the data structures, but none of the working JavaScript. That's probably the best place to start if you are following along. After that, the directories are named after their chapter numbers.

To run the code, you need a few dependencies:

The code uses Ruby version 3.0, although use of 3.0 features are minimal, and I think anything from 2.6.0 and up should work if you update the .ruby_version file and change the version number in the Gemfile. I recommend installing a Ruby version manager such as RVM,[8] rbenv,[9] or chruby.[10]

---

6.   https://tailwind_url
7.   https://pragprog.com/book/nrclient
8.   https://rvm.io
9.   https://github.com/rbenv/rbenv
10. https://github.com/postmodern/chruby

The code uses PostgreSQL,[11] so you'll need to have that set up on your machine. And you'll need Node (versions 10.x, 12.x, or 14.x should work)[12] and Yarn (version 1.22 is preferable; the 2.0 version doesn't work as I write this)[13] to help set up the Node packages.

A number of the tools used in this book are still in active development as I write this. Here's the combination of the most important versions that back the code in this book:

- Hotwire-Rails 0.1.3
- Rails 6.1.3.1
- Ruby 3.0
- Stimulus 2.0.0
- React 17.0.2
- Turbo 7.0.0-beta4
- Turbo-Rails 0.5.9
- TypeScript 4.2.3
- Webpacker 6.0.0-beta.6 (Be particularly careful with this one; the Webpacker team has been changing the API)

To install this application, you need to be able to install Ruby and a Rails application on your machine. I'm assuming that you are broadly familiar with setting up Rails and its connection to the PostgreSQL database.

The sample code is split into a number of different directories, each corresponding to a different stage of the app in the book. Examples in the book will specify which directory is being used at any time.

From the downloaded code, you can run bin/setup within any of the individual application directories. (You need to be on a system that runs a Unix-style shell, like Bash or Zsh. You may also need to make bin/setup executable with chmod +x bin/setup.)

The setup script will do the following:

- Install bundler.

- Run bundler install.

- Run Yarn install.

---

11. https://www.postgresql.org/download
12. https://nodejs.org/en/download
13. https://yarnpkg.com/getting-started/install

- Run rails db:prepare—this creates the database and generates a bunch of random data for the application.

- Run rails restart.

With the app set up and the main branch running, run it using rails s. You should hit http://localhost:3000 where you'll see the schedule page with a bunch of dates at the top, a search field in the middle, and a lot of schedule information at the bottom, with each scheduled day having a kind of ugly button labeled "Hide." If you click any of the concert names, you'll be taken to a concert page that shows basic data as well as a grid of sets for the show. Neither of these pages has any interactivity at the moment.

From the login link, you can log in with username "areader@example.com" and password "awesome." Doing so will take you back to the schedule page, with an additional option to make each concert a favorite.

The schedule page should look something like this (your randomized data will be different):

If you want to keep following along, each separate step in the application is a different directory in the sample code download, and you can move from one to another to see the entire application at different steps.

There are a lot of ways to do client-side coding, but Rails is here to help. Let's start by taking a look at the tools it provides.

Part I

Getting Started

In this part, we'll explore adding interactivity to our application, first using Hotwire, then JavaScript without a framework, then using Stimulus, and then React. We'll also look at some CSS tools and how they work with Rails and JavaScript.

Getting Started with Client-Side Rails

Every modern web application uses client-side features in an effort to improve the end-user experience. Even though Rails is a server-side framework, it has always offered tools that made it easier to deliver client-side code to the browser. From the very beginning of Rails, its ability to make client-side coding easier has been a selling point.

Over time the client-side tools have become more powerful, which is great, and more complicated, which is less great. One thing that hasn't changed, though, is that Rails still has opinions about how to deal with the client tools.

In this book, we're going to take a basic Rails application and add client-side interactivity. The JavaScript ecosystem includes a lot of tools that allow you to work with Rails; for our purposes, we're going to focus two patterns that work well with Rails. In one pattern, the server communicates with the client by sending HTML, and the client's job is mostly to direct that HTML to the correct part of the page and add some client-only interactions. In the other pattern, the server communicates by sending data (usually in JSON format), and the client is responsible for the logic to covert that data into HTML and is responsible for client-only interactions.

To demonstrate the first pattern, we'll use the Hotwire family of tools, which comes from Basecamp and is a more or less official add-on to Rails.[1] Hotwire consists of Turbo,[2] a library that manages user navigation and communication with the server without needing custom JavaScript, and Stimulus,[3] which supports client-side interactions written in JavaScript. Stimulus is designed to be written as an extension to the HTML markup you are already writing

---

1. http://hotwire.dev
2. https://turbo.hotwire.dev
3. http://stimulusjs.org

and is well suited to small interactions that don't need to manage a lot of state, or where the majority of the state is managed by the server application. A third tool, Strada, which manages interactions with native mobile devices, has not yet been released as I write this.

Many frameworks support the JSON interaction pattern and create their own markup on the client. We'll use React to represent those tools.[4] React replaces your HTML markup with a custom hybrid of JavaScript and HTML called JSX. React automatically updates the DOM when data changes, and is suited for interactions where a lot of state is stored on the client.

In addition, we'll use two other tools that are more foundational. The code we'll write will be in TypeScript, which is a language that extends JavaScript by allowing us to specify the type of any variable, class attribute, function argument, or function return value.[5] I like using TypeScript because there are a whole bunch of mistakes I normally make in JavaScript that TypeScript catches for me. TypeScript's syntax is JavaScript with a few extra features. The first few chapters cover the TypeScript syntax as we need it, and then we'll discuss TypeScript itself in more detail in Chapter 6, TypeScript, on page 115 and Chapter 14, Validating Code with Advanced TypeScript, on page 269.

Finally, we'll use Webpacker to put all of these pieces together.[6] Webpacker is a Rails tool that provides sensible defaults and useful conventions for the webpack build tool.[7] webpack allows us to take all the code we write, whether it is JavaScript, TypeScript, CSS, or even static images, and write it in a structure of our choosing and then package everything in a way that is easy for the browser to manage.

We'll start by installing these tools and showing how much Hotwire and Turbo allow you to do without custom JavaScript. But first, before we dive in and write code, let's talk about web applications, Rails, and JavaScript for a second.

Managing State and Front-End Development

A lot of the decisions about program structure in web applications are about how to manage *state*, which is the data that controls the interactions between the user and the application. Managing state includes both the location of that data itself and the location of the logic that manipulates that state.

---

4.   http://reactjs.org
5.   https://www.typescriptlang.org
6.   https://github.com/rails/webpacker
7.   https://webpack.js.org

The Structure of Web Applications

One of the main questions we'll be dealing with is how to structure your web application so as to best manage your state. The goal is to avoid having multiple sources of truth, both by avoiding duplicating data as well as avoiding writing the same logic on both the client and the server side. We also want to make the program as easy as possible to understand and change.

A consistent problem in web development is that as far as the browser and HTTP server are concerned, the interaction for each page view is "stateless." Being stateless means that each interaction is completely self-contained. As far as the web server is concerned, each request has no relation to or memory of previous requests.

This lack of state is quite useful if you are a web server because it makes your life much easier not to have to keep track of any state. If you are a user of the web, however, the lack of state is annoying because the web server never remembers anything about you. Web applications depend on maintaining your state to remember who you are and what you are doing, so developers have created different solutions to manage the state of a user's interaction with a web server.

Almost since the beginning of the web, a technical solution to this problem has been *cookies*. A cookie is a small amount of data—which often consists of a random string of characters—generated by the server and managed by the browser. The cookie allows the browser to identify itself, and an application server can use that identification to remember the user's state for each request. Over time, interaction patterns were created where nearly all state would be managed on the server, and the browser's job was largely to ask for new pages or new parts of pages, receive the result of the state change, and display it to the user.

Designing Around Basic Web Actions

Ruby on Rails is a framework for managing the state of a web application on the server. Rails is, to a large extent, built around the idea that most web interactions involve a very small set of operations. This set of actions is often abbreviated CRUD: Create, Read, Update, and Delete. In Rails, these actions are represented by the seven operations provided for a standard resource (create, new, show, index, edit, update, and delete).

One of the great insights of Rails is that once you've settled on this set of basic actions, you can remove a lot of repetitive boilerplate and assume common behavior no matter what shape the data is in. In Rails, this default behavior is often defined by the scaffolding that Rails creates for new resources.

If you are dealing with these basic actions, it turns out web browsers can offer you a lot of help. Browsers can provide data input elements, manage the state of form elements, and maintain a list of historical actions. Working hand in hand with a browser makes the Rails' core actions more powerful.

In fact, the basic set of Rails interactions is so powerful that it starts to be worthwhile to take things that are not necessarily basic resource interactions and model them as if they were. Take, for example, Twitter. Twitter, which was originally built partially using Rails, can be modeled as a system where a tweet is a resource, and the user has actions to create one, show one or more, and delete one.[8] (But not edit, which is an argument I'm not getting into here.) Is that the best way to model Twitter's user interaction? I don't know. Probably not. But it's at least a pretty good way to model Twitter, and doing so gives you a big head start because you can take advantage of the power of Rails and the browsers.

The server-side model has many advantages, but ten years ago, it was pretty limited in terms of user interaction. This created problems when users began to expect web applications to have the same rich and complex interactions as desktop interactions. Client-side logic was one response to this problem. Another was making the browser markup, particularly CSS, more powerful to allow browsers more access to complex interactivity.

Designing Around Client Logic

As a web application begins to act more like a desktop application, the application needs to maintain a lot of state and logic that only pertains to the user interface (UI). It doesn't always make sense to manage the client-only information and logic on the server, so JavaScript applications in the browser became more and more complex.

The interactions a user has that are managed by JavaScript may be harder to model as CRUD resources and actions. Single-page application JavaScript frameworks often have a different set of actions. As a result, these frameworks have structured themselves quite differently from server-side Rails applications. For example, a primary concern of JavaScript application frameworks is managing the state of the objects and data being interacted with on the client (for example, which items are active), and the frameworks often

---

8.   http://twitter.com

emphasize having a lot of relatively small constructs that manage the data and logic for a small part of the page. Therefore, a problem in a lot of client-side app frameworks is sharing common state information among otherwise unrelated small components across the page or the app.

On the server side, sharing common state is not a concern in the same way. A server-side Rails app stores global state in the database and generally doesn't worry about the mutability of individual instances because they don't last beyond a single request. How, then, would we structure an application that combines a lot of server-side logic that is Rails-shaped with a lot of client-side interaction that is JavaScript-shaped?

One option is to do as little in JavaScript as possible. In this paradigm, the server generates rendered HTML and the client manipulates the existing DOM. When the client wants to update all or part of the page, it makes requests to the server, receives HTML, and inserts that HTML directly into the DOM. This was more or less the original Web 2.0 paradigm and was the interaction supported by early versions of Rails via helper methods that made remote calls and inserted the returned HTML into a DOM element with a given ID.

These days, Hotwire and Turbo allow a more powerful version of this paradigm to create very interactive client experiences while writing little to no JavaScript. Again, it also helps that many client-side flourishes can now be done in CSS.

On the other extreme, you have a single-page JavaScript app that does the maximum amount of work on the client. After sending the original JavaScript, the server is limited to sending data back and forth, probably using JSON, while the client converts that data to DOM elements using templates or JSX or something. The client also manages the state of the application, including the address the browser displays in the address bar, and the way the browser's Back button works. The client is responsible for making sure the server is informed of any data change that needs to be persisted.

Both of these options have their benefits and drawbacks. There's also a middle ground, where individual web pages might have their own rich interactions, but we let the server handle the transition between pages.

Patterns of Web Applications

To make this architecture discussion more concrete, let's look at how these decisions might play out in a specific web app. Slack is a real-time collaboration and chat application that runs in a browser.[9] Later in the book we'll look

---

9. http://www.slack.com

at how an application might handle real-time chat notification. For now, let's focus on two user interactions: (1) when users click in the sidebar to remain in chat but change the Slack channel they are looking at, and (2) when users click to view their profiles, which completely takes away the chat interface and replaces it with something more like a form.

When the user clicks on a different channel, the basic UI stays in place, but all the displayed data changes. Very broadly speaking, there are a few ways to handle this change. Clicking on a channel could trigger an entire page refresh, making a normal HTTP request to the server and redrawing the entire page. This would usually cause the page to flicker, leading to a poor user experience, although in theory, when using default Rails, the Turbo Drive part of the Turbo library prevents flickering. This is the solution with the least JavaScript.

Clicking on a channel could trigger sending a request to the server, where the server handles the rendering logic and returns the HTML of the part of the page that changes. The client side integrates that HTML into the page. There is a little bit of UI cleanup, such as changing the active status of channels in the sidebar. This would either be done in the client-side code, or, alternately, the server could return a JavaScript script that both updated the HTML and did the UI cleanup or return multiple chunks of HTML that manage the cleanup. This is the JavaScript interaction pattern that many early Rails applications used and which you see a new version of in the Hey[10] email app and other apps that use Turbo Frames and Turbo Streams.

Clicking on a channel could also trigger sending a request to the server that returns data in JSON format. The JavaScript code is responsible for using that data to update, which different frameworks handle in different ways. The data update would trigger changes to the DOM, and the specific updated DOM elements would be redrawn. This is the interaction pattern that React and most JavaScript applications use these days.

When we switch to the profile page, we have the same options, plus we now have one more kind of state to deal with—the name of the entire page that we are looking at. In an older Rails app, switching to a new profile page would be a request to a different URL, and the routing table in the Rails app would handle the decision of what view templates to render and send back to the browser.

---

10. http://hey.com

In a single-page application, the routing happens on the client, and the client's routing table intercepts the click, determines what components are displayed and what data needs to be retrieved from the server to render that data. This routing is slightly more complicated because it splits one step (call the server) into two (navigate internally, then make calls to the server).

Single-page applications often come at a high complexity cost. They can be effective in cases where the interaction pattern is different from the typical CRUD set of actions. Over time, the single-page frameworks have been hard at work lowering the cost of duplicating browser functionality.

For the most part, in this book we'll deal with apps where the server side determines what page is drawn, but each page might have its own interactivity that is managed by a smaller page-level set of components that run in the browser.

Now that we have our structure in mind, it's time to start adding client interaction to the pages of our North By application. Let's begin with the schedule page using the tools that will help us implement all these designs, starting with Webpacker.

Configuring Webpacker

A Rails 6.1 app installs Webpacker as part of the default app creation; however, you need to make some configuration changes up front to install Hotwire, and make sure that CSS and TypeScript are properly integrated.

Webpacker is a Rails gem, so the default install puts it into your Gemfile:

```
gem "webpacker"
```

As I write this, Webpacker 6.0 is in beta. This book uses Beta 6—hopefully it will be released by the time you read this.

Webpacker creates a number of local configuration files, including the package.json manifest of JavaScript libraries to use, and then retrieves those JavaScript libraries using the Yarn package manager.[11]

The default installation of Webpacker does not integrate with TypeScript or with CSS libraries. We'll add those integrations now, per the Webpacker documentation,[12] and we'll get to installing React later on.

To allow Webpacker to manage CSS, we need to add a few packages:

---

11. https://yarnpkg.com
12. https://github.com/rails/webpacker

```
yarn add css-loader mini-css-extract-plugin css-minimizer-webpack-plugin
```

Webpacker also recommends adding a few lines to base.js configuration (this listing also has a TypeScript addition):

chapter_01/01/config/webpack/base.js
```
const { webpackConfig, merge } = require("@rails/webpacker")
const ForkTSCheckerWebpackPlugin = require("fork-ts-checker-webpack-plugin")

const customConfig = {
  plugins: [new ForkTSCheckerWebpackPlugin()],
  resolve: {
    extensions: [".css"],
  },
}

module.exports = merge(webpackConfig, customConfig)
```

We'll also use the PostCSS and Sass extensions:

```
yarn add postcss-loader sass sass-loader
```

Next, we're going to take a second to install Tailwind for CSS, since it supports the styling of the site, but we won't get into the specifics of Tailwind much:

```
$ yarn add tailwindcss@latest postcss@latest autoprefixer@latest
$ yarn add @tailwindcss/forms
$ npx tailwindcss init
```

Now we need to update the postcss.config.js to this:

chapter_01/01/postcss.config.js
```
module.exports = {
  plugins: [
    require('postcss-import'),
    require('postcss-flexbugs-fixes'),
    require('postcss-preset-env')({
      autoprefixer: {
        flexbox: 'no-2009'
      },
      stage: 3
    }),
    require('tailwindcss'),
    require('autoprefixer')
  ]
}
```

And update the app/javascript/packs/application.scss to this:

chapter_01/01/app/packs/entrypoints/application.scss
```
@import "tailwindcss/base";
@import "tailwindcss/components";
@import "tailwindcss/utilities";
```

For TypeScript, most of the support is already there. We just need to add one extension to the Babel JavaScript preprocessor to make it work:[13]

```
yarn add typescript @babel/preset-typescript
```

And then we need to add a tsconfig.json file. We'll talk more about that file in Chapter 6, TypeScript, on page 115. For now, you can find the default on GitHub.[14] As you saw earlier, we also added a plugin to the Webpacker configuration. This plugin allows Webpacker to use TypeScript information during compilation.

Webpacker uses about a dozen files, plus we added a new directory, node_modules, which contains umpteen zillion JavaScript modules. Right now, we're going to look at what some of these new files do for us. Later in Chapter 8, Webpacker, on page 149, we'll take a deeper dive into what Webpacker install does.

The first batch of files we are going to look at are the ones that manage JavaScript packages.

Package Managers and Modules

Many programming languages have ways for useful libraries of code to be shared as well as tools that manage the dependencies between those libraries. The goal is for the set of the exact same versions of libraries in use to be reproduced when setting up the application. In Ruby, we have Ruby Gems, which are managed with Bundler.[15] Bundler works via two files: the Gemfile, which is a manifest of the gems in use, and the Gemfile.lock, which is a list of the actual versions of all gems and their dependencies being loaded by the application.

In JavaScript, the libraries are called *packages*. You'll also sometimes hear them called *modules*, which is technically not correct, even if the directory that Yarn puts all these packages in is called node_modules. There are a few different package managers, of which the first one was the Node Package Manager (npm).[16] Webpacker uses Yarn, which was designed by many of the people who helped build Bundler and is somewhat similar in structure. Yarn was created to respond to limitations in npm; however, since then, npm has fixed most of those limitations. Our choice to use Yarn here is largely due to it being the default choice for Rails.

---

13. https://babeljs.io
14. https://github.com/rails/webpacker#integrations
15. https://bundler.io
16. https://www.npmjs.com

The manifest file for our JavaScript packages is package.json. Let's take a look at the one that Webpacker has created for us:

chapter_01/01/package.json

```json
{
  "name": "north-by",
  "private": true,
  "dependencies": {
    "@babel/preset-typescript": "^7.12.7",
    "@rails/actioncable": "^6.0.0",
    "@rails/activestorage": "^6.0.0",
    "@rails/ujs": "^6.0.0",
    "@rails/webpacker": "6.0.0-beta.6",
    "@tailwindcss/aspect-ratio": "^0.2.0",
    "@tailwindcss/forms": "^0.2.1",
    "@tailwindcss/typography": "^0.3.1",
    "autoprefixer": "^10.1.0",
    "css-loader": "^5.0.1",
    "css-minimizer-webpack-plugin": "^1.1.5",
    "fork-ts-checker-webpack-plugin": "^6.2.0",
    "mini-css-extract-plugin": "^1.3.3",
    "postcss": "^8.2.1",
    "postcss-flexbugs-fixes": "^5.0.2",
    "postcss-import": "^14.0.0",
    "postcss-loader": "^4.1.0",
    "postcss-preset-env": "^6.7.0",
    "sass": "^1.30.0",
    "sass-loader": "^10.1.0",
    "tailwindcss": "^2.0.2",
    "turbolinks": "^5.2.0",
    "typescript": "^4.1.3",
    "webpack": "^5.11.0",
    "webpack-cli": "^4.2.0"
  },
  "version": "0.1.0",
  "devDependencies": {
    "@tailwindcss/custom-forms": "^0.2.1",
    "@typescript-eslint/eslint-plugin": "*",
    "@typescript-eslint/parser": "*",
    "@webpack-cli/serve": "^1.3.1",
    "eslint": "^7.16.0",
    "eslint-config-prettier": "*",
    "eslint-plugin-prettier": "*",
    "prettier": "^2.2.1",
    "webpack-dev-server": "^3.11.2"
  },
```

```
  "babel": {
    "presets": [
      "./node_modules/@rails/webpacker/package/babel/preset.js"
    ]
  },
  "browserslist": [
    "defaults"
  ]
}
```

The package.json file has similar information to the Gemfile, but in JSON format. The important part of the file for us right now is the dependencies part, which lists all the packages our run-time code depends on. At the moment, we've got a bunch of Rails-specific packages, including actioncable, activestorage, webpacker itself, and the classic @rails/ujs, which is the package for Rails's default interactive behavior (like data-confirm fields). We've also got typescript, which is the TypeScript compiler itself, and @babel/preset-typescript, which configures the Babel transpiler tool to allow it to use the TypeScript compiler. Plus we have a lot of packages related to Tailwind and CSS processing.

At the bottom of the file is the devDependencies section, which has all of the dependencies we use in development and not during run time. Right now the most important one is webpack-dev-server, which you'll learn more about in Chapter 7, webpack, on page 133.

You can put other things in the package.json file. In our case, the Babel transpiler is using it to store the location of its preset file. Babel is used to convert newer versions of JavaScript into older versions that are usable by more browsers, and the preset file tells us what JavaScript features we can safely use. The default preset, which is provided by Webpacker, ensures that language features that Stimulus, TypeScript, and React depend on are available.

The Browserslist tool is using package.json to define that we're targeting the default set of current browsers.[17] Babel and PostCSS both use that information to specify what is generated when they convert our code to its browser-ready version.

Webpacker also creates a yarn.lock file, which is the equivalent of Gemfile.lock, but *way* more verbose. It has the versions of all our dependencies, and all our dependencies' dependencies, and so on. Part of the complexity is that, unlike Bundler, if two separate dependencies themselves depend on two different versions of the same library, Yarn allows both libraries' modules to

---

17. https://github.com/browserslist/browserslist

depend on their own required version rather than limiting itself to just one version of the common dependency.

The actual packages are stored in the node_modules directory, which, just from this basic setup, contains well over 700 packages. Unlike Ruby gems, the JavaScript packages are stored with each individual project. Thankfully, the install has also updated our .gitignore to not include the node_modules directory. The fact that we already have more than 700 packages might give some insight into the need for, and complexity of, a JavaScript build tool.

Configuration Files

The next category of files contains the configuration of webpack and Webpacker. (We'll talk way more about these files in Chapter 7, webpack, on page 133.) There is a YAML file called config/webpacker.yml, which has some general Webpacker options, including where to look for input files, where to put output, and so on.

Webpacker introduces a Rails-like concept of environment. It maintains a common environment file, config/webpack/base.js, and then separate additional files for different environments, which allows for different behavior in development versus production. This directory also keeps track of *loaders*, which are the bits of code that attach particular file types with the webpack extension that processes them. Webpacker uses a loader for PostCSS processing, which we'll talk about more in Chapter 5, Cascading Style Sheets, on page 91.

Webpacker also generates a series of configuration files at the top level of the application to configure various other tools it uses along the way. We have the tsconfig.json file, which configures how TypeScript is converted to browser-friendly JavaScript. (More about that file in Chapter 6, TypeScript, on page 115.) And we have the postcss.config.js file, which manages the PostCSS tool for processing CSS.

Two executable scripts are added into the bin directory: webpack and webpack-dev-server. Both of these allow you to invoke webpack to build your code. We don't actually need to use either of these explicitly right now, but we'll come back to them later on.

Finally, we get to the actual code in our app.

Code Files

Webpacker, at its most basic level, makes a very clear bargain. For every file we put in the app/packs/entrypoints directory, it will compile that file, along with any other files referenced by it, into what Webpacker calls a *pack*. It will, by default, place that pack in the public/packs directory, and you can access it in your view files using the helper method javascript_pack_tag.

Webpacker generates a default pack for us, which it places in app/packs/entry-points/application.js. As I write this, there's a discrepancy between what Rails creates as the default pack and what Webpacker creates as the default in version 6.0. I've combined the two here, because Rails loads some libraries of its own, but if you start from scratch, your file will likely look different:

chapter_01/01/app/packs/entrypoints/application.js

```
import "channels"
import "core-js/stable"
import "regenerator-runtime/runtime"
import * as ActiveStorage from "@rails/activestorage"
import Rails from "@rails/ujs"
import Turbolinks from "turbolinks"

Rails.start()
Turbolinks.start()
ActiveStorage.start()
```

That file loads and starts the Rails UJS library, which handles basic Rails Ajax functionality and also standard Rails confirmation dialogs. We've also got Turbolinks, ActiveStorage, and Channels, which is ActionCable. Right now we're just going to let this file stay as it is. (Turbolinks will be replaced by Hotwire and Turbo in just a little bit.)

We've also created an application.scss file, which right now just handles our Tailwind imports:

chapter_01/01/app/packs/entrypoints/application.scss

```
@import "tailwindcss/base";
@import "tailwindcss/components";
@import "tailwindcss/utilities";
```

Typically, these top-level pack files act like manifests and primarily contain a list of other files to include in the pack. But that's not required. For better or for worse, Webpacker doesn't make any assumptions or place any limitations on how you structure your code; although later you'll see that different frameworks have opinions on the subject.

Using Webpacker

With Webpacker installed, let's take it for a spin and build something.

First, let's make sure everything is working. To connect the Webpacker build to our app, we need to add two helper method calls to the app/views/layouts/application.html.erb file, like so:

```
chapter_01/01/app/views/layouts/application.html.erb
<!DOCTYPE html>
<html>
  <head>
    <title>North By North East</title>
    <meta name="viewport" content="width=device-width,initial-scale=1">
    <%= csrf_meta_tags %>
    <%= csp_meta_tag %>
    <%= stylesheet_pack_tag(
          "application",
          media: "all",
          "data-turbolinks-track": "reload"
        ) %>
    <%= javascript_pack_tag("application", "data-turbolinks-track": "reload") %>
  </head>
  <body>
    <section class="py-12 px-6">
      <%= render "layouts/nav" %>
      <div class="container mx-auto">
        <div class="mt-6">
          <p class="notice"><%= notice %></p>
          <p class="alert"><%= alert %></p>
          <%= yield %>
        </div>
      </div>
    </section>
  </body>
</html>
```

The Webpacker specific helpers are stylesheet_pack_tag and javascript_pack_tag.

Next we'll start up the server with rails s and hit the localhost:3000 web page in our browser. Everything will look normal except that the Rails log will have a couple of extra lines:

```
[Webpacker] Compiling…
[Webpacker] Compiled all packs
        in /Users/noel/code/github/noelrappin/north_by/public/packs
```

followed by the results of the compilation.

Webpacker is telling us that it has converted our application.js file to new files that live in public/packs. Specifically, public/packs/js/application-786ca3f8a9651f4cc4d4.js. (That last part with all the numbers is a digital fingerprint marking the version of the file, so if you are running this at home, your file name will be different.) There's also a public/packs/manifest.json file, which webpack uses to keep track of the different packs.

And there are .js.map files, which are *source maps*. Source maps allow the browser's development tools to display our code as it was written before

Webpacker compiled. This is valuable if you are using a tool, like TypeScript, that compiles to ordinary JavaScript. The debugger messages will point to our TypeScript code rather than the compiled JavaScript, making it easier for us to associate bugs with specific lines of code.

If we reload the page in the browser, we don't get the "Compiling..." message in the log. If we change the application.js file, however, Rails and Webpacker will recompile the file when you reload the page.

This is great. It means we don't need to do anything special to make sure our front-end code is recompiled when we visit pages in development. That said, having the compilation wait until we actually hit the page can be slow. There's another way, using webpack-dev-server, that we'll go over in more detail in Chapter 8, Webpacker, on page 149.

What's Next

In this chapter, we installed Webpacker and TypeScript. Next, we're going to use Hotwire and Turbo to see how to add a lot of dynamic behavior without actually writing our own JavaScript.

CHAPTER 2

Hotwire and Turbo

In the last chapter we got up and running with Webpacker and TypeScript. In this chapter, we're going to start creating front-end applications with Rails by doing something that may seem odd. We're going to add front-end features without writing JavaScript. In fact, we are going to *not* write a lot of JavaScript. And by that I mean we are going to add a lot of dynamic features to our page that you'd expect would require a bunch of JavaScript, but we're not going to write any, at least not at first. Instead, we're going to use Hotwire and Turbo to build client-side interactivity into our page without writing JavaScript.

The Hotwire Way

Hotwire is the generic name for the client-side toolkit written by the Basecamp team to power the Hey email application.[1,2] The goal of Hotwire is to support an application where most of the dynamic nature happens by making normal HTTP requests to the server, receiving HTML for a part of the page, and inserting that HTML in the correct place in the DOM for a page update. (The name *Hotwire* is derived from the phrase, "HTML over the wire.")

The idea is that by moving all the logic to the server, you can replace a lot of complicated and specific client-side code with a small set of generic client-side actions that handle retrieving and managing HTML from the server. You still have to write the logic server side, but the bet here is that, at least some of the time, by making the server the source of truth, you are preventing duplicate logic on the client and the server. In particular, Turbo allows you to reuse and repurpose view code that you have already written for greater interactivity. The intention is that writing the complex logic in Ruby and Rails will be easier than writing it in the JavaScript ecosystem. Your mileage may

---

1. http://hotwire.dev
2. http://hey.com

vary on that last part, but you are reading a book about Rails development, so it is my hope that it does become easier for you.

The big picture idea here is:

- The server communicates with the client by sending rendered HTML, not raw data. This HTML response may contain some metadata about where to put it when it arrives.

- Any business logic the application might need should be on the server, not on the client.

- Specific client logic should be limited only to interface items that the server won't care about.

- Where possible, client logic should be handled through the addition and removal of CSS classes. Doing so allows for a lot of client logic to be written in a generic manner.

The Hotwire team claims that about 80 percent of their client interaction is manageable via HTML over the wire, and I'd guess that at least half of the client-side code is just manipulating CSS. Looking at your application through that lens will result in much less client-side complexity, and you'll be able to leverage Rails features to keep the overall complexity low. Hotwire works particularly well if you use Rails conventions for partial-view files, and especially if you use the ActiveRecord naming convention for partial files.

Installing Turbo

Hotwire currently consists of two parts: Turbo, which manages HTML requests to the server and directs the responses correctly, and Stimulus, which is a minimal JavaScript library well suited to the interactions Turbo can't handle.

Turbo is the successor to Turbolinks, and its purpose in life is to make it trivially easy to direct user actions into server requests that then return partial HTML, which Turbo then inserts into the page or part of the page.

Hotwire and the Asset Pipeline

 The Hotwire team put a bit of effort into making Hotwire work with or without a JavaScript build tool. We use Webpacker in this book to support TypeScript and React, but if you want to use Hotwire with the older Rails asset pipeline, you can still do so via the hotwire-rails gem. If Webpacker is not installed, the gem installs Turbo and Stimulus using the asset pipeline, including the Stimulus auto-load behavior we'll talk about later. There is also a gem

Hotwire and the Asset Pipeline

> called tailwindcss-rails that will do a default Tailwind installation
> in the asset pipeline or in Webpacker. For a simple app, this is a
> low-overhead way to go.

To install Hotwire, we use a gem called hotwire-rails, which is aware of whether
you are using Webpacker or not, and adjusts its installation accordingly.

1. In the Gemfile, replace the turbolinks gem with hotwire-rails.
2. Run bundle install.
3. Run rails hotwire:install. This will install Hotwire (both Stimulus and Turbo)
   via npm and Webpacker if Webpacker is installed (which it is).

Specifically, the hotwire:install command does the following:

- Adds @hotwired/turbo-rails and stimulus to our package.json and removes turbolinks.

- Runs yarn to install the new package.

- Makes a configuration change to ActionCable that we'll talk about in
  Chapter 10, Immediate Communication with ActionCable, on page 187.

- Changes our application.js file to remove Turbolinks, add the turbo-rails gem,
  and import the controllers directory that Stimulus uses. Following is an
  edited version; the installer puts the import controllers at the end of the file:

chapter_02/01/app/packs/entrypoints/application.js
```
import "@hotwired/turbo-rails"
import "channels"
import "controllers"
import "core-js/stable"
import "regenerator-runtime/runtime"
import * as ActiveStorage from "@rails/activestorage"
import Rails from "@rails/ujs"

Rails.start()
ActiveStorage.start()
```

We'll talk more about this file in Chapter 3, Stimulus, on page 37, when we
start writing JavaScript.

And we're off!

Well, almost. I do want to say a quick word about Turbo Drive, since, for the
most part, we're going to let it work in the background and not trouble ourselves with it.

What Is Turbo Drive?

Turbo Drive is the new name for what used to be known as Turbolinks. When Turbo Drive is active, it captures every clicked link or form submission on a page, receives the response in the background, extracts the body of the request, and replaces the existing page body with the new response. It also does some behind-the-scenes bookkeeping to keep the Back button working and manage caches and whatnot.

The goal is that by using Turbo Drive, page navigation is both actually faster, because large assets in the header of the page aren't reloaded, and also perceived as faster by the user because the page doesn't flicker or go blank. If you look at the chapter_01/01 version of our page and try the "Make Favorite" feature, you probably will find it quite responsive even though there is no special client-side behavior at the moment; it's just Turbo Drive redrawing the page without much flicker.

There is a downside to Turbo Drive, and this downside is the reason why a lot of Rails applications have historically chosen not to use Turbolinks. Because the browser does not see a Turbo Drive change as a full page load, it does not send page-load related events, so Turbo Drive can interfere with other JavaScript libraries or code that depend on the page-loaded or DOM-loaded events. Turbo does have its own page-load event that you can watch for called turbo:load, but it can be tricky to integrate with existing JavaScript libraries that depend on document load.

Turbo Drive is nice, but it's not nearly enough to build an exciting application on its own. For that, we need to turn to Turbo Frames and Turbo Streams.

Adding Interactivity with Turbo Frames

We are now going to add new functionality to our app's schedule page. We're going to allow a user to edit concert data inline on the schedule page. When users hit the Edit button, the display will be replaced by a form, and when they hit the Submit button on the form, the updated data is there in place. (We're not going to worry about authentication very much here. If you are using the existing code, the sign-in links work, and you can sign in with the email areader@example.com and the password awesome.)

Oh, and we're going to do this without writing a single line of JavaScript. Instead, we are going to use Turbo Frames.

A *Turbo Frame* is a custom HTML tag, <turbo-frame>, that wraps part of our page. Turbo Frames capture navigation. Within a Turbo Frame, any link clicks or form submissions will, by default, capture the server response, look for a Turbo Frame in that response with the same ID, and redraw only that Turbo Frame with only the new Turbo Frame portion of the response. To put it another way, Turbo Frames allow a small part of the page to behave the way Turbo Drive treats the entire page.

Let's use our edit in place as an example.

The display of a single line of concert data is managed by a partial at app/views/concerts/_concert.html.erb. To wrap the entire partial, add this line to the top:

<%= turbo_frame_tag(dom_id(concert)) do %>

and close it with an <% end %> appended to the end.

The turbo_frame_tag method is a helper added by the turbo-rails gem and available anywhere in Rails views. It generates a <turbo-frame> custom HTML element with the contents coming from the block, similar to many other Rails tag-building helper methods.

Do the same thing with the app/views/concerts/_form.html.erb partial. The new first line is <%= turbo_frame_tag(dom_id(concert)) do %> and the new last line is <% end %>. Yes, the edit and display partial turbo frames have the same DOM ID, but that's not going to cause a problem because they will never be on the page at the same time.

In the ConcertsController, we need to change the behavior of a successful update to just return the partial and not the entire page:

```
chapter_02/01/app/controllers/concerts_controller.rb
def update
  respond_to do |format|
    if @concert.update(concert_params)
      format.html do
        render(@concert)
      end

      format.json { render(:show, status: :ok, location: @concert) }
    else
      format.html { render(:edit) }

      format.json do
        render(json: @concert.errors, status: :unprocessable_entity)
      end
    end
  end
end
```

The render call in the successful branch now looks for the partial rather than redirecting to the show page.

Refresh the page. (If you haven't restarted the server since installing Turbo, you also need to do that first. You may also need to re-log in as areader@example.com with the password awesome.)

Click "Edit" on any of the concerts. You should see the form display inline, and submitting the form should result in the updated data appearing back inline.

This works. We now have inline editing with no custom JavaScript written. We've barely even written any Rails; mostly we've just added a couple of tags to the HTML output we were already generating.

What's happening here?

By putting our HTML inside the <turbo-frame> tag, we are allowing Turbo to control both the request to the server and the response from the server.

When we click the Edit button, we make an ordinary Rails GET request—in this case for the ConcertController#edit action. Rails handles this request normally (almost). If you look in the browser network tab, you can see that the return value is the entire edit page, including the <h1>Editing Concert</h1> header. Turbo inserts a Turbo-Frame header into the request, and Rails recognizes that frame and optimizes by not rendering the layout in the return value, since presumably the part that the receiving Turbo Frame is interested in is not in the layout.

When the response comes back to the browser, Turbo intercepts it and looks for the part of the response that contains a Turbo Frame tag with the matching ID. This is why the Turbo Frame in the form partial and one in the display partial had to have the same DOM ID. Turbo extracts that Turbo Frame from the response and replaces the existing Turbo Frame's contents with the contents from the incoming response's Turbo Frame.

If the incoming response does not contain a matching Turbo Frame, the existing Turbo Frame is replaced with blank contents. It seems to disappear, though you will get an error message in the console saying, Response has no matching <turbo-frame id="concert_15"> element. If you have a link inside a Turbo Frame and it appears to vanish, check the Rails log to see if an error was thrown, or check the Network tab on the browser inspector to see what is actually being returned. It's likely you are not getting a Turbo Frame with a matching ID.

The same process happens again when we submit the form. The submission is an ordinary Rails POST request—Turbo adds one item to the Accept header so that Rails can identify the request as a Turbo Stream. The response renders a single partial that contains the display for that concert, which has a Turbo Frame with a matching ID, and Turbo takes that display and replaces the Turbo Frame contents that contain the form.

Strictly speaking, we did not need to change the controller's update method to return only the one partial display. We could have redirected it to display the entire schedule page, and Turbo would still have extracted the single Turbo Frame with the matching DOM ID to replace the form. But doing so would have forced a lot more database activity. For performance reasons, we choose to render as little as possible.

TurboFrames and Tables

 One side effect of Turbo Frames being custom HTML elements is that browsers don't know anything about them, which can occasionally lead to trouble. In particular, browsers are very particular about what elements can be inside a table, and attempting to use turbo-frame to surround table rows or cells won't work; the browser will rearrange the tags so that the turbo-frame is outside the table. (If the Turbo Frame tag is only inside a single td, that'll work fine.) The workarounds are to either wrap the entire table or use CSS grids for table behavior.

We can polish this interaction by supporting a Cancel button in the form and also by properly handling submission errors. This is all standard Rails, made just a tiny bit more complicated by the fact that I've set up the application to have two different concert displays: the inline one that we see on the schedule page, and the actual concert show page that you can see at a URL like http://localhost:3000/concerts/58.

To make this work, we need to make two changes to the concert form.

The error display for the form is currently at the bottom of the form, and we want to move that to the top of the form, right after the call to simple_form_for:

chapter_02/02/app/views/concerts/_form.html.erb
```erb
<% if f.object.errors.present? %>
  <div class="text-red-500 border-red-800 font-bold border-2 p-2 mb-2">
    <%= f.error_notification %>
    <%= f.error_notification(
        message: f.object.errors.full_messages.to_sentence
      ) %>
  </div>
<% end %>
```

If there are errors, Rails will put them in the view inside the div, which will show up with a red outline.

At the end of the form, where the Submit button is, we need to add a cancel link (this can just be a regular anchor tag, since the cancel is just a GET request to go back to the server for a show action):

```
chapter_02/02/app/views/concerts/_form.html.erb
<div class="col-span-1 text-xl my-10">
  <%= f.input :ilk, collection: Concert.ilks, label: false %>
  <%= f.input :access, collection: Concert.accesses, label: false %>
  <%= f.button :submit %>
  <%= link_to(
      "Cancel",
      concert_path(@concert, inline: true),
      class: "#{SimpleForm.button_class} py-2 mt-4"
    ) %>
</div>
```

We're passing inline: true to the controller on the cancel request so that the controller can differentiate between the inline display and the separate full-page display.

The controller method looks like this:

```
chapter_02/02/app/controllers/concerts_controller.rb
def show
  if params[:inline]
    render(@concert)
  end
end
```

If the inline parameter is passed, it renders the inline display partial; otherwise, it continues on and performs the default action of rendering the normal show.html.erb page. (A Rails default action checks to see if render has already been called, so this code does not result in a double render error.)

Oh, and it'll be useful to add a validation to the Concert model so that we can easily trigger a validation error: validates :name, presence: true.

And that's that. The Cancel button triggers a request that returns the inline display. An invalid form redirects to redisplay the form with the error message, and again Turbo grabs the matching Turbo Frame and extracts the form into the page.

Navigating Outside a Turbo Frame

If you've been clicking around the schedule page as it exists after adding the edit functionality, you've probably noticed that we moved fast and broke things. Specifically, the links on each concert name that led to the concert show page and the Make Favorite button both appear to be broken. Clicking the concert name does nothing but make the concert display disappear, and clicking the Make Favorite button updates the concert display but not the Favorites section.

Both of these problems have the same cause: the links are now inside a Turbo Frame but are trying to change parts of the page outside that frame. Turbo Frames, by default, only captures the part of the response that matches the ID of the Turbo Frame that the request came from. In the case of the concert name link, there is no corresponding Turbo Frame, so the existing frame is replaced by nothing. In the case of the Make Favorite link, the response is the entire page, which happens to contain a Turbo Frame for the concert you favorited, and Turbo updates that frame and that frame alone.

It's common to need to break out of a Turbo Frame for navigation for one reason or another, and Turbo Frames provides for it in two ways.

First, we can set the default target for the entire frame by setting the target= attribute of the HTML <turbo-frame> tag, or the target: argument of the tur-bo_frame_tag helper method. The target is the DOM ID of a different Turbo Frame. By adding the target attribute, you are changing the behavior or all links within the frame to redraw the target frame rather than the frame that the link originates from. This isn't the behavior we need for our fixes; the intended use for this is something like a navigation bar where the links would all redraw a content frame rather than redraw the navigation bar itself.

What we want to do is change the behavior of some individual links within a frame in case most of the links in the frame still just work within that frame. To do that, Turbo Frames allows you to set the data-turbo-frame attribute on a link or form to the DOM ID of a different Turbo Frame. When doing so, the link looks for and redraws the Turbo Frame specified in the data-turbo-frame attribute.

In both the target and the data-turbo-frame case, the special value _top refers to the entire page rather than a specific frame.

We want the concert name links to change the entire page to the full concert show page, so we can do that by adding data-turbo-frame=_top to that link. Or like this in Rails helper:

chapter_02/03/app/views/concerts/_concert.html.erb
```erb
<%= link_to(
    concert.name,
    concert,
    data: {"turbo-frame": "_top"}
  ) %>
```

And those links work again.

Getting the Favorite buttons to work is a slightly more involved process. I mean, we could also make those links _top links as well, but I'd rather actually just redraw the Favorites part of the page. Not only does that have better performance, but also it will eventually allow us to add CSS animations to the redraws and keep any statuses on the single page.

As of right now, the Favorites page is not a Turbo Frame, so the first thing we need to do is fix that.

The entire Favorites part of the page is in a partial. Let's wrap that in a Turbo Frame:

chapter_02/03/app/views/favorites/_list.html.erb
```erb
<%= turbo_frame_tag("favorite-concerts") do %>
  <section class="my-4">
    <div class="text-3xl font-bold">Favorite Concerts</div>
    <div class="text-xl font-bold" id="no-favorites">
      <% if current_user.favorites.empty? %>
        No favorite concerts yet
      <% end %>
    </div>
    <div id="favorite-concerts-list">
      <% current_user.favorites.each do |favorite| %>
        <%= render(favorite) %>
      <% end %>
    </div>
  </section>
<% end %>
```

While we're at it, let's also create a Favorites index page that just draws the partial:

chapter_02/03/app/views/favorites/index.html.erb
```erb
<%= render "favorites/list" %>
```

And a blank index method added to the controller as well. Just def index; end should do it. This will allow us to refer to this in a redirect or as a render helper.

Notice that the call to render the concert inside the list just calls render(favorite). This draws the view partial at app/views/favorites/_favorite, which is (slightly) different from the regular concert partial, but will make it easier to distinguish between the favorite display and the concert display later on.

Now, we need to change the behavior of the Make Favorite and Remove Favorite buttons to have the data-turbo-frame attribute:

chapter_02/03/app/views/concerts/_concert.html.erb
```erb
<% if current_user.favorite(concert) %>
  <%= button_to(
        "Remove Favorite",
        favorite_path(id: current_user.favorite(concert)),
        method: "delete",
        form: {data: {"turbo-frame": "favorite-concerts"}},
        class: SimpleForm.button_class
      ) %>
<% else %>
  <%= button_to(
        "Make Favorite",
        favorites_path(concert_id: concert.id),
        method: "post",
        form: {data: {"turbo-frame": "favorite-concerts"}},
        class: SimpleForm.button_class
      ) %>
<% end %>
```

Note here that the data-turbo-frame attribute has to be on the form created by button_to, not on the button itself, which is why we use the form: argument in the method.

And we need to change the FavoritesController to only return the partial with the list of favorites when a favorite is created or removed:

chapter_02/03/app/controllers/favorites_controller.rb
```ruby
class FavoritesController < ApplicationController
  def index
  end

  def create
    Favorite.create(user: current_user, concert_id: params[:concert_id])
    render(partial: "favorites/list")
  end

  def destroy
    @favorite = Favorite.find(params[:id])
    @favorite.destroy
    render(partial: "favorites/list")
  end

  private def favorite_params
    params.require(:concert_id)
  end
end
```

And this works, sort of. Clicking the Make Favorite or Remove Favorite buttons does update the Favorites section, but only the Favorites section. The concert display line does not change, which means the button label and action doesn't change.

What we really want to do is allow our request to respond in such a way that Turbo will update both the Favorites section and the concert display line, while leaving the rest of the page alone.

We want to use Turbo Streams.

Extending Our Page with Turbo Streams

Turbo Streams is the next step in using Turbo to make pages more dynamic without writing any custom JavaScript. I encourage you to think of this development process as successive enhancement. We started with a working page that we thought needed to be more interactive. We added inline editing, we added more responsive updates to part of the page, and now we're going to add updating multiple parts of a page from a request.

Turbo Streams allows you to send an arbitrary amount of HTML content to the page and have that content replace or augment existing content in multiple arbitrary locations on the page. It's designed for exactly our situation, where we want multiple parts of the page to update from a single request. Turbo Streams is also designed to work really well with WebSockets via ActionCable, which we'll talk about later in Chapter 10, Immediate Communication with ActionCable, on page 187.

A Turbo Stream is another custom HTML tag, <turbo-stream>, which has two attributes and a child tag of template. Generically, a Turbo Stream element looks like this (an HTTP response can contain an arbitrary amount of Turbo Stream tags):

```
<turbo-stream action="<ACTION>" target="<TARGET>">
  <template>
    OUR HTML GOES HERE
  </template>
</turbo-stream>
```

The two attributes, which are required for the Turbo Stream to work, specify the target, which is the DOM ID of the element of the page being changed, and the action, which specifies what to do with the incoming HTML. There are five actions:

- append: The body of the template is added at the end of the target, and the existing contents are maintained.

- prepend: The body of the template is added at the beginning of the target, and the existing contents are maintained.

- remove: The element with the target ID is removed. In this case, the turbo-stream does not need to have any contents.

- replace: The body of the template will completely replace the existing element with the target ID. Typically the body of the template is a new element with the same ID.

- update: The body of the template will replace the content of the target, but not the element itself.

When the Turbo Stream response is evaluated, each separate Turbo Stream element has its action performed on its target.

Turbo Streams are evaluated on form submissions, or on receipt of ActionCable broadcasts. When a form is submitted inside a Turbo app, Turbo intercepts the request to insert into the Accept header, text/vnd.turbo-stream.html. You can verify that the header is attached by looking at the Network tab of your browser inspector for the form submission. The information will also show up in the Rails log, where the line will say, Processing by ConcertsController#edit as TURBO_STREAM.

What we need is to respond to the create and delete favorite requests with a Turbo Stream that updates the Favorites display and also updates the inline display of the concert. Since we can, let's not update the entire Favorites display but just append or remove the concert in question.

A feature that makes using Turbo Streams easier from the controller side is that Rails recognizes turbo_stream as a format in the same way it recognizes html and json. The Rails controller can then use respond_to. Within your respond_to block, Rails recognizes turbo_stream as a format. As a format, that means that you can use format.turbo_stream to specify response behavior specific to Turbo requests. Rails will also automatically use a file with turbo_stream as the format, the way it does for HTML and JSON, so it looks for a file named <action>.turbo_stream.erb. When Rails recognizes that the request is a Turbo Stream, it does not use the layout when it returns the response on the theory that a Turbo response will only be interested in the body part of the page anyway. This is a small but helpful performance benefit.

And it turns out that nearly all we need to do is create those ERB files and point the controllers at them.

Here's what the controller looks like:

```
chapter_02/04/app/controllers/favorites_controller.rb
class FavoritesController < ApplicationController
  def index
  end

  def create
    @favorite = Favorite.create(
      user: current_user,
      concert_id: params[:concert_id]
    )
    respond_to do |format|
      format.turbo_stream
    end
  end

  def destroy
    @favorite = Favorite.find(params[:id])
    @favorite.destroy
    respond_to do |format|
      format.turbo_stream
    end
  end

  private def favorite_params
    params.require(:concert_id)
  end
end
```

Both the create and destroy methods have a similar structure. In the first part, we do the actual creating or destroying of the favorite record, then we use the standard Rails respond_to to direct turbo_stream responses to the default Rails behavior, which is to look for create.turbo_stream.erb or destroy.turbo_stream.erb. Strictly speaking, since this is all default behavior, you could leave out the respond_to block entirely as the controller would by a default search for the same <action>.<format>.erb file anyway; whether you do so depends on whether there are other formats you want to deal with. This structure makes it easy to do something different with a regular html request versus a turbo_stream request.

The ERB files use a new Rails helper to create Turbo Streams. Let's look at the create file first:

```
chapter_02/04/app/views/favorites/create.turbo_stream.erb
<%= turbo_stream.append("favorite-concerts-list", @favorite) %>
<%= turbo_stream.replace(dom_id(@favorite.concert), @favorite.concert) %>
<%= turbo_stream.update("no-favorites") do %>
   
<% end %>
```

This code uses a set of helpers defined by turbo-rails and based off of turbo_stream: one helper for each action. The first argument is the target DOM ID for the Turbo Stream, and the remaining arguments are passed through to render. Anything you can do in a controller render you can do here. Alternately, the method can take a block, where the contents of the block are the children of the Turbo Stream, similar to how blocks work in other Rails helpers like form_with, link_to or content_tag.

In this case, we are using the append action to append one favorite view to the favorite-concerts-list. We are passing @favorite to use the default favorite partial view we've already created. Then we are using the replace action to overwrite the existing concert display given its new status as a favorite. Finally, we're taking out the text "No favorite concerts yet," because, by definition, there is now a favorite concert, so we're just passing a blank space to the div that displays that text.

The destroy file is similar:

```erb
chapter_02/04/app/views/favorites/destroy.turbo_stream.erb
<%= turbo_stream.remove(dom_id(@favorite)) %>
<%= turbo_stream.replace(dom_id(@favorite.concert), @favorite.concert) %>
<% if current_user.favorites.empty? %>
  <%= turbo_stream.update("no-favorites") do %>
    No favorite concerts yet
  <% end %>
<% end %>
```

The second part with the replacement is the same, but we're starting with a remove action to get the favorite version of the display off the page, and finishing by dynamically setting the "No favorite concerts yet" text if the user has no favorites after the removal.

And that, once again, is that. Reload the page and the Make Favorite and Remove Favorite buttons will work as expected.

Again, we have written zero lines of JavaScript and made only minor changes to our server-side Ruby.

Turbo Frames vs. Turbo Streams

A quick guide to the difference between Turbo Streams and Turbo Frames is shown on page 34.

Turbo Frames	Turbo Streams
A response can only change one DOM element.	A response can change an arbitrary number of DOM elements.
A response will update the inner HTML of the element.	A response can append, prepend, remove, replace, or update the affected elements.
The affected element must be a turbo-frame with the same DOM ID.	Affected elements can be any type of HTML with a matching DOM ID to the target of the stream.
Turbo Frames are evaluated on any navigation inside a turbo-frame element.	Turbo Streams are evaluated on form responses or ActionCable broadcasts.

Lazy Loading a Turbo Frame

Let's stretch this a little. Let's add one more feature: a count of the number of favorited items in the header. You can think of this as being broadly analogous to a shopping cart. And along the way, I'll show you one more Turbo feature: lazy loading.

Lazy loading allows us to separate the static and dynamic parts of a page so that the static part can be cached and the dynamic part automatically fills itself in when the page is loaded. If the dynamic part is slow, then this technique can also make the rest of the page appear faster and give the user a loading sign or something while the slow part of the page catches up.

To make this work, we want an entry in the navigation bar that is a placeholder for the favorites count:

```erb
chapter_02/05/app/views/layouts/_nav.html.erb
<div class="flex justify-items-end text-gray-300
            px-3 py-2 text-sm font-bold">
  <span>Favorite Count:</span>
  <%= turbo_frame_tag(
      "favorites-count-number",
      src: favorites_path(count_only: true)
    ) do %>
    <span id="favorites-count" class="ml-2">
      ?
    </span>
  <% end %>
</div>
```

There are two odd things about this. The first is that it doesn't actually display the favorites count; it just displays a question mark. (Which is mostly there so that it's clear that something is happening. In actual practice, I'd probably leave it blank or put in some kind of loading spinner.) The second is that we've added a src argument to the turbo_frame_tag helper, which results in a src="" attribute in the eventual <turbo-frame> tag.

When a turbo-frame has a src attribute, Turbo will automatically update the contents of the frame once by calling the src url. So the page will load with the question mark and then immediately call favorites_path(count_only: true) to fetch the contents of that frame.

We need to make the following minor change in the index method to allow for a count-only display. I'm justifying putting this in the index method on the maybe-dubious grounds that the count is a kind of display of the entire set of favorites. But if you wanted to create a FavoritesCount controller, that would work too.:

chapter_02/05/app/controllers/favorites_controller.rb
```ruby
def index
  if params[:count_only]
    render(partial: "favorites/count")
  end
end
```

That method calls a new partial if the count_only parameter is set:

chapter_02/05/app/views/favorites/_count.html.erb
```erb
<span>Favorite Count:</span>
<%= turbo_frame_tag("favorites-count-number") do %>
  <span id="favorites-count" class="ml-2">
    <%= current_user&.favorites&.count || 0 %>
  </span>
<% end %>
```

This partial has the same structure as the fragment from the nav partial except that it actually displays the favorites count. Critically, it has a Turbo Frame with a matching ID as the Turbo Frame in the navigation—favorites-count-number.

Also—and this is *very* important—this version of the tag does *not* have an src attribute set. If you fetch a version with an src attribute, Turbo will assume it is another lazy load, and will try to fetch it again. This can easily lead to an infinite loop where Turbo just continually fetches the same src. Ask me how I know that.

Anyway, the placeholder is loaded with the original page and then Turbo loads the real version. Then Turbo matches the Turbo Frame IDs, extracts the matching segment of the return, and replaces the placeholder version.

If you want the loading to be even lazier, adding the attribute loading=lazy will delay the turbo frame from fetching its source until the frame is actually visible. This is useful for menus or "more detail" frames that might be hidden on first page load.

To finish making this work, the update and delete turbo_frame.erb Turbo Streams also need to update this number. All both files need is the following call:

```
chapter_02/05/app/views/favorites/create.turbo_stream.erb
<%= turbo_stream.update(
    "favorites-count",
    plain: current_user.favorites.count
  ) %>
```

Here we're adding a Turbo Stream update call to the DOM ID favorites-count with just the text of the new value. If you look at the earlier code snippets, you'll see that favorites-count is just the inner span with the value, not the Turbo Frame. By using update instead of replace, we can just send the number rather than the entire HTML structure.

And again, this now works and we've still not written any JavaScript.

What's Next

In this chapter, we explored Turbo Frames and Turbo Streams and used them to add quite a bit of interactivity to our page without needing to write any custom JavaScript for our client side.

That can't go on forever. There's still some interactivity that's better to build on the client. This is where Stimulus comes in.

Stimulus

In the last chapter, we saw how Turbo allows us to build a lot of interactivity into a web application without any JavaScript. Still, some things can either only be done on the client, like animations, or are display-only changes that the server doesn't need to know about. For those, we turn to the other part of the Hotwire HTML story: Stimulus. Stimulus is a JavaScript tool that integrates with HTML and is particularly designed to adapt to new HTML as it changes the DOM, which means it's specifically good at dealing with the DOM changes that come from Turbo Frames or Turbo Streams.

In this chapter, we're going to use the Stimulus library to start adding features to our schedule page. Along the way, we'll explore Stimulus's basic concepts and then combine those concepts to build complex functionality into our app.

What Is Stimulus?

Stimulus is a tool with small goals.[1] Its own website describes it as "a modest JavaScript framework for the HTML you already have." Where React tries to replace your entire view layer, Stimulus allows you to handle a common JavaScript pattern quickly and without much extra complication. That pattern is, "an event happens, and I'd like to update the DOM in response to it."

Stimulus's main concepts simplify the process of creating the relationship between an event and the code that gets invoked in response. If you weren't using Stimulus, you'd likely try to handle these interactions with jQuery or just using native DOM methods without a framework at all. Stimulus, like Rails, was originally built by Basecamp, and has many convention-over-configuration design features that are reminiscent of the way Rails works.

---

1.   https://stimulus.hotwire.dev

Stimulus is particularly good for interactions that are relatively small and are expansions of existing browser capabilities. Stimulus is great at adding contained areas of interactivity to your application, like augmented forms, or simple navigation, and it works well as an enhancement to Turbo. We're going to use Stimulus here to implement our Show/Hide button, and we'll use it for filters and to support search within our page.

A few concepts in Stimulus describe how your HTML markup relates to your JavaScript code. All of these items are inserted into your application by adding specific data attributes to DOM elements in the HTML markup that you send to the browser. When the page is loaded, Stimulus looks for these special attributes and uses them to set up event listeners behind the scenes. These listeners dispatch events to the controller method specified in your actions.

Controllers

Controllers are where your Stimulus JavaScript code goes. They contain methods that are called in response to events that happen.

Actions

Actions declare that you are interested in having Stimulus do something in response to an event on the page.

Targets

Targets are DOM elements that are of interest to a controller, typically because the controller is using the element to determine the state of the page or because the controller is using the state of the page to change the element.

Data maps and values

Data maps and values are state that is stored in the DOM that is of interest to a controller. Stimulus allows you to declare the types of these values in your controller, though, as you'll see, doing so conflicts a little bit with TypeScript.

Classes

A common use of data maps and values is to represent CSS classes. Stimulus provides a special mechanism for managing updating CSS classes on DOM elements.

Stimulus and React represent two different sides of a long-standing debate over how to structure a web application. (We'll take a look at React in Chapter 4, React, on page 63.) Stimulus is of the opinion that a web application primarily is based on the server and the role of the client is to provide some interactivity, but on top of the markup that is rendered on the server. Stimulus makes extensive use of HTML markup to specify the interaction between HTML and JavaScript. This is unlike React, which uses its own JSX markup, and also unlike jQuery, which tries to keep JavaScript logic outside the HTML markup.

Installing Stimulus

We've already installed Stimulus as part of the hotwire-rails gem install. However, Stimulus depends on static class attributes, which are not a part of standard JavaScript. That works fine with the default setup if we were writing JavaScript, but in order to get the class attributes to run in TypeScript, we need to change the Babel setup in package.json to this:

```
"babel": {
    "presets": [
      [
        "./node_modules/@rails/webpacker/package/babel/preset.js"
      ],
      ["@babel/preset-typescript"]
    ]
  }
```

I'm honestly not 100 percent sure why this is necessary (the TypeScript preset is already loaded in the default file), but I think it might have something to do with the order in which presets are loaded.

Let's look at the code we have generated in the main pack file. (As I mentioned earlier, the default code generated by Rails and Webpacker is still not settled for Webpacker 6 as I write this, so your generated code might look different.)

```
chapter_03/01/app/packs/entrypoints/application.js
import "@hotwired/turbo-rails"
import "channels"
import "controllers"
import "core-js/stable"
import "regenerator-runtime/runtime"
import * as ActiveStorage from "@rails/activestorage"
import Rails from "@rails/ujs"

Rails.start()
ActiveStorage.start()
```

We haven't looked at this file closely yet; let's do so now. Because of how Webpacker works, this file creates a Webpacker pack called application, which we then use in our layout with the javascript_pack_tag helper.

Typically these top-level files in the packs are manifests that import and, in some cases, install libraries that the pack will use. In this case, application.js was generated by Rails and includes some Rails specific start-up.

A few standard libraries are imported:

- @rails/activestorage: ActiveStorage is the Rails library that handles file uploads. This library provides client-side support for upload-related activities. We're not going to be dealing with it in this book after this paragraph ends. The ActiveStorage.start() command turns on ActiveStorage.

- @rails/ujs: UJS stands for Unobtrusive JavaScript, which was a big buzzword phrase about JavaScript development around 2007. Somewhat oversimplified, "unobtrusive" relates to the practice of putting event handlers in separate JavaScript files rather than putting the event handlers directly in the HTML markup. At one time, this practice was uncommon; now it's ubiquitous. The Rails UJS library dates back to when Rails started to structure its normal client-side activities using unobtrusive principles. This library provides what you'd think of as normal Rails behavior, like Ajax calls when data-remote is true or alert boxes when data-confirm has a value. With Hotwire installed, the data-remote behavior is deprecated and shouldn't be used—it interferes with Turbo—but the data-confirm behavior is still available, as are some Ajax events it defines. If you don't already have legacy code using it, I'd recommend not relying on Rails UJS at all beyond the default features it provides and implementing its features with Hotwire. The Rails.start() command turns on UJS.

- @hotwired/turbo-rails: This is Turbo, which we just spent a chapter talking about (see Chapter 2, Hotwire and Turbo, on page 19).

- channels: Channels is the client-side portion of the ActionCable WebSockets framework. You'll see this in action later in Chapter 10, Immediate Communication with ActionCable, on page 187, when you learn how to use WebSockets and ActionCable to send information from the server to the live browser.

- "controllers": This is where we are putting our stimulus code.

- "core-js/stable": An npm module that includes *polyfills* for newer JS features. A polyfill is an implementation of a new feature so it can be used in browsers that don't support the feature.[2]

---

2. https://github.com/zloirock/core-js

- "regenerator-runtime": An npm module that is a polyfill for JavaScript's yield functionality.[3]

By calling import "controllers", we're assuming a module at app/packs/controllers. The import call automatically loads an index.js file in that directory if it exists, and that's where we're putting the Stimulus initialization code. I've made one change to the default file to have the pattern for the require statement support both .js and .ts files:

chapter_03/01/app/packs/controllers/index.js
```
import { Application } from "stimulus"
import { definitionsFromContext } from "stimulus/webpack-helpers"

const application = Application.start()
const context = require.context("controllers", true, /_controller\.[jt]s$/)
application.load(definitionsFromContext(context))
```

This starts the Stimulus application, and sets up an autoload, where any file in the controllers directory that ends in .js or .ts is loaded without needing to be explicitly imported by this file. As set up, we can write Stimulus controllers in JavaScript or TypeScript. We'll use TypeScript.

The default Hotwire install added a sample controller at app/packs/controllers/hello_controller.js, which I have deleted.

Stimulus uses static class-level variables, which is a newer JavaScript feature that the Babel JavaScript preprocessor needs to know about. This is all taken care of by the default babel preset in the package.json file, but you should look at the Stimulus installation instructions if you are not using the default preset.[4]

Okay, we're now ready to write some Stimulus code.

Adding Our First Controller

The first thing we're going to do with Stimulus is make a Show/Hide button that will toggle the contents of the favorite concerts block on our page.

The bulk of your Stimulus code will go into a *controller*, which is similar to your Rails controller in that it's where the responses to events are stored, but different in that there's much less structure and fewer expectations around a Stimulus controller than a Rails controller.

---

3. http://facebook.github.io/regenerator/
4. https://stimulus.hotwire.dev/handbook/installing

To invoke a controller, we add an attribute named data-controller to a DOM element on your page. The value of the attribute is the name of the controller. If we added an attribute data-controller="toggle", then Stimulus attaches it to a ToggleController, which it expects will be at controllers/toggle_controller.ts (or .js).

If the controller's name is more than one word, you use dash case, so it would be fancy-color, not fancyColor. The controller has the same scope as the DOM element it's attached to. This means that any events you want dispatched to the controller need to happen inside the controller's DOM element. Any elements you designate as targets for the controller also need to be inside the controller's DOM element.

In our app we want to have a Show/Hide button, so we want to be able to press the button, hide the list of favorite concerts, and change the text of the button. This means our Stimulus controller needs to be attached to a DOM element that encompasses both the button and all the favorite concerts.

Happily, we have such a DOM element. It's the parent <section> element in our favorites/_list partial. We want to give it a data-controller attribute:

chapter_03/01/app/views/favorites/_list.html.erb
```erb
<section class="my-4"
         data-controller="favorite-toggle">
```

Here we are adding the DOM attribute data-controller and giving it the value favorite-toggle. By itself this doesn't do much. But when the page is loaded, Stimulus will look for a matching controller. Using convention over configuration, that controller should be in the file app/javascript/controllers/favorite_toggle_controller.ts.

Here's a basic controller that doesn't do anything yet:

chapter_03/01/app/packs/controllers/favorite_toggle_controller.ts
```ts
import { Controller } from "stimulus"

export default class FavoriteToggleController extends Controller {
  connect(): void {
    console.log("The controller is connected")
  }
}
```

The first line uses ES6 module syntax to import the Controller class from the stimulus module. We will talk about this more in Chapter 7, webpack, on page 133, but for now, just know that using webpack allows this import statement to be reconciled against the Stimulus module living in our node_modules directory.

Next we declare our class, again using ES6 module keywords. The export keyword means that the thing about to be defined is publicly visible to other files that might import this file. The default keyword means the thing about to be defined is the default item exported if the importing module does not specify what it wants.

Inside the class, we define one method: connect(): void. Don't get too attached to it because we're not going to keep it. The connect() method is automatically called by Stimulus when a controller is instantiated and connected to a DOM element. I included it here only to allow us to see that the controllers are, in fact, instantiated when the page is reloaded. The :void is our first part of TypeScript-specific syntax and just tells TypeScript that the connect method doesn't return a value. (TypeScript can actually figure that out for itself, but it prevents some errors if you get in the habit of specifying whether or not you expect a return value in the function declaration.)

Okay, reload the page and look at the browser console. You'll see that the message has been printed to the console.

The Stimulus library searches the DOM for data-controller attributes, and every time it finds one, it attempts to find a matching controller for it using the name of the controller to find the matching file. This is true no matter when the DOM is changed; Stimulus connects on initial page load, and it also recognizes DOM changes once the page has loaded, no matter what the source of the change is.

At this point it's worth making a couple of points that aren't necessarily important now but are important to keep in the back of your mind because of the way they will inform how we structure Stimulus code going forward.

First, you can declare the same controller an arbitrary number of times in a single document. You can use the same name over and over again to get separate instances of the same controller. You can even have the same controller nested inside itself:

```
<div data-controller="thing">
  <div data-controller="thing">
  </div>
</div>
```

This works just fine—anything declared as part of a thing controller is connected to its nearest matching ancestor in the DOM tree.

Also important to keep in mind is that a single element can be attached to multiple controllers, separated by spaces:

```
<div data-controller="color size shape">
</div>
```

This element instantiates three different controllers: ColorController, SizeController, and ShapeController (assuming the controllers have actually been defined in app/packs/controllers). Inside the element, targets and actions can be directed at any of the controllers.

These two features make Stimulus great for small, generic, composable controllers.

Controllers are great, but they don't do much on their own; they need to be attached to actions.

Creating an Action

In Stimulus, an *action* is what connects a DOM event to the controller code that you want executed when that event happens. Like controllers, Stimulus actions are defined using a data attribute in the markup: you add the attribute to the DOM element whose events you want to watch. In our case, we want to add a button that says "Hide":

```
chapter_03/02/app/views/favorites/_list.html.erb
<div class="text-3xl font-bold">
  Favorite Concerts
  <button class="<%= SimpleForm.button_class %> py-1 text-xl font-semibold"
          data-action="click->favorite-toggle#toggle">
    Hide
  </button>
</div>
```

The new line defining the actions is data-action="click->favorite-toggle#toggle". The data-action is the attribute name that signals to Stimulus that an action is being defined. The value of the data-action attribute is a mini-language to define the connection between the event and the code.

The mini-language, which Stimulus calls an *action descriptor*, has three parts:

- The first element is the name of the event being watched for, which in our case is click, followed by an arrow (->).

- The second element is the name of the controller, spelled exactly the way the name is spelled where the controller is defined, meaning that it's dash-case. For us, that's favorite-toggle. This element ends with a hashtag (#).

- The last element is the name of the method to be called on the controller when the event happens. This needs to be the exact name of the method, which usually means it's in camelCase. (I'm not sure why Stimulus chooses not to translate from dash-case to camelCase here). Our method name is toggle.

This is a three-part sentence of action, controller, and method. When Stimulus sees a data-action attribute, it sets up a listener on the event, which executes the named method on the controller when the event fires. If there are multiple instances of controllers with that name, the instance representing the closest ancestor to the element triggering the event is the instance that executes the method.

Default Events

I don't recommend it, but Stimulus allows you to leave off the event name for the "default" event of specific elements. If your element is a, button, or input[type="submit"], then the default action is click, and you can respond to a click event with just the controller name and method, as in "day-toggle#toggle". If the element is any other kind of input, a select, or a textarea, then the default event is change, and for a form, the default event is submit. I find the consistency of keeping the event around to be worth the extra typing, however.

Having created an action descriptor that references a toggle method, we need to write a corresponding toggle method in our controller:

chapter_03/02/app/packs/controllers/favorite_toggle_controller.ts

```
import { Controller } from "stimulus"

export default class FavoriteToggleController extends Controller {
  toggle(): void {
    console.log("Click!")
  }
}
```

Here we removed the connect method and replaced it with a toggle that similarly writes to the console. Now if you reload the page, clicking the new Hide button for favorites will cause the output to be written to the console. This is nice but isn't quite what we're hoping for. What we need is a way to identify the DOM element we want to hide. We can use DOM IDs for that, but Stimulus gives us a shortcut: targets.

Stimulus Action Names

Before we get to targets, there are a couple more useful facts about Stimulus actions. First, the event name in the action descriptor can be anything you want, including custom events. Custom events can be a useful way to communicate between controllers. You can also capture global events on the window or document by adding @window or @document, as in ready@document. Typically you'd add these global descriptors to the same DOM element that the controller is defined in.

Second, as with controllers, you can define multiple actions on the same DOM element by adding multiple event descriptors to the same attribute, separated by spaces. This is quite common and is a great way to split up behavior into small controllers and small methods. One nice feature is that if you have multiple responses to the same event, Stimulus guarantees the controller methods will be invoked in the same order the action descriptors are displayed, which allows you to rely on the behavior of the first method already having taken place when you call the second method.

We don't show it in our toggle method, but Stimulus does pass one argument to the methods it calls. For TypeScript purposes, this argument is of type CustomEvent, and it allows you access to the target, which is the element that actually hosted the event, and the currentTarget, which is the element that contains the data-action attribute. The two might differ if, say, the click actually happened on an element nested within the element with the data-action. You also have access to normal DOM event methods, such as preventDefault() and stopPropagation().

Adding a Target

In client-side coding, it is fairly common to have to mark a particular DOM element as being of interest to the code. Typically this means either you are reading the DOM element's state to determine what to do or you are changing the DOM element's state as a result of some other event. In our case, it's the latter: we want to add the DOM class hidden to an element to hide it, and eventually we want to change the text of the button itself.

In a world without a framework, or in jQuery world, we would identify these elements using a DOM ID or DOM class. However, because those DOM attributes are also used to manage CSS styling, it can be confusing as to what DOM ID or class elements are styling and which are used by JavaScript.

Stimulus allows you to explicitly identify DOM elements of interest by marking them as *targets*. A target is identified using a specially named attribute of the format data-<controller name>-target attribute on a DOM element. The value of the attribute is the name of the target. Target names need to be in camelCase in the HTML attribute.

Our target element is the element we want to hide. In this case, that's the body of the list, which is currently not its own div element. Let's make it so:

chapter_03/03/app/views/favorites/_list.html.erb
```erb
<div data-favorite-toggle-target="elementToHide">
  <div class="text-xl font-bold" id="no-favorites">
    <% if current_user.favorites.empty? %>
      No favorite concerts yet
    <% end %>
  </div>
  <div id="favorite-concerts-list">
    <% current_user.favorites.each do |favorite| %>
      <%= render(favorite) %>
    <% end %>
  </div>
</div>
```

We've surrounded the display with a div element that we have given a target attribute of data-favorite-toggle-target="elementToHide". This attribute declaration sets up the FavoriteToggle controller to have a target named elementToHide.

That declaration sets up the target on the HTML side, but we also need to declare the target in the controller, and the mechanism is a little different depending on whether you are using TypeScript or JavaScript. Here's the way it works in TypeScript:

chapter_03/03/app/packs/controllers/favorite_toggle_controller.ts
```ts
import { Controller } from "stimulus"

export default class FavoriteToggleController extends Controller {
  static targets = ["elementToHide"]

  elementToHideTarget: HTMLElement

  toggle(): void {
    this.elementToHideTarget.classList.toggle("hidden")
  }
}
```

Stimulus requires that any targets in use from the controller need to be declared in a static variable called targets, as in our line static targets = ["elementToHide"]. Once that declaration is in place, Stimulus defines three properties on the controller you can use:

- targetNameTarget (as in elementToHideTarget): This property returns the first DOM element in the scope of the controller that declares this target. If there is no such element, accessing the property raises an exception.

- targetNameTargets (as in elementToHideTargets): This property returns an array of all the DOM elements in the scope of the controller that declare this target.

- hastargetNameTarget (as in hasElementToHideTarget): This property returns a Boolean value—true if there is a elementToHideTarget, false otherwise. You'd typically use this method to avoid the exception raised by elementToHideTarget.

As with other Stimulus features, a DOM element can declare multiple target descriptors, separated by a space, and multiple DOM elements can declare the same target name, in which case you use the plural version of the property to access all of them.

If you are using TypeScript—and only if you are using TypeScript—you need to declare any of these properties that you plan on using so that the TypeScript compiler knows they are there. This is a pain and removes some of the convenience of having the properties automatically defined. We do this with the line elementToHideTarget: HTMLElement, which is a TypeScript-visible declaration of the property. Perhaps someday, Stimulus will do these declarations automatically.

It's worth taking a moment here to say that these TypeScript lines declare what the properties of the class are and what type they are. If we attempt to invoke a property of a class that's either not defined in this list or is a method in the class body, such as this.banana, TypeScript will flag that nonexistent property and won't compile. Further, if we attempt to use one of the properties we have declared but call a nonexistent property on them, such as this.filterButton.flavor, TypeScript will also flag that as an error. Since the file has a .ts extension, our Webpacker build will compile it using the TypeScript compiler, which ensures that we use the types as declared. We'll talk more about this in Chapter 6, TypeScript, on page 115.

The rest of our controller now implements the toggle method to use the elementToHideTarget and change its class list to swap in and out the hidden Tailwind CSS class. At this point, if you load the page, it will work, and the Hide button of the favorites will work to hide the selection but doesn't yet change the text.

Yay for Stimulus!

 I want to take a moment here to point out that we've written this in about two lines of code, and we didn't have to deal with event listeners or do anything particularly special to get it to work.

Using Values

Our code is pretty simple so far, but it's still missing a bit of functionality. We're not yet changing the text of the button from "Hide" to "Show." On a more structural level, we don't have a place in the code that explicitly stores the state of the button. We have to infer the state from the presence or absence of the hidden class, which is not a terrible thing to have to do, but it's better to explicitly have the state of the controller available.

We can do all of these things using another Stimulus concept: *values*. In Stimulus, values are a bit of syntactic sugar that allows us to use data attributes to store data that is specifically associated with a controller, and gives the controller some methods to manipulate that data directly without dealing with the DOM dataset itself.

To declare a value, we use a similar pattern to what we've been using for targets. The attribute name itself has multiple parts: data-, the dash-case controller name followed by another hyphen (-), the name of the attribute, then -value.

We want to start with one data HTML attribute for the visibility state of the element. This means our attribute name will be data-day-toggle-visible-value. Note that in this case, the attribute name is in dash-case in the HTML but will be camelCase in the JavaScript.

You typically add the value attributes to the same DOM element that declares the controller, though technically they can be attached to any DOM element inside the controller. Most of the time you want them with the controller declaration so that the data references are easy to find. That gives us:

```
chapter_03/04/app/views/favorites/_list.html.erb
<section class="my-4"
         data-controller="favorite-toggle"
         data-favorite-toggle-visible-value="true">
```

In our case, a "visible" value, where visible is true, means that the target is not hidden.

To use values, we also have to declare them in our controller. Again, sigh, twice. The declaration is another static property, values, but rather than an array like the other ones we've seen, the values property contains an object with the type of each individual value we want to use; at the moment ours looks like this:

```
chapter_03/04/app/packs/controllers/favorite_toggle_controller.ts
static values = { visible: Boolean }
visibleValue: boolean
```

The key in this object visible means we've declared a visible value in the markup, and the Boolean means we expect the visible value to be a Boolean, so Stimulus will automatically convert the string value to a Boolean one.

The types that Stimulus makes available are Array, Boolean, Number, Object, and String. Boolean and Number are converted from the string using the toString method, while Array and Object are converted using JSON.stringify. If a value isn't specified, the default is an empty object, array, or string; the number 0; or Boolean false.

Declaring a value gives you three properties, similar to what we've seen for targets and classes. For the singular (non-array) properties, there's a property, <valueName>Value, that can be used as a getter and also as a setter, as in visibleValue = true. There's also an has<valueName>Value, which returns true or false depending on whether the attribute is actually present in the DOM. The array properties are the same but plural: <valueName>Values and has<valueName>Values.

These properties need to be declared in TypeScript, so we'd have visibleValue: boolean. Yes, Stimulus capitalizes Boolean in its type declaration and TypeScript doesn't.

Here's how we might use the value in our controller to change the button text. We want to take the element whose text we want to change and also make it a target:

```
chapter_03/04/app/views/favorites/_list.html.erb
<button class="<%= SimpleForm.button_class %> py-1 text-xl font-semibold"
        data-favorite-toggle-target="elementWithText"
        data-action="click->favorite-toggle#toggle">
  Hide
</button>
```

The controller looks like this:

```
chapter_03/04/app/packs/controllers/favorite_toggle_controller.ts
import { Controller } from "stimulus"

export default class FavoriteToggleController extends Controller {
  static targets = ["elementToHide", "elementWithText"]
  elementToHideTarget: HTMLElement
  elementWithTextTarget: HTMLElement

  static values = { visible: Boolean }
  visibleValue: boolean
```

```
connect(): void {
  this.updateHiddenClass()
  this.updateText()
}

toggle(): void {
  this.flipState()
  this.updateHiddenClass()
  this.updateText()
}

flipState(): void {
  this.visibleValue = !this.visibleValue
}

updateHiddenClass(): void {
  this.elementToHideTarget.classList.toggle("hidden", !this.visibleValue)
}

newText(): string {
  return this.visibleValue ? "Hide" : "Show"
}

updateText(): void {
  this.elementWithTextTarget.innerText = this.newText()
}
}
```

The code has gotten a lot longer, in part because I've been a little aggressive about splitting off small methods, but it's only a small step more complex than the last version.

We start by declaring two targets: the button text and the element to hide. We also declare one Stimulus value, visible, and its associated TypeScript property visibleValue.

Our action method is toggle, which does three things: flip the state, update the hidden class, and update the text. We need to flip the state first because the target and text change depend on the new state.

The flipState method uses the value to set the visibility value of the button to its Boolean opposite. The updateHiddenClass method uses the class list method toggle in its two-argument form, meaning that the class name will be added to the class list if the second argument, this.visibleValue, is true, and removed otherwise. The updateText method similarly sets the innerText of that DOM element to "Show" or "Hide" based on whether the toggle is active.

Finally, we're using the connect method to ensure that the initial state of the toggle is valid. The connect method adjusts the target and the text based on the initial state of the active data map key—since connect doesn't also call flipState, the state as it's specified in the markup is the basis of the initial adjustment to the target and text. By using connect, we could start the controller in the hidden state by changing the initial value of data-favorite-toggle-active-value to false in the markup.

And now we have a working button that changes both the show/hide behavior and the text of the button.

Automating Value Changes

Another useful feature of the Stimulus Values API is that the API includes a callback method called <value name>Changed, which is automatically called after a Stimulus value is changed. In other words, we could rewrite our toggle controller as follows:

chapter_03/05/app/packs/controllers/favorite_toggle_controller.ts

```
import { Controller } from "stimulus"

export default class FavoriteToggleController extends Controller {
  static targets = ["elementToHide", "elementWithText"]
  elementToHideTarget: HTMLElement
  elementWithTextTarget: HTMLElement

  static values = { visible: Boolean }
  visibleValue: boolean

  toggle(): void {
    this.flipState()
  }

  flipState(): void {
    this.visibleValue = !this.visibleValue
  }

  visibleValueChanged(): void {
    this.updateHiddenClass()
    this.updateText()
  }

  updateHiddenClass(): void {
    this.elementToHideTarget.classList.toggle("hidden", !this.visibleValue)
  }

  newText(): string {
    return this.visibleValue ? "Hide" : "Show"
  }

  updateText(): void {
    this.elementWithTextTarget.innerText = this.newText()
  }
}
```

Now the flipState() method automatically causes visibleValueChanged to be invoked because it changes the value of visibleValue. Inside that method we adjust the target and text. What's nice about this mechanism is that it will keep the target and text in sync with the value no matter where in the controller we change it—if we change the value outside the controller, we still have to separately manage the other changes.

An especially cool feature of using the changed mechanism is that it operates even if the DOM data element is changed directly. You can show this in the JavaScript console. Reload the page, then in the JavaScript console type the following:

```
> fav = fav = document.querySelector("[data-controller=favorite-toggle]")
    <THE ELEMENT>
> fav.dataset.favoriteToggleVisibleValue = "false"
    "False"
```

When you enter the second line, Stimulus will notice the DOM change, trigger the visibleValueChanged method, and hide the Favorites section. What's nice about this ability is that it means that Stimulus controllers can cascade effects just by changing data attributes in other elements. This gives us very reactive behavior, where we can redraw the DOM automatically in response to the state of the data changing.

Any changed method that you have in the controller is automatically called when the controller is initialized using either the initial value given in the markup or the default, which is why we were able to remove our connect method and still get our startup behavior.

Stimulus Has Class

In our current code we are using the hidden CSS class to denote hidden status, and we are hard-coding the class name inside our controller. For a short class name like hidden, that's unlikely to change. That's not really a big deal, but it's better practice to not tightly couple the class name to the controller and specify the exact CSS classes only in the view. Eventually, we'll want our controller to have more generic behavior.

Stimulus has a mechanism for this, where we can store the class name as a special data attribute. Essentially, this is a special case of the values attributes. The name of the data attribute has the form data-<controllerName>-<descriptor>-class, and the value of the attribute is the name of the CSS class being described—typically you'd use a descriptor that describes the role of the CSS class. These class descriptors are usually added to the same DOM element as the controller.

Note this currently doesn't work very well with utility CSS tools like Tailwind, where you are likely to have a set of CSS classes rather than a single one, but there is an unreleased change to Stimulus that has already been made, so I expect the set behavior may be available by the time you read this.

What we do is use a special attribute to register the CSS class in the DOM:

```
chapter_03/06/app/views/favorites/_list.html.erb
<section class="my-4"
         data-controller="favorite-toggle"
         data-favorite-toggle-visible-value="true"
         data-favorite-toggle-hidden-class="hidden">
```

Here we have a new attribute, data-favorite-toggle-hidden-class, with

- data
- The controller name: favorite-toggle
- A description of the role of the class: hidden
- class

As with targets, we have to declare the class in the controller and we get a getter and an existence property. Then we can use those properties in place of the hard-coded class.

Our new version of the controllers looks like this:

```
chapter_03/06/app/packs/controllers/favorite_toggle_controller.ts
import { Controller } from "stimulus"

export default class FavoriteToggleController extends Controller {
  static classes = ["hidden"]
  hiddenClass: string

  static targets = ["elementToHide", "elementWithText"]
  elementToHideTarget: HTMLElement
  elementWithTextTarget: HTMLElement

  static values = { visible: Boolean }
  visibleValue: boolean

  toggle(): void {
    this.flipState()
  }

  flipState(): void {
    this.visibleValue = !this.visibleValue
  }
```

```
visibleValueChanged(): void {
  this.updateHiddenClass()
  this.updateText()
}
updateHiddenClass(): void {
  this.elementToHideTarget.classList.toggle(
    this.hiddenClass,
    !this.visibleValue
  )
}
newText(): string {
  return this.visibleValue ? "Hide" : "Show"
}
updateText(): void {
  this.elementWithTextTarget.innerText = this.newText()
}
}
```

We added a new static declaration of our known classes, static classes = ["hidden"], and, alas, the associated TypeScript declaration hiddenClass: string. Stimulus creates a hasHiddenClass: boolean property that we're not using in this example. Then, in our updateHiddenClass method, we can replace the direct usage of hidden with the indirect reference to this.hiddenClass and everything works as before. (By the time you read this, there will probably also be a hiddenClasses plural that returns a space-delimited list of classes.)

Why would you do this since it seems to be making the code slightly more complex? There are a few reasons:

- The code is now decoupled from the CSS class name, so if the CSS class name changes, the code doesn't have to also change. This makes it harder to have a bug because you forgot to change the name somewhere.

- The CSS class name is now in the view, which is valuable if you have designers who don't want to deal with JavaScript working on the app.

- The CSS class name is now in the view, which means it's controlled by Rails. Which also means it's much easier to have a dynamic CSS class name, for example, if the CSS class name depended on internationalization or some other property of the Rails side of the site.

In addition to all of those reasons, being able to put all this data in the markup allows us to have generic, reusable Stimulus controllers. In much the same way Turbo allows us to add a lot of functionality without writing much custom JavaScript, writing generic Stimulus controllers can allow us to add a lot of functionality without adding a lot of custom JavaScript.

Going Generic

In our case, what do generic Stimulus controllers look like?

What we have now is one controller that responds to a click by showing or hiding a target element and by changing the text of a target.

Let's think a bit more abstractly, and what we have here are two separate actions that respond to a click: one that adds and removes a CSS class and one that changes the text of a button. we're going to split those into two separate controllers to show how Stimulus allows for composition of small, generic pieces of action.

Now, there's an obvious downside here, which is that the code and the HTML are going to get more verbose. Let's look at the code and then talk about the upsides.

Both the generic Stimulus controllers are mostly subsets of our previous controller. Here's the text one:

```
chapter_03/07/app/packs/controllers/text_controller.ts
import { Controller } from "stimulus"

export default class TextController extends Controller {
  static targets = ["elementWithText"]
  elementWithTextTarget: HTMLElement

  static values = { status: Boolean, on: String, off: String }
  offValue: string
  onValue: string
  statusValue: boolean

  toggle(): void {
    this.flipState()
  }

  flipState(): void {
    this.statusValue = !this.statusValue
  }

  statusValueChanged(): void {
    this.updateText()
  }

  newText(): string {
    return this.statusValue ? this.onValue : this.offValue
  }

  updateText(): void {
    this.elementWithTextTarget.innerText = this.newText()
  }
}
```

We've got three values: the status of the controller, text for when the status is "on," and text for when the status is "off." When the status changes, the "on" text is used if the status is true; otherwise, the "off" text is used. Both the text values are expected to be defined in the HTML markup as data attributes.

The CSS controller is similar:

chapter_03/07/app/packs/controllers/css_controller.ts
```typescript
import { Controller } from "stimulus"

export default class CssController extends Controller {
  static classes = ["css"]
  cssClass: string

  static targets = ["elementToChange"]
  elementToChangeTarget: HTMLElement

  static values = { status: Boolean }
  statusValue: boolean

  toggle(): void {
    this.flipState()
  }

  flipState(): void {
    this.statusValue = !this.statusValue
  }

  statusValueChanged(): void {
    this.updateCssClass()
  }

  updateCssClass(): void {
    for (const oneCssClass of this.cssClass.split(" ")) {
      this.elementToChangeTarget.classList.toggle(
        oneCssClass,
        this.statusValue
      )
    }
  }
}
```

The CSS controller only expects one value to add or remove that value, but it allows the value to be multiple CSS classes separated by a space. The updateCssClass method splits the value and adjusts the CSS list for each entry. (Again, a future version of Stimulus will likely do this for us.)

Now we can do a lot just in our HTML without writing more JavaScript. Here's what the Show/Hide button looks like in the favorites list:

```
chapter_03/07/app/views/favorites/_list.html.erb
<%= turbo_frame_tag("favorite-concerts") do %>
  <section class="my-4"
           data-controller="css"
           data-css-css-class="hidden"
           data-css-status-value="false">
    <div class="text-3xl font-bold">
      Favorite Concerts
      <button class="<%= SimpleForm.button_class %> py-1 text-xl font-semibold"
              data-favorite-toggle-target="elementWithText"
              data-controller="text"
              data-text-target="elementWithText"
              data-text-status-value="false"
              data-text-off-value="Hide"
              data-text-on-value="Show"
              data-action="click->css#toggle click->text#toggle">
        Hide
      </button>
    </div>
    <div data-css-target="elementToChange">
      <div class="text-xl font-bold" id="no-favorites">
        <% if current_user.favorites.empty? %>
          No favorite concerts yet
        <% end %>
      </div>
      <div id="favorite-concerts-list">
        <% current_user.favorites.each do |favorite| %>
          <%= render(favorite) %>
        <% end %>
      </div>
    </div>
  </section>
<% end %>
```

The outer section declares the css controller and specifies that it will use hidden
as the class to toggle. The inner span for the actual button declares the text
controller, the off value of "Hide," and the on value of "Show." The button also
declares itself as the target of the text controller, meaning it is the element
whose text changes, and it declares that clicking on it triggers the toggle action
in both the CSS and text controllers. Below, the div surrounding the actual
value declares itself the target of the CSS controller, meaning it is the element
that gets the hidden class added and removed from it. One other change here
is that the button does not actually have HTML text in it—the Stimulus controller will call its statusValueChanged method when it connects and will set the
text for us.

This works, and we can now adapt it around the page.

We can add a similar structure to the buttons for each day of the schedule, allowing those to be shown or hidden:

```erb
chapter_03/07/app/views/schedule_days/_schedule_day.html.erb
<section data-controller="css"
         data-css-css-class="hidden"
         data-css-status-value="false">
  <h2 class="text-3xl font-bold">
    <%= schedule_day.day.by_example("Monday, January 2, 2006") %>
    <span class="<%= SimpleForm.button_class %> py-1 text-xl font-semibold"
          data-controller="text"
          data-text-target="elementWithText"
          data-text-status-value="false"
          data-text-off-value="Hide Day"
          data-text-on-value="Show Day"
          data-action="click->css#toggle click->text#toggle">
    </span>
  </h2>
  <% if show %>
    <section data-css-target="elementToChange">
      <% schedule_day.concerts.sort_by(&:start_time).each do |concert| %>
        <%= render(concert) %>
      <% end %>
    </section>
  <% end %>
</section>
```

This has nearly the same structure, with an outer element declaring the CSS controller and an inner button declaring the text controller and the actions. This now also works, with no additional JavaScript.

The calendar dates at the top of the page are meant to be part of a filter system that we'll define more in Chapter 11, Managing State in Stimulus Code, on page 211. But we do want to be able to show whether the filter is active with, say, a red border:

```erb
chapter_03/07/app/views/schedules/show.html.erb
<div class="text-center border-b-2 border-transparent"
     data-controller="css"
     data-css-css-class="border-red-700"
     data-css-status-value="false"
     data-css-target="elementToChange"
     data-action="click->css#toggle">
  <%= schedule_day.day.by_example("Jan 2") %>
</div>
```

This element declares the CSS controller, with a CSS class of border-red-700, and it declares itself the target and the action. And now, clicking on one of those dates gives you a thin red border. Again, no new JavaScript.

The benefit of these small, generic controllers is that a very large amount of common, boilerplate interactions can be added to your site without any new JavaScript. This approach isn't perfect. You might not like the use of data attributes, though I find I like the explicitness of them. Stimulus doesn't currently support two instances of the same controller on the same element, so if you have multiple CSS actions on the same element, that's going to be more complicated (nested elements might also be a problem). Like a lot of the Rails aesthetic, the goal here is to be able to do simple, common things with little to no code so that you can focus your code and time more precisely on the complex and uncommon things.

Stimulus Quick Reference

Stimulus is small, but the conventions need to be hit exactly for it to work. I find that a short, quick reference table helps a lot. The basics of Stimulus can fit in the simple table that follows, with the naming conventions mimicking the expected case of the value.

Item	Attribute	Naming Convention
Controller	data-controller	controller-name
Action	data-action	event->controller-name#method-Name
Target	data-controller-name-target	targetName
Value	data-controller-name-attribute-name-value	value
Class	data-controller-name-description-class	value

And some notes on semantics:

- A controller declared as controller-name assumes the existence of a file app/packs/controller/controller_name_controller.ts (or .js), which exports a class that extends Stimulus's Controller class.

- An action assumes the existence of methodName on the associated controller, and that method is invoked when the event is triggered.

- A target needs to be declared in a static variable array of strings called targets in the associated controller. Doing so creates three methods: targetNameTarget, targetNameTargets, and hasTargetName. In TypeScript, those methods need to be declared as properties before use.

- Value attributes are usually declared with their associated controller. Values need to be declared in a static object of strings and data types called values in the associated controller. Doing so creates valueNameValue,

valueNameValue=, and hasValueNameValue (or for arrays: valueNameValues, value-NameValues=, and hasValueNameValues).

- Class attributes are usually declared with their associated controller. Classes need to be declared in a static variable array of strings called classes in the associated controller. Doing so creates classNameClass and hasClassNameClass properties. (By the time you read this, there may also be classNameClasses, which is an array of the space-delimited class names).

What's Next

Stimulus is a small framework that can help make it easier to insert relatively simple JavaScript interactions into a project. We'll explore more complex interactions in later chapters. First, though, let's look at a bigger library—React—and see what it can do for us in our Rails application.

React

React has emerged as the most popular of the current JavaScript frameworks. It has a huge user base and a large ecosystem. Structurally, React is the polar opposite of Stimulus. It is more complex, and its design reflects fundamentally different assumptions about how best to manage state and logic in a JavaScript program. Specifically, a React application expects to get data from the server and manages state and HTML by managing the DOM on the client using a custom HTML-generation language called JSX.

For our purposes in this book, we will only use a fraction of React's capabilities; our focus here will be on using React to support interactivity on a single page while working with our Rails application. We will not focus on using React for a single-page application. A single-page application is a perfectly reasonable thing to write in some circumstances, but it is more complex and less likely to benefit from Rails as the back end. We're going show simpler use cases.

All of this is to say that there are many, many opinions on how to write and structure React apps, and I'm not going to attempt to catalog them all here. This is one way to write React applications for Rails, but it's not meant to be *the* way.

What Is React?

React is a JavaScript client-side framework that allows you to enhance HTML markup with custom JavaScript to allow for complex user interactions.[1] React uses a mini-language called JSX to allow you to write HTML-style markup inside your JavaScript or TypeScript code.

---

1.   https://reactjs.org

React is designed using a fundamentally different model of interaction than Stimulus. Stimulus is designed to allow you to add interactivity to HTML markup that you are already writing or have already written. In React, the markup is written using React's own JSX language, and React completely controls what is written to the DOM within its boundaries.

The two tools also handle internal state differently. In Stimulus, we keep state using the DOM itself or on the server and are responsible for updating the page when state changes. In React, state is kept within the React system. When state changes, the React run-time loop updates the DOM automatically to reflect the new state.

React's approach to displaying values is called *declarative* or *reactive*. Both terms refer to the same process. When it comes to displaying information in React, it is the developer's job to declare in code what the output should look like and the system's job to react to changes in values by redrawing the page.

React manages this process by maintaining its own virtual DOM and using that virtual DOM to update only the parts of the actual DOM that change when a state value changes. However, in order to allow the DOM to automatically change, React needs to be made aware when you change a value that is relevant to the display in the browser. Because of this, you can only change state in React using specific functions provided by the framework, which trigger the resulting browser display changes. As we'll see, React allows you to declare a specific value as being part of the changeable state, and when you do so, React provides you with a custom setter function that changes that value. When you use these setter functions, React notices the state change and updates the parts of the DOM that are affected by the change in values.

Most of the code you write in React will be in a *component*. A React component is a function that behaves something like a template, combining data with markup written using JSX that results in the HTML that is sent to the DOM. As we'll see, JSX allows you to mix JavaScript logic with HTML tags and calls to other React components.

Let's install React and then talk more about components and JSX.

Installing React

We're going to use React to build up the individual pages for each concert. These pages will contain a seating diagram and will allow you to put together a ticket order. Normally I wouldn't use Stimulus and React in the same app—I'd pick one and stick with that choice—but it's far from the most ridiculous thing I've ever done in an app, and I decided that keeping them together would be less confusing than trying to keep track of separate Stimulus and React apps.

Webpacker is already set up to handle React if React's webpack loader is set up, so let's do that:

```
$ yarn add react react-dom @babel/preset-react @types/react @types/react-dom
```

This command adds several packages to the package.json file. In addition to the react package, we get react-dom, which contains React's DOM-specific features. We get a Babel package, which allows our build to compile JSX files. We also get the @types packages, which contain TypeScript definitions for React and React-DOM (we'll talk more about what these modules contain in Chapter 14, Validating Code with Advanced TypeScript, on page 269).

We need to change the tsconfig.json file to include the line

```
"jsx": "react",
```

which makes that file look like this:

chapter_04/01/tsconfig.json
```
{
  "compilerOptions": {
    "declaration": false,
    "emitDecoratorMetadata": true,
    "experimentalDecorators": true,
    "lib": ["es6", "dom"],
    "jsx": "react",
    "module": "es6",
    "moduleResolution": "node",
    "baseUrl": ".",
    "paths": {
      "*": ["node_modules/*", "app/packs/*"]
    },
    "sourceMap": true,
    "target": "es5",
    "noEmit": true
  },
  "exclude": ["**/*.spec.ts", "node_modules", "vendor", "public"],
  "compileOnSave": false
}
```

I want to make a couple of additional changes here. We've been using ESLint in the background to allow for style checking and format consistency in our TypeScript code. We'd like to have that for our React code as well. There's a ESLint extension for React, which we can add with yarn add --dev eslint-plugin-react, and there's an associated change to the .eslintrc.js file:

```
chapter_04/01/.eslintrc.js
module.exports = {
  parser: "@typescript-eslint/parser",
  extends: [
    "eslint:recommended",
    "plugin:react/recommended",
    "plugin:@typescript-eslint/recommended",
    "prettier/@typescript-eslint",
    "plugin:prettier/recommended",
  ],
  env: {
    browser: true,
    es6: true,
    amd: true,
  },
  parserOptions: {
    ecmaVersion: 2018,
    sourceType: "module",
  },
}
```

Adding Our First Component

Let's take a second and talk about what we are going to use React to do. The concert display page was quietly part of our original Rails app, but we haven't looked at it closely yet. It currently has a grid of seats that we'd like to use to allow people to select what seat they want to purchase at the particular concert being displayed.

Right now, it's a grid of squares in an HTML table:

```
chapter_04/01/app/views/concerts/show.html.erb
<table class="table">
  <tbody>
    <% @concert.venue.rows.times do |row| %>
      <tr>
        <% @concert.venue.seats_per_row.times do |seat| %>
          <% ticket = @concert.find_ticket_at(
               row: row + 1,
               number: seat + 1
             ) %>
          <td>
            <%= link_to(ticket_path(ticket.id),
                  method: :patch) do %>
              <div class="<%= ticket.color_for(current_user) %>
                          p-4 m-2 border-black border-4 button
                          hover:bg-blue-300 text-lg">
                <%= seat + 1 %>
              </div>
            </div>
          <% end %>
```

```
        </td>
      <% end %>
    </tr>
  <% end %>
  </tbody>
</table>
```

Plus the page has a pull-down menu to select the number of tickets, but we'll get to that later.

The first thing we are going to do is convert this code to give React control of that part of the page. Eventually we are going to add interactivity to allow a user to select seats, show a running total, and show the current status of seat purchases. But first we're going to simply draw the table in React.

This feature has great potential for React because it is interactive but doesn't use traditional browser form elements that might already have a lot of built-in functionality in the browser.

React encourages splitting your page into small components. To draw this section of the page, we're going to have three components: one for each individual seat, one for each row that contains a row's worth of seats, and one for the venue itself, which combines all the rows.

Here's a screenshot of the page with the boundaries of our eventual React components—Venue, Row, and Seat—marked:

Let's work from the most inside component up, which in our case is the Seat component. I've decided to put all our React components in their own subdirectory of app/packs, which I have creatively named components. Here's what the Seat component file looks like:

```
chapter_04/02/app/packs/components/seat.tsx
import * as React from "react"

interface SeatProps {
  seatNumber: number
}

const Seat = (props: SeatProps): React.ReactElement => {
  return (
    <td>
      <span
        className="p-4 m-2 border-black border-4 button
                   hover:bg-blue-300 text-lg">
        {props.seatNumber + 1}
      </span>
    </td>
  )
}

export default Seat
```

The core of this file is the actual component, which is the constant function Seat. You'll notice that the syntax inside the Seat function does not look like standard JavaScript or TypeScript. Instead we have this weird <td> there, and it looks like we dropped HTML directly into our TypeScript file, and somehow it's all working.

That syntax is JSX. JSX is an extension to JavaScript that allows HTML-like elements inside angle brackets to be included in JavaScript or TypeScript code. React uses JSX to define HTML tags that are part of our React components, and also as a way of calling React components from other React components. The React JSX parser converts our .jsx and .tsx files to plain JavaScript or TypeScript. This conversion has already been set up for us by Webpacker using a mechanism we'll discuss in more detail in Chapter 7, webpack, on page 133 and Chapter 8, Webpacker, on page 149.

Functional vs. Class Components

React components can be either functions that return a JSX element or a class that contains a render method that returns a JSX element. Until recently, only class components could maintain internal state, but that changed in React 16.8 with the introduction of *hooks*. It seems to be the clear direction of the React team that

Functional vs. Class Components

functional components are the future, so that's what we'll deal with here, but if you look at a lot of older React code, you'll see a lot of class components.

Looking at our Seat function, we see that it takes one argument called props and does nothing but return an element that uses JSX to describe an HTML table cell. The return value encloses the JSX in parentheses, which is a common idiom for returning multi-line JSX elements, allowing you to start the JSX element on the line after the return statement and preserve logical indenting.

The returned value starts with <td>. When a JSX file sees an angle bracket, it looks to convert the expression contained by that angle bracket element to a React element using an internal React function. (JSX is mostly a shortcut for calling React's tag creation functions all over the place, which would be horribly verbose.) If the initial text inside the angle brackets, in this case td, starts with a lowercase letter, React assumes it is an HTML element. If it starts with an uppercase letter, React assumes it's another React component.

Using JSX, we can include HTML attributes in our React components almost identically to how we would in normal HTML markup. You can see one of the main exceptions in this code. Since class is a reserved word in JavaScript, DOM classes are added to elements using the attribute name className.

Inside our span element we have {props.seatNumber}. This syntax uses two parts of React, *props*, and the use of the curly brace. The curly brace is React's interpolation marker, similar to the way <%= %> is used in ERB. Inside curly braces, arbitrary JavaScript expressions are executed and passed through to the resulting element. In this case, we're taking the seat number and rendering each Seat component using its actual seat number.

Which brings us to *props*. Props—short for "properties," presumably—is React's term for the attributes of a component that are meant to be stable, meaning that the component cannot change its own props by itself. Props are passed into a component as a single argument when the component is created and are the only argument to a component. We could name the argument anything we want when defining the function; using props is a convention.

We're also using TypeScript to declare the type of our incoming props. In our case, we've declared SeatProps to say that the props object is expected to have only one key, seatNumber, and we expect that value to be a number. By declaring this interface, we allow TypeScript to do compile-time type checking to ensure that the necessary values are passed to our components. We can then use the props object, as we do here, by interpolating props.seatNumber into our JSX. We'll talk more about TypeScript interfaces in Chapter 6, TypeScript, on page 115.

Destructuring

 You'll also often see JavaScript destructuring syntax used to declare a component, in which case our declaration would be written as export const Seat = ({ seatNumber }). And then we could use that value in the component directly, with <span className="button">{seatNumber}</span>, since the incoming props object will have been deferenced directly to seatNumber.

The most important fact about props in a component is that a component cannot change its own props once the component is instantiated. Changeable values in React components are called *state* and are handled differently. In the next section you'll see how props are passed to a component, and then you'll see one of the mechanisms by which React allows us to change stateful values.

And that is our first component. We added an export default statement to allow the Seat function to easily be imported by other files. As written, this actually prevents us from exporting the SeatProps type, but we don't need it by name outside this file.

Composing Components

Now that we have a component for each seat, we want to combine multiple seats into a row and then combine multiple rows into a venue. Invoking a component from another component normally involves a JSX call that looks as though the component was an HTML tag with the name of the component first and the props following with the same syntax used to write HTML attributes.

So if we want to use our Seat component, we'd call it with syntax like <Seat seatNumber={seatNumber} />. The first part of the tag is our component name, and then we assign the prop as if it were an HTML attribute using the curly bracket notation to send the value of the seat number. If the value being sent is a string, you can use a string literal rather than the brackets, as in <Seat description="front row center" />.

We don't want to add just one Seat, though; we want to add an entire row of them. For the moment, we can assume that the seat numbers are just incremental integers, but even so, our Row component needs to create a Seat component corresponding to each seat number.

Here's what the Row component looks like. Look at the code first, and then we'll talk about what's weird here:

```
chapter_04/02/app/packs/components/row.tsx
import * as React from "react"
import Seat from "components/seat"

interface RowProps {
  rowNumber: number
  seatsPerRow: number
}

const Row = (props: RowProps): React.ReactElement => {
  const seatItems = Array.from(Array(props.seatsPerRow).keys()).map(
    (seatNumber) => {
      return <Seat key={seatNumber} seatNumber={seatNumber} />
    }
  )
  return <tr className="h-20">{seatItems}</tr>
}

export default Row
```

The basic structure of the component is similar to Seat. We have a props interface with two fields—one for the row number and one for the number of seats. We have a function named Row that returns some JSX that contains an HTML tr tag. There are a couple of differences. We need to import the Seat component from its file—a component needs to be visible in order to be used.

The biggest oddity, though, is that rather than include each Seat inside a loop in the returned JSX, the way we might expect a templating language like ERB to work, we're instead creating all the Seat components as an array of components using JavaScript's map function. We start with Array.from(Array(props.seatsPerRow)), an obscure JavaScript idiom which turns the number 5 into the array [0, 1, 2, 3, 4]—it's the closest we can get to a Ruby range object without writing some helper functions. Then we use map to create a new array by sending each of those numbers to a function that takes that number and converts it to a React element by returning JSX: return <Seat key={seatNumber} seatNumber={seatNumber} />. This code demonstrates an important part of JSX—JSX creates regular JavaScript objects that can be returned and managed like any other JavaScript object.

As a result of that map call, the seatItems variable is set to an array of JSX elements, which we then include in our return value online 15 using more curly brackets: return <tr>{seatItems}</tr>. The array of items are rendered inside the table row, and all ends up as we expect.

Why do we need to go through this indirection rather than include a for loop inside the <tr> tag the way the original ERB did?

The reason is that inside a JSX element, you can only include JavaScript expressions that return values. In Ruby, every statement, including if and each statements, is also an expression, meaning that every statement returns a value. (This is why x = if y == true then 3 else 4 end is legal Ruby.) JavaScript works differently. if and for in JavaScript are statements but not expressions. Since if and for don't return values, they can't be included directly into JSX expressions. We have to use those features a different way.

In the case of a loop, a common way is to use map as we are doing to convert the array into an array of JSX expressions. For if statements, one option is to use the ternary operator, which is an expression in JavaScript:

```
return (
  <div>
    (x === true) ? <span>True</span> : <span>False</span>
  </div>
)
```

Another common pattern is to use an if statement to assign a value, similar to what we just did with our array:

```
let spanItem
if (x === true) {
  spanItem = <span>True</span>
} else {
  spanItem = <span>False</span>
}
return <div>{spanItem}</div>
```

In a case where the component is only rendered if the Boolean condition is true, the and operator is often used:

```
return (
  <div>
    {condition && <AnotherComponent />}
  </div>
)
```

In this case, if the condition is false, the code inside the curly braces short-circuits and returns null. If the condition is true, then the AnotherComponent is rendered.

In both the array and if cases, if the logic gets complicated, separating out to another function or possibly another component makes it clearer. You can nest functions in JavaScript, so you could do something like this:

```
const Conditional = (props) => {

  function spanItem {
    return (props.x === true) ? <span>True</span> : <span>False</span>
  }

  return <div>{spanItem()}</div>
}
```

There's one other React quirk that you need to know about when you are generating lists of items. If you look at our creation of the Seat component, you'll see that the call looks like this:

```
<Seat key={seatNumber} seatNumber={seatNumber} />
```

The seatNumber goes into the props for the component, but the key is new. The key is an internal property used by React to enable the React run time to differentiate between elements in a list and render only the ones that have changed. The exact value of the key doesn't much matter for our purposes right now. The only thing that matters is that each element's key is unique. If you render a list without a key, React will place a warning in the browser console at run time, so that's something to look out for.

So far the JSX tags we've written have all been self-closing, ending in />. But you can have beginning and ending tags with arbitrary expressions inside the tags. These expressions can be a string, like <Tag>Fred</Tag>; one or more JSX elements, like <Header><Nav/><Nav/></Header>; or an arbitrary expression, like <DisplayUser>{user}</DisplayUser>. In all these cases, the value inside the tags is available as props.children, and the parent receiving them is responsible for doing whatever makes sense with the props.children value so that the child elements are used.

TypeScript and Child Props

 In TypeScript, if you are going to use props.children, you can declare children as part of the interface object that is the type of the props argument. If you know the internal value will be a string, you can use children?: string, or use children?: React.ReactNode if it's getting an internal element—the question mark indicates that the value is optional, which protects you in the case where the component is called without anything inside it. If you aren't sure, you can always do children?: any, which lets any element pass.

One other quick thing about JSX: sometimes you will just want to render a set of JSX elements that don't really have a parent element, and you don't want to return them as an array. Since a React component expects to return a single JSX item, you need a little trick to return a set—React calls this a Fragment, and it has a convenient shortcut:

```
return (
  <>
    <div>One thing</div>
    <div>Another thing</div>
  </>
)
```

That empty tag, <>, and empty close tag, </>, indicate a fragment, and let you return your set of otherwise unrelated items together as a bundle.

Connecting to the Page

As we combined Seat components into a Row, we also need to combine Row components into a Venue. Our Venue component is similar to Row:

chapter_04/02/app/packs/components/venue.tsx
```
import * as React from "react"
import Row from "components/row"

interface VenueProps {
  rows: number
  seatsPerRow: number
}

const Venue = (props: VenueProps): React.ReactElement => {
  const rowNumbers = Array.from(Array(props.seatsPerRow).keys())
  const rowItems = rowNumbers.map((rowNumber) => {
    return (
      <Row
        key={rowNumber}
        rowNumber={rowNumber}
        seatsPerRow={props.seatsPerRow}
      />
    )
  })
  return (
    <table className="table">
      <tbody>{rowItems}</tbody>
    </table>
  )
}

export default Venue
```

There's a minor difference in that the Venue returns an HTML table, and the props type is a little different, but basically the structure is similar: we still use map to convert a list of row numbers to a list of row items.

We do cheat here a little bit in that the list of row numbers is hard-coded. This is because we haven't looked at ways to get the information about how many rows are in a venue from Rails to React. We'll talk more about that in Chapter 9, Talking to the Server, on page 161.

With all our components done, we need to connect them into the page so that React is invoked to control the section of the page we want it to draw. Since we are using Webpacker, that means we want a top-level pack we include in our page that will embed the React components into the existing DOM. This is slightly different from many React apps that take over the entire page. In our case, React is, at least for the moment, only managing our grid of seats.

Here's our pack file:

```
chapter_04/02/app/packs/entrypoints/venue_display.tsx
import * as React from "react"
import * as ReactDOM from "react-dom"
import Venue from "components/venue"

document.addEventListener("turbo:load", () => {
  if (document.getElementById("react-element")) {
    ReactDOM.render(
      <Venue rows={10} seatsPerRow={10} />,
      document.getElementById("react-element")
    )
  }
})
```

It starts by installing React and ReactDOM, which is the library that allows React to interact with the actual browser DOM. It also imports our Venue component.

Then there's a standard DOM event listener, which is waiting for the turbo:load event to signify that the DOM has completely loaded for the page. Since we are using Turbo Drive, we won't get an ordinary DOM page load event because the page doesn't technically load; Turbo Drive just inserts the body into the DOM. Turbo Drive provides the turbo:load event as an equivalent.

When the event fires, it checks to see if the DOM element we want to connect to exists, which in our case is a DOM element with the ID react-element. If so, the code calls the ReactDOM.render method, which takes two arguments: a component to render (for us, the Venue, with some props to start us off) and a component to render into, which is the same react-element element. The method will give React control over the DOM element that is the second argument and will use the first argument as the top-level component to draw.

To connect this to the page, we need a DOM element with the react-element ID, which we can get by taking the app/views/concerts/show.html.erb file and replacing the part that was rendering the seats with <div id="react-element" />.

We also need to load the pack on the page. We're going to add it to the layout file app/layouts/application.html.erb by changing our call:

```
chapter_04/02/app/views/layouts/application.html.erb
<%= javascript_pack_tag(
    "application",
    "venue_display",
    "data-turbo-track": "reload"
  ) %>
```

Now our javascript_pack_tag includes both packs. (Note: As I write this, having two separate calls to javascript_pack_tag triggers an error due to Turbo being loaded twice. Hopefully, by the time you read this, it'll be fixed.)

This is not necessarily a final decision. On the one hand, this means that the React code will be part of every page download, but on the other hand, Turbo Drive means that Rails won't actually reload the header more than once per session, plus webpack will do some optimization. Still, putting all the packs in the header all the time isn't ideal from a performance perspective. We'll talk more about how webpack optimizes pack loading in Chapter 7, webpack, on page 133.

Interactivity, State, and Hooks

At this point, React has taken over part of our page and is drawing the seats, which is nice enough, but we'd like it to, you know, *react* to something. We'd like to have a little interactivity.

In React, you can use JSX to specify event handlers on React elements in much the same way you would when writing old-school JavaScript embedded in HTML. The problem is how to make changes to our components as a result of those events. As mentioned, the props we pass into each component are immutable, which means if we want to change something about a component, we can't use props. React uses the term *state* to refer to the parts of a component that change and trigger an update to how the component is displayed when they are changed.

To be clear, although a component can't change its own props, changing the state of a component can cause that component to rerender child components with new props.

Because state changes are used by React to trigger a redrawing of the page, React requires you to register them with the system; you can't just change the value of a variable and be done with it. React allows you to designate a value as being part of the state and gives you a special setter for that value using a mechanism called *hooks*.

Hooks are new in React as of version 16.8. Before then, components defined as functions could not manage changing state (components defined as classes always could manage state using a different mechanism). As mentioned earlier, the React core team has said that hooks and functional components are the way of the future, which is why we will be focusing on using hooks to manage state in this book.

Here's the code for the Seat component that changes status when clicked:

chapter_04/03/app/packs/components/seat.tsx

```
import * as React from "react"

interface SeatProps {
  seatNumber: number
  initialStatus: string
}

const Seat = ({
  seatNumber,
  initialStatus,
}: SeatProps): React.ReactElement => {
  const [status, setStatus] = React.useState(initialStatus)

  function changeState(): void {
    if (status === "held") {
      setStatus("unsold")
    } else {
      setStatus("held")
    }
  }

  function stateDisplayClass(): string {
    if (status === "held") {
      return "bg-green-500"
    } else {
      return "bg-white hover:bg-blue-300"
    }
  }

  const cssClass = "p-4 m-2 border-black border-4 text-lg"

  return (
    <td>
      <span
```

```
35          className={`${cssClass} ${stateDisplayClass()}`}
            onClick={changeState}>
            {seatNumber + 1}
        </span>
      </td>
40    )
  }

export default Seat
```

The first new React-specific line here is line 12, const [status, setStatus] = React.useState(props.initialStatus). We are calling the React method useState, which is a React *hook* method. It's called a hook because it allows our component to "hook into" the React rendering life cycle to allow the component to change the larger system. React defines several different default hooks, plus you can create your own.

Right here, right now, we're calling useState. What useState does is register a given value as being a part of React state such that changing that value triggers a rerender. The argument to useState is the initial value of the new state object in question—in our case, we're taking the value from an initialState passed in as a prop. (We'll need to change the row.tsx component so that its call looks like this: <Seat key={seatNumber} seatNumber={seatNumber} initialStatus="unsold" />.)

The useState method has kind of a weird return value; it returns a two-element array, which you typically capture into two different variables using Java-Script's destructuring syntax. Here we are capturing the values into variables named status and setStatus. The first return value, in our case, status, is a property that has the current value of our state. The second return value, setStatus, is our state setter—a function that we can call later in our component to change the value of the state and trigger a redraw.

The useState Hook Initial Value

 One important gotcha to keep in mind here is that the argument passed to useState is only used the first time the component is rendered. On subsequent rerenders, the component keeps track of the existing state and does not need or use the initial value.

This is great—we now have a mechanism for both getting and setting the value of the changing state of our component, which we can then use through the rest of our component.

Let's jump to the JSX return value of the component. Two things about this value have changed:

- the className now includes a call to a stateDisplayClass() function, and
- we've added another prop to the span, namely onClick={changeState}.

The onClick prop is how React does event handling: you create a prop whose name is on followed by the event; the value of that prop is a function that is called when the event happens. In our case, we're using {changeState}. (For a complete list of event names supported by React, check out the official docs on the React website.)[2]

When the button is clicked, the onClick event fires, which causes us to go to the changeState function inside our component. Within that function we do a check on the value of status—the same status variable that was defined by the call to useState. We then change the value of status based on the current value of status using the setState function, also the one defined by useState, to officially register the change with React.

Using setState triggers a redraw of the element, which takes us back to the return value and the call to stateDisplayClass(), which is used to change the background color of the item based on the current status. Clicking once changes the status to held, which then causes the display class to be bg-green-500—Tailwind-speak for "make the background green." Clicking again calls setStatus("unsold"), and the rerender changes the display class to bg-white hover:bg-blue-300, or "make the background white but change it to light blue when we hover the mouse pointer over it." There are a couple of logistical issues with React hooks to keep in mind:

- Hooks can only be used in components that are defined as functions and can only be declared at the top level of the function—not inside a nested function, loop, or if statement.

- If you want to manage more than one value in state, you can make multiple calls to useState to get setters for each of them, or you can have the initial value be an array or object. If the value gets more complicated, there may be other hooks that will be easier to use, which we'll talk more about in Chapter 12, Managing State in React, on page 227.

- If it bothers you that the status takes strings as values but only has a limited number of valid string values, never fear, TypeScript has a mechanism for that, and we'll take a look at it in Chapter 14, Validating Code with Advanced TypeScript, on page 269.

---

2.   https://reactjs.org/docs/events.html

Sharing State

Hooks and useState work cleanly when the state is completely encapsulated inside one component, but often components have to share state. Sometimes state is shared among just one subtree of DOM elements on the page, but sometimes state is shared across a page. We'll talk more about more complex state patterns in Chapter 12, Managing State in React, on page 227, but here we will cover the simplest version of one common scenario where state is shared among parent and child components.

In this React pattern, when there is a common parent to all the components that need that state, the state is typically owned by the common parent. The parent sends the raw values down to the child components as props and typically also sends a function that the child components should call to change the parent state. When the child components call that function, the parent state changes. Then the parent component rerenders, causing the child components to rerender with new prop values. This pattern is often called "lifting state up" and "passing state down."

As an example, let's imagine we can use a pull-down menu to determine the number of seats we want to purchase at a time and that clicking on a seat also selects seats to the right of the seat clicked on such that a matching number of seats is purchased. If that number of seats is not available to the right, then the seat is marked unavailable and clicking it has no effect.

This feature adds one new piece of state: the number of seats being purchased via the pull-down menu. It also requires that Seat components need to know something about the other seats in their row to determine their status. In the first case, the state for the number of seats being purchased should be owned by the common parent of all the components that use it, which here would be Venue. Similarly, we need to lift the state of an individual seat up to the Row so that the Row can determine which seats are valid for purchase given the number of seats desired.

When the value in the pull-down menu is changed, that state change needs to trigger a redraw of each row because the set of valid seats changes. When a Seat is clicked on, the Row needs to update the status of the nearby seats.

Here's what that looks like in code.

First we need to remember to remove the select tag from the existing HTML in the app/views/concerts/show.html.erb file; otherwise, we'll get two pull-down menus and only one of them will work.

Let's start from the top with the new version of the Venue component:

```
chapter_04/04/app/packs/components/venue.tsx
import * as React from "react"
import VenueBody from "components/venue_body"
import VenueHeader from "components/venue_header"

interface VenueProps {
  rows: number
  seatsPerRow: number
}

const Venue = ({ rows, seatsPerRow }: VenueProps): React.ReactElement => {
  const [ticketsToBuyCount, setTicketsToBuyCount] = React.useState(1)

  return (
    <>
      <VenueHeader
        seatsPerRow={seatsPerRow}
        setTicketsToBuyCount={setTicketsToBuyCount}
      />
      <VenueBody
        seatsPerRow={seatsPerRow}
        rows={rows}
        ticketsToBuyCount={ticketsToBuyCount}
      />
    </>
  )
}

export default Venue
```

I've done a refactoring here, splitting the Venue into a VenueHeader and a Venue-Body. The header is structurally a different thing, and in React, the general principle is to keep components small and split them up as you add new DOM elements.

We're adding one piece of state to the Venue, which is the number of tickets we're buying at a time. So we need to both manage that state and provide an interface to update it.

We start managing the state right off in the beginning of the component with const [ticketsToBuy, setTicketsToBuy] = React.useState(1). This gives us a property—ticketsToBuy—with an initial value of 1, and a setter function, setTicketsToBuy. The method setTicketsToBuy is a setter function, and we pass it as a prop to the VenueHeader component.

Here's the whole VenueHeader component.

```
chapter_04/04/app/packs/components/venue_header.tsx
import * as React from "react"

interface VenueHeaderProps {
  seatsPerRow: number
  setTicketsToBuyCount: (n: number) => void
}

const options = (seatsPerRow) => {
  const arrayOfNumbers = Array.from(Array(seatsPerRow).keys())
  return arrayOfNumbers.map((i) => (
    <option key={i + 1} value={i + 1}>
      {i + 1}
    </option>
  ))
}

export const VenueHeader = ({
  seatsPerRow,
  setTicketsToBuyCount,
}: VenueHeaderProps): React.ReactElement => {
  const setTicketsOnChange = (event: React.SyntheticEvent): void => {
    const target = event.target as HTMLSelectElement
    setTicketsToBuyCount(parseInt(target.value, 10))
  }

  return (
    <div>
      <span>How many tickets would you like?</span>
      <span className="select">
        <select onChange={setTicketsOnChange}>
          {options(seatsPerRow)}
        </select>
      </span>
    </div>
  )
}

export default VenueHeader
```

The incoming props are declared first. The props are the number of seats in a row and the setTicketsToBuy function, getting passed down from the parent class so it can be invoked from the header.

Then, we build up the list of <option> tags the same way we needed to build up the list of rows. We do that with a map function that returns a JSX representation of the option, including a key because it's a React list.

The return value of the component is the JSX for the header—some text and a <select> tag containing our previously created options. The select item has an onChange event handler, which triggers a setTicketsOnChange function.

In that function, which is nested inside the component so it has access to the setTicketsToBuy prop, we extract the new value of the select tag and pass it to our setTicketsToBuy setter function, which, since it's a useState setter function, triggers a change in state.

The VenueBody component calls the list of rows as before, except we are passing the number of tickets to buy as a new prop in the object. Because ticketsToBuy is passed as a prop, changing its value with the setTicketsToBuy setter will cause those components to rerender. Keep in mind that calling the component function again with new prop values does not re-initialize React's internal state as seen by useState, so the default value passed to useState is not reused.

chapter_04/04/app/packs/components/venue_body.tsx

```tsx
import * as React from "react"
import Row from "components/row"

interface VenueBodyProps {
  rows: number
  seatsPerRow: number
  ticketsToBuyCount: number
}

const rowItems = (
  rows: number,
  seatsPerRow: number,
  ticketsToBuyCount: number
) => {
  const rowNumbers = Array.from(Array(rows).keys())
  return rowNumbers.map((rowNumber) => (
    <Row
      key={rowNumber}
      rowNumber={rowNumber}
      seatsPerRow={seatsPerRow}
      ticketsToBuyCount={ticketsToBuyCount}
    />
  ))
}

export const VenueBody = (props: VenueBodyProps): React.ReactElement => {
  return (
    <table className="table">
      <tbody>
        {rowItems(props.rows, props.seatsPerRow, props.ticketsToBuyCount)}
      </tbody>
    </table>
  )
}

export default VenueBody
```

The Row component has gotten a lot more functionality, some of which has been taken from the Seat component. In this version of the code, the status of a seat depends on the status of the seats next to it—if the tickets to buy number is two, then a set with an already sold seat to its right is not available. Because an individual seat can no longer contain all the data needed to ascertain its status, the status for the entire row now needs to be stored in the Row component.

Here's the Row code:

```
chapter_04/04/app/packs/components/row.tsx
import * as React from "react"
import Seat from "components/seat"

interface RowProps {
  rowNumber: number
  seatsPerRow: number
  ticketsToBuyCount: number
}

const Row = (props: RowProps): React.ReactElement => {
  const [seatStatuses, setSeatStatuses] = React.useState(
    Array.from(Array(props.seatsPerRow).keys()).map(() => "unsold")
  )

  function isSeatValid(seatNumber): boolean {
    if (seatNumber + props.ticketsToBuyCount > props.seatsPerRow) {
      return false
    }
    for (let i = 1; i < props.ticketsToBuyCount; i++) {
      if (seatStatuses[seatNumber + i] === "held") {
        return false
      }
    }
    return true
  }

  function validSeatStatus(seatNumber): string {
    if (seatStatuses[seatNumber] === "held") {
      return "held"
    } else {
      return isSeatValid(seatNumber) ? "unsold" : "invalid"
    }
  }

  function newState(oldStatus: string): string {
    if (oldStatus === "unsold") {
      return "held"
    } else if (oldStatus === "held") {
      return "unsold"
    } else {
```

```
      return "invalid"
    }
  }

  function onSeatChange(seatNumber: number): void {
    if (validSeatStatus(seatNumber) === "invalid") {
      return
    }
    setSeatStatuses(
      seatStatuses.map((status, index) => {
        if (
          index >= seatNumber &&
          index < seatNumber + props.ticketsToBuyCount
        ) {
          return newState(seatStatuses[seatNumber])
        } else {
          return status
        }
      })
    )
  }

  const seatItems = Array.from(Array(props.seatsPerRow).keys()).map(
    (seatNumber) => {
      return (
        <Seat
          key={seatNumber}
          seatNumber={seatNumber}
          status={validSeatStatus(seatNumber)}
          clickHandler={onSeatChange}
        />
      )
    }
  )

  return <tr className="h-20">{seatItems}</tr>
}

export default Row
```

This component does two important things: First, it keeps track of the seat statuses in an array. Second, it defines a click handler to be executed when a seat is clicked. To make that work, the Row component passes that handler function as a prop to the Seat component, namely clickHandler.

The first thing that we need to do is call the useState hook again, this time to create an array of seat statuses. The initial value, which is the argument to the useState call, is an array of unsold values, one for each seat in the row.

Using an array or an object as the value of the state in a useState call, rather than an individual value, works differently than you might expect. It is important to keep in mind that the argument to the useState method is only applied to the state value the first time the component is drawn. When the component rerenders, that value is ignored.

An implication of that rule is that you generally don't want the argument to the useState method to be dynamic. In our case, it's just a static array of unsold values since we don't expect the number of seats in the row to change. (Later, in Chapter 9, Talking to the Server, on page 161, we'll see what to do when you do want the state to update on rerender, which we'll use to get the server status of each seat into the system.)

It's also important to keep in mind that in order to trigger a rerender based on changing the state of an array value, you need to create a new array. Just updating an element in the array won't do it.

In our implementation, the Row is going to store in the state value whether each seat is unsold or held, and it's going to calculate separately if the seat is valid. In our admittedly contrived business logic, a seat is valid if you can buy the currently expected number of seats starting at the seat and moving right without hitting the end of the row or another held seat.

We start with one ticket to buy and all the seats valid. If we change the ticketsToBuy to 2, we expect the rightmost seat in each row to be invalid because you can't buy a second seat to the right of the end of the row. If ticketsToBuy becomes 3, we expect the two rightmost seats in each row to become invalid. Clicking on a seat causes the seat and the correct number of seats to its right to become held, and a similar number of seats to the left to become invalid.

I can suggest a principled argument for making the unsold or held status of a seat part of the underlying state and calculating validity on the fly. The server or whatever is storing the data eventually is only going to deal with the seats the user actually selects, whereas validity is only a concern of the UI while the user is picking seats. It's generally a good idea to separate data concerns from UI concerns.

Let's move down to the end of the component and look at the return value, which is an array {seatItems}. If we look a little bit further up at the line defining the seatItems array, we see that we are now sending four props to each seat. We sent the key and the seatNumber before; we're making sure each seat has a distinct number. Then we send a status, which is calculated by the validSeatStatus function (more about that in a moment). Our last prop is actually a function clickHandler={onSeatChange}—we're sending the function object onSeatChange itself, not calling the function.

This pattern—a parent component holding on to state for all its child components and sending functions down as props to the children to receive events that change state—is a common way in React to manage shared state. It works best if the component hierarchy isn't very deep and when the state is easily encapsulated in as set of components.

Our Row component has two functions for determining the status of a seat based on its number: validSeatStatus and isSeatValid. The isSeatValid function returns true or false based on how close the seat is to either the edge of the row or a held seat, while validSeatStatus converts that Boolean to a status string to send to the Seat component. Basically, a held seat is always held while an open seat might be unsold or invalid depending on its context.

We also have two functions that manage the new state of a seat after it is clicked. One of them, newState, was moved from the Seat component now that the state is managed here, and it just toggles state from unsold to held and vice versa. The actual click handler onSeatChange is a little more complicated.

The first thing onSeatChange does is if you click an invalid seat, the function just returns without doing anything. If we click on a valid seat, we then need to change the seat statuses in such a way that React will trigger rerender.

Our partner here is setSeatStatuses, the function created by the useState hook at the beginning of the component. In order to call this function in such a way as to trigger React, we cannot use the existing seatStatuses array with values changed; React will not recognize that as a new value.

Instead, we have to build a completely new array and pass the new array to setSeatStatuses. We do this by using the map function to create a new array from the old array. For each seat, if the seat number is either the seat that was clicked or a seat to its right based on the number of tickets being bought, we toggle its state. Otherwise, we just pass the state through. The result of this map is that we wind up with a new array with new values for the affected seats, but the same value for the unaffected seats.

Rerendering the row causes all the Seat components to be redrawn. Now that Seat no longer manages its own state, the component is somewhat simpler:

chapter_04/04/app/packs/components/seat.tsx
```tsx
import * as React from "react"

interface SeatProps {
  seatNumber: number
  status: string
  clickHandler: (seatNumber: number) => void
}
```

```
export const Seat = ({
  seatNumber,
  status,
  clickHandler,
}: SeatProps): React.ReactElement => {
  function stateDisplayClass(): string {
    if (status === "unsold") {
      return "bg-white hover:bg-blue-300"
    } else if (status === "held") {
      return "bg-green-500"
    } else {
      return "bg-red-500"
    }
  }

  function changeState(): void {
    clickHandler(seatNumber)
  }

  const cssClass = "p-4 m-2 border-black border-4 text-lg"

  return (
    <td>
      <span
        className={`${cssClass} ${stateDisplayClass()}`}
        onClick={changeState}>
        {seatNumber + 1}
      </span>
    </td>
  )
}

export default Seat
```

We have an interface that defines the props, including the clickHandler prop, which is defined as a function that takes a number and does not have a return value. When we declare the Seat, we use JavaScript destructuring to assign the props to values directly rather than use a props object.

We define two functions: the first converts the seat's status to a Tailwind CSS class to draw the background color. It's what we had before plus a new entry for invalid seats. On a click, we now call the second function, changeState, which itself calls our clickHandler prop. Remember, the clickHandler is the function defined by Row and passed into the seat's props. So when the seat is clicked, the OnClick is invoked, the clickHandler function is called, and control goes back to the Row, where the statuses are updated and the row redrawn.

Although this pattern of passing handlers down and therefore passing state up a component tree is common, it can quickly become complicated as the state or the page gets larger. In Chapter 12, Managing State in React, on page

227, we'll look at more options for managing state in React, including the important concept of a *reducer*.

What's Next

In this chapter, we used React to create a series of components and add interactivity to a web page. Now that we have some real markup on our pages, it's a good time to talk about how to style them. In the next chapter, we'll discuss some CSS tricks, including how to load CSS stylesheets and image assets into our build, how to add CSS animations, and how to integrate CSS styling into our React components.

Cascading Style Sheets

It's hard to talk about front-end web development without talking about Cascading Style Sheets (CSS) and their ability to alter and improve the user experience. As CSS has gotten more powerful over the years, it's made it possible to create amazing layouts and effects with less JavaScript code and more CSS styling. Because of the power of CSS, integration with CSS has become an increasingly important part of front-end development. In this chapter, we're going to take a look at how we can make CSS part of our build and use it to add neat effects, and further make our components self-contained.

CSS is a big topic, and covering all of it is well beyond the scope of this book. As such, I'm going to assume you are familiar with the rough basics of how CSS works and spend this chapter focusing on three issues:

• How to integrate CSS with our Webpacker build and with the PostCSS tool that Webpacker integrates with to process our CSS

• How to use CSS animations to augment the interactivity of our JavaScript

• How to declare our CSS inside our JavaScript tools, especially in React, where it can be useful to scope CSS to React components

Don't worry; if you don't feel fully versed on how CSS works, Learn CSS Layout has a lot of exercises that show how CSS spacing works.[1] Also try the ezine Hell Yes, CSS.[2]

---

1. http://learnlayout.com
2. https://wizardzines.com/zines/css

Building CSS in webpack

In this section, we're going to focus on using CSS in webpack. (For more details on exactly what our tools do when we load them, see Stylesheets and Assets, on page 153.) Initially, CSS was a little tricky to load from Webpacker, but there have been continual improvements, and it's now about the same complexity as using Sprockets.

Webpacker allows you to add support for CSS as well as css processors like PostCSS, and CSS variant languages like Sass and SCSS.[3] Sass and SCSS are valuable extensions to basic CSS, including an easier syntax for variables and nested selectors. The SCSS version of the syntax is similar to original CSS, while Sass is a minimalist syntax that is similar to HAML. We'll be using SCSS for examples in the book, though I expect that most of them will also work as plain CSS.

If you look at our codebase so far, we've been using the Tailwind CSS framework. Let's talk about how CSS and Tailwind was installed. (There is also a tailwind-rails gem in progress that will simplify this process.) All of this has already been done in the codebase as part of setting up the site. For more detailed information on installing Tailwind, see the Tailwind documentation and the book *Modern CSS with Tailwind*.[4,5]

Webpacker needs a couple of packages imported to load CSS files. Most of this setup was already done in Chapter 1, Getting Started with Client-Side Rails, on page 3.

```
$ yarn add css-loader mini-css-extract-plugin
$ yarn add css-minimizer-webpack-plugin
$ yarn add sass sass-loader
$ yarn add postcss-loader
```

Plus, we need to update the config/webpack/base.js file to allow for CSS files to be resolved:

```
chapter_05/01/config/webpack/base.js
const { webpackConfig, merge } = require("@rails/webpacker")
const ForkTSCheckerWebpackPlugin = require("fork-ts-checker-webpack-plugin")

const customConfig = {
  plugins: [new ForkTSCheckerWebpackPlugin()],
  resolve: {
```

---

3.   https://sass-lang.com
4.   https://tailwindcss.com/docs
5.   https://pragprog.com/titles/tailwind/modern-css-with-tailwind

```
      extensions: [".css"],
  },
}
```

```
module.exports = merge(webpackConfig, customConfig)
```

Tailwind can be imported as a node module, along with a few other utility tools like PostCSS, autoprefixer, and a few useful PostCSS utilities.

```
$ yarn add tailwindcss@latest postcss@latest autoprefixer@latest
$ yarn add postcss-import postcss-flexbugs-fixes postcss-preset-env
```

And we need a posts.config.js file to reflect these tools:

chapter_05/01/postcss.config.js
```
module.exports = {
  plugins: [
    require('postcss-import'),
    require('postcss-flexbugs-fixes'),
    require('postcss-preset-env')({
      autoprefixer: {
        flexbox: 'no-2009'
      },
      stage: 3
    }),
    require('tailwindcss'),
    require('autoprefixer')
  ]
}
```

Now, we can load Tailwind by adding its main definitions to an app/packs/entry-points/application.scss file:

chapter_05/01/app/packs/entrypoints/application.scss
```
@import "tailwindcss/base";
@import "tailwindcss/components";
@import "tailwindcss/utilities";
```

Here are the contents of the file:

@import is a Sass statement that imports a file.

You need to separately add the stylesheet to the application layout using stylesheet_pack_tag:

```
<%= stylesheet_pack_tag("application") %>
```

And we're set.

We can now add custom CSS rules to the application.scss file, or we can import other files into the application.scss file. Webpacker doesn't have any opinions on how you structure your custom CSS. As with JavaScript packs, it's pretty common to have the top page be basically a manifest of other pages and to then split those other pages such that each file has a relatively focused batch of CSS rules, one for say, button styling, or one for typography, or for colors.

Our application now processes CSS using a tool called PostCSS.[6] PostCSS provides our SASS/SCSS parsing, but it can also do a lot of other post-processing of CSS, which we're not using at this point, but you should check the docs for features that could be useful on larger projects.

Adding CSS and Assets to webpack

You might want to use a lot of static file assets via Webpacker, such as images or fonts, in your code or CSS. To get those assets into our pack file we have to import them, and then Webpacker gives us some helper methods to be able to access the files. We need helper methods here because bundling the images into the pack changes the name of the file, so we can't just use the raw file name.

First we need to import the static files. To do so, we need to add the following code to our application.js. This code is boilerplate from the Webpacker gem, which I removed along the way; we can put it back now:

chapter_05/01/app/packs/entrypoints/application.js
```
const images = require.context("../images", true)
const imagePath = (name) => images(name, true)
```

The first line is the important one: it uses the webpack require.context method to add the entire ../images directory into our pack—that's the relative name for the app/packs/images directory. One important piece here is that the app/packs/images directory must actually exist, or TypeScript will fail to compile.

Any files placed inside that subdirectory are then available to the pack when the pack is compiled. We can do separate require.context calls for other directories if we want to add items like fonts, or video, or whatever.

The last line creates a method called imagePath that you can then export or use in other JavaScript code to get the name of the file.

At this point, we have a few ways to access any image file in that images subdirectory.

From JavaScript code, we can use that imagePath function we just defined, which looks like imagePath("./arrow.png") (you need the ./ for the method to work).

---

6.   https://postcss.org

We can also import the image file as import FileName from "images/file_name.svg" and then use the imported name as the source of an image file.

From our SCSS files, we can reference the image directly, relative to the file we are in, and webpack will handle the reference correctly. If we wanted to use an image as a background image in a style defined in our packs/application.scss file, it'd look like background-image: url("../images/arrow.svg");. We can directly reference the image file relative to application.scss.

Inside a Rails view, Webpacker defines two helper methods: asset_pack_path, which takes in the location of a file in the file system and returns its Webpacker name, and image_pack_tag, which is a replacement for image_tag, as in image_pack_tag("arrow.png").

Animating CSS

CSS is a powerful tool, and one of the powers it has is that many CSS properties can be animated. You can animate the color, position, and even the shape of a CSS element. This gives you the ability to make your site more dynamic and interesting by just adding and removing CSS classes.

Three somewhat overlapping CSS concepts allow you to animate the display of existing elements with CSS:

- transform is a CSS property that instantly changes the values of other CSS properties by changing the size, position, or orientation of the element being drawn.

- transition specifies a CSS property and a duration. When the specified property changes, the change happens gradually over the specified duration of time, rather than instantaneously.

- animation is a more general form of a transition that allows you to specify multiple stopping points between the start and end value as well as more complex timing and repeating behavior.

To show how these properties work, we're going to go back to our original Show/Hide button on the schedule page of our app and turn it into something that looks more like the triangle widget in the MacOS finder—both the button and the text will gradually change their positions.

First, we need the image. I've put a raw image in app/packs/images/chevron-right.svg. (Technically, I copied the SVG chevron-right image from http://heroicons.com and made the fill color gold so that it would show against both the black and white backgrounds of the button.)

Then, we need to adjust our view to display that image instead of the "Show" or "Hide" text. Here's a temporary change I've made to the button in the app/views/favorites/_list.html.erb file (in a moment, we'll make a more permanent change to allow Stimulus to draw the button):

```
chapter_05/01/app/views/favorites/_list.html.erb
<button class="<%= SimpleForm.button_class %>"
        data-action="click->css#toggle">
  <%= image_pack_tag(
        "chevron-right.svg",
        width: 25,
        height: 25,
        class: "inline mb-3"
      ) %>
</button>
```

We've removed the text Stimulus controller, which we're going to replace in a moment, and we've added an image tag that displays the new image. You need the inline class so that Tailwind displays the image without giving it its own new line and the mb-3 just places the image inside the button more centrally.

It looks something like this:

The image displays, but that arrow points right; we want it to point up and down. This is where our CSS transforms come in. Here's a SCSS file that implements those transforms:

```
chapter_05/01/app/packs/entrypoints/application.scss
@import "tailwindcss/base";
@import "tailwindcss/components";
@import "tailwindcss/utilities";
```

Note for those who are interested: yes, you can also do the transformations with Tailwind utilities, but we're going to stick to plain CSS for the moment.

We've added two new CSS classes: .is-open and .is-closed. Our new classes have only one CSS property: transform. The transform property can be defined as having one or more *transform functions*. In this case, we're using the transform function rotate.

There are lots of transformation functions. The ones you'll use most often are:

- rotate: Rotates the element around its center point by default. The argument to rotate is the amount of turn, clockwise, and can be in degrees (deg), radians (rad), gradients (grad), or just turn.

- scale: Changes the size of the element. If it takes one argument, that scale is used in both the x and y dimension. If there are two arguments, the first is the x scale and the second is the y scale.

- skew: Transforms the element by performing a shear transformation on it. If there is one argument, it's the angle of the shear in the x dimension. If there is a second argument, it's the angle in the y dimension.

- translate: Moves an element. The first argument is the amount to move the element in the x dimension. The optional second argument is the amount to move in the y dimension.

A full list of all the transformation functions can be found online.[7]

So, we've got an is-open class that rotates our image 90 degrees clockwise, leaving it pointing down, and an is-closed class that rotates the image 90 degrees counter-clockwise, leaving it pointing up. Those classes will affect their underlying DOM element once they are attached to the element, so now, instead of changing the text of this image based on the state of the controller, we're now changing the CSS class, and the CSS renderer will transform the image appropriately.

This is not exactly like our existing CSS controller because we're not taking a CSS class in and out; we're swapping between two different CSS classes. We need a slightly different CSS controller:

chapter_05/02/app/packs/controllers/css_flip_controller.ts
```
import { Controller } from "stimulus"

export default class CssFlipController extends Controller {
  static classes = ["on", "off"]
  onClass: string
  offClass: string

  static targets = ["elementToChange"]
  elementToChangeTarget: HTMLElement

  static values = { status: Boolean }
  statusValue: boolean

  toggle(): void {
    this.flipState()
  }
```

---

7.   https://developer.mozilla.org/en-US/docs/Web/CSS/transform

```
flipState(): void {
  this.statusValue = !this.statusValue
}

statusValueChanged(): void {
  this.updateCssClass()
}

updateCssClass(): void {
  for (const oneCssClass of this.onClass.split(" ")) {
    this.elementToChangeTarget.classList.toggle(
      oneCssClass,
      this.statusValue
    )
  }

  for (const oneCssClass of this.offClass.split(" ")) {
    this.elementToChangeTarget.classList.toggle(
      oneCssClass,
      !this.statusValue
    )
  }
}
}
}
```

This is something of a merger between our existing CSS controller and our existing text controller. It expects "on" and "off" classes to be registered in the HTML, and when the status changes, if the status is true, the "on" classes are added to the DOM class list and the "off" ones are removed. If the status is false, the reverse happens.

The ERB file changes to the following:

```
chapter_05/02/app/views/favorites/_list.html.erb
<button class="<%= SimpleForm.button_class %>"
    data-controller="css-flip"
    data-css-flip-status-value="true"
    data-css-flip-off-class="is-closed"
    data-css-flip-on-class="is-open"
    data-action="click->css#toggle click->css-flip#toggle">
  <%= image_pack_tag(
      "chevron-right.svg",
      width: 25,
      height: 25,
      class: "inline mb-3",
      "data-css-flip-target": "elementToChange"
    ) %>
</button>
```

And so we have a button that instantly flips the image when clicked. But what if we didn't want that transition to be instantaneous?

Adding CSS Transitions

When we add the new CSS class to our elements in the previous example, the transform property changes the orientation of the element on the screen. However, we can change the element in other ways. Our new classes could specify a background color, change the margin, add a border, and so on. There are many, many properties of a DOM element that can change with the addition of new CSS classes. Generically, we can call these property changes *transitions.*

CSS provides what you can think of as a meta-property called transition. The transition property allows you to describe the behavior of the CSS element when one of its display properties changes. The default behavior is that the property changes instantly.

It doesn't take much syntax to use the transition property to make our arrows move; all we need to do is add one new CSS class to our SCSS (again, Tailwind can do this for us, too, but we'll keep using plain CSS):

chapter_05/03/app/packs/entrypoints/application.scss
```
.slow-transition {
  transition: all 0.5s ease-in-out;
}
```

The new line here is transition: all 0.5s ease-in-out;, which specifies that we want properties to transition.

The syntax of the transition property has up to four elements:

- The first is the name of the property being observed, or the special words all or none. The rotation angle, strictly speaking, doesn't have a property, so it can only be captured using all. But if you only wanted to transition on changes to background-color or margin, for example, you could limit the change by only including one property. There's a specific list of what changes can be transitions, but the short of it is that basically anything where you could potentially list all the steps between values is fair game. That means that properties that have discrete enumerated values, like display, can't be transitioned, and you also usually can't transition to or from magic values like height or width auto.

- The second element is the amount of time you want the transition to take, which is defined either in seconds (s) or milliseconds (ms).

- The third element is a timing function that determines the rate at which the value changes across the transition. The default is linear, meaning the rate is the same for the entire time. Our code uses ease-in-out, which slows the rate of change at the beginning and end of the transition, and speeds it up across the middle. There are other timing functions, should you want to investigate.[8]

- The last element, which our code doesn't have, is a delay—the amount of time to wait before starting the transitions.

What our code is saying is that when any property in our DOM element changes, spread that change out over 0.5 seconds, and use an ease-in and ease-out function to manage the rate of that change.

If we add the new CSS class to the image_pack_tag call that is displaying the image, then just like that, when we click that button, the transition from down to up and back is animated. This effect is a little hard to get across in a screenshot, but trust me on this.

chapter_05/03/app/views/favorites/_list.html.erb
```
<%= image_pack_tag(
    "chevron-right.svg",
    width: 25,
    height: 25,
    class: "inline mb-3 slow-transition",
    "data-css-flip-target": "elementToChange"
) %>
```

Animation Side Effects

 A fun side effect of the current implementation is that the initial transition from the basic image pointing right to the initial down state might also be animated, leading to all the arrows turning down at page load. I find this kind of charming, but you could also get rid of it by either starting with a real down-pointing image or only adding the transition to the DOM element after the page has loaded.

Transitions don't have to be paired with transformations. Any change in values can be transitioned. A common use of this is to change a value on the hover pseudo-element. For example, let's add this definition:

chapter_05/04/app/packs/entrypoints/application.scss
```
.blue-hover {
  transition: all 0.3s ease-in-out;

  &:hover {
    background-color: blue;
  }
}
```

---

8.   https://developer.mozilla.org/en-US/docs/Web/CSS/transition

Then add the .blue-hover CSS class to the span around our button:

chapter_05/04/app/views/favorites/_list.html.erb
```
<button class="<%= SimpleForm.button_class %> blue-hover"
        data-controller="css-flip"
        data-css-flip-status-value="true"
        data-css-flip-off-class="is-closed"
        data-css-flip-on-class="is-open"
        data-action="click->css#toggle click->css-flip#toggle">
  <%= image_pack_tag(
      "chevron-right.svg",
      width: 25,
      height: 25,
      class: "inline mb-3 slow-transition",
      "data-css-flip-target": "elementToChange"
    ) %>
```

With this change in place, when the mouse hovers over the button, the background color turns blue, and it does so with a gradual transformation over 0.5 seconds (which, admittedly, is a subtle effect).

We'd also like to have the actual item that we show and hide—all the concert information—gradually hide itself as well. This is a little bit harder. One of the first things you might think to try is to transition max-height from 100 percent to 0 percent. However, this doesn't work reliably because the max-height property changes if the width of the element changes, which I think means that if you resize the browser, the element won't transition correctly.

That said, if you have an explicitly set max-height that works, you can try it. Here's some CSS for the concerts part of the page:

chapter_05/05/app/packs/entrypoints/application.scss
```
.resizer {
  transition: all 1s ease-in-out;
  max-height: 1000px;
  overflow: hidden;

  &.shrink {
    max-height: 0px;
  }
}
```

The shrink transitions the max-height down to zero, which, combined with the overflow: hidden, will cause the item to appear to fade away—it's not actually leaving the DOM; it's just not taking up any space. We're giving this a 1-second timing.

SCSS Ampersands

The ampersand (&) prefix is a reference to the parent CSS class in the nested definition. The effect in this case is to make the styles apply on an element that has both resized and shrink. Without the &, the style would apply when there are nested DOM elements, the outer of which has resized and the inner of which has shrink.

This works perfectly well with two small changes in the view in app/views/favorites/_list.html.erb—we need to add the resizer class to our elementToChange target, and we need to change the data-css-css-class from hidden to shrink. Same toggle controller, but now it adds and removes the shrink class from the target rather than hidden. Another change made with no new JavaScript.

However, because the max-height is bigger than most of the elements, there appears to be a delay if the list is small (because it takes longer for the shrinking height value to get to the point where it's overtaking the text). It's also possible we might have an entire day's list of concerts bigger than 1000px, in which case the current implementation would cut it off, which is not ideal. In practice, I'd probably use Animate.css to make managing the animation a little easier.

Animating Turbo Streams with Animate.css

All this animation talk makes me wonder about the transitions we built in Chapter 2, Hotwire and Turbo, on page 19 with Turbo Streams, where we have new elements appearing in our favorites list and old ones being removed. It'd be cool to be able to animate those transitions.

Turns out we can do this, though managing the outgoing transitions takes a little bit more work.

I'm going to call in a helper for the animation, rather than continuing to code the transitions by hand. The Animate.css library adds quite a few useful little CSS animations that are just a couple of CSS classes away.[9]

The install process consists of two steps. First, add the package using yarn:

```
$ yarn add animate.css
```

Second, include the line @import "animate.css/animate.css"; in app/packs/entrypoints/application.scss.

---

9. https://animate.style

Now we can animate our transitions just by adding the CSS class animate__animated to any element and then following that with one of the several specific animation classes that Animate.css provides, like animate__fadeInUp.

Going back to our Turbo Streams example, when we add something to the favorites list, we'd like it to animate in. All we need to do in that case is add the Animate.css classes to the response HTML that the Turbo Stream sends back when we make a concert a favorite.

Here's how I did it—this snippet has changes for both the animate in and animate out in the _favorite partial:

```
chapter_05/06/app/views/favorites/_favorite.html.erb
<article class="my-6 animate__animated animate__slideInRight"
         id="<%= dom_id(favorite) %>"
         data-animate-out="animate__slideOutRight">
```

For animate in, I've added the CSS classes animate__animated animate__slideInRight to the article tag that surrounds the favorite listing. A side effect of this code as written is that on an ordinary page load, all the existing favorites will slide in from the right. If that bothers you, then you need to add another local variable so you can distinguish between "on page load" and "on turbo stream request" and add the animate classes conditionally.

This works. When you make a new favorite concert, the article will appear to slide in from the right.

Halfway there.

The problem with animating the removal of the concert is that we need to make sure the animation happens before Turbo Stream removes the element; otherwise, nobody will be able to see our snazzy animation.

To make that happen, we need to capture the Turbo Stream event before it is rendered. Then we can add the CSS classes and trigger the DOM removal ourselves after the animation completes.

Turbo provides an event hook for just this purpose called turbo:before-stream-render. The event is triggered after a Turbo Stream response is returned to the client but before Turbo Stream does anything with that response, which is perfect for us.[10]

Here's code that does what we want. To start, if you look at the earlier code, I added a "data-animate-out": "animate__slideOutRight" to the turbo-frame tag. This makes the choice of animation data-driven and also allows us to distinguish

---

10. https://turbo.hotwire.dev/reference/events

between Turbo Stream removals where we want an animation, which will have this data element defined, and those where we don't want an animation, which won't.

Here, I'm adding an event listener for turbo:before-stream-render:

```
chapter_05/06/app/packs/entrypoints/application.js
document.addEventListener("turbo:before-stream-render", (event) => {
  if (event.target.action === "remove") {
    const targetFrame = document.getElementById(event.target.target)
    if (targetFrame.dataset.animateOut) {
      event.preventDefault()
      const elementBeingAnimated = targetFrame
      elementBeingAnimated.classList.add(targetFrame.dataset.animateOut)
      elementBeingAnimated.addEventListener("animationend", () => {
        targetFrame.remove()
      })
    }
  }
})
```

(This code is based on sample code Nick Goodall posted to the Hotwire discussion board.)[11]

The event is passed to the callback function by Turbo; the event target is the code being returned. You get one of these callbacks for each Turbo Stream, so if your HTML response combines multiple requests, as ours does, you'll call this event multiple times.

The first thing we do is check the action of the stream event.target.action, which is the action= attribute of the incoming stream. We only care about removals for this part, so we only proceed if the action equals remove.

Next up we pull in the target frame ID, which is the target attribute of the event.target or event.target.target. Remember, the Turbo Stream looks like <turbo-stream action="remove" target="fav_concert_40">. We use document.getElementById to get the actual element on the page with that DOM ID, which is the Turbo Frame element we are planning to remove.

If the Turbo Frame element has a data-animate-out attribute, we know we want to animate it. Inside that if block, we first preventDefault(). Doing so keeps the event from being propagated, which in our case prevents Turbo from removing the element before we're done with it.

We then grab the element referenced by the target frame—in our case that's the article element that already has animate_animated added to it. (It's an

---

11. https://discuss.hotwire.dev/t/are-transitions-and-animations-on-hotwire-roadmap/1547

assumption of this code that the element being removed will be both a top-level element containing the entire contents of the frame and will already have animate__animated.)

We take the value of targetFrame.dataset.animateOut, which we set to animate_slide-OutRight, and we add it to the child element. We also add a listener to that element for the event animationend, which is fired by the DOM when an animation ends, and inside that listener we remove the targetFrame from the DOM by ourselves, which is what Turbo would have done with it anyway.

This works. When we hit the button to remove a favorite, an HTTP request is sent and the response is a Turbo Stream, which fires the turbo:before-stream-render event. Our listener captures that event, verifies the data, adds the correct CSS animation class to the top-level element of the stream data, listens for the end of the animation, and finally, removes the element.

This code is reusable. Anywhere we think a Turbo Stream might remove a frame, we can augment that frame with a data-animate-out attribute, and this listener will apply that animation on removal.

Using CSS and React Components

Where Stimulus encourages using the markup you are already writing, therefore keeping CSS in its own separate files, React encourages thinking about CSS and code together. Once you get in the habit of thinking of your page as made up of a number of different React components, it's only a small step to imagine those components as containing their own CSS for features that are specific to that component.

Including CSS with React code is such a common thought that there are oodles of libraries that handle this. I'm going to talk about one of these libraries that has an interesting way to insert CSS into your React code: styled-components.

What Is the styled-components Library?

The styled-components library allows you to define React components that include CSS styles inside the definition of the component.[12] When the component renders, the styled-components library generates CSS code with definitions for these styles and uses those generated CSS class names in the rendered HTML markup.

In practice, what this means is that we are not attaching CSS definitions to the React components we've already defined. Instead the internal markup of

---

12. https://styled-components.com

the components, such as div and span tags, is replaced with styled-components that contain their own CSS.

Why would you do such a thing? Isn't CSS good enough? CSS is great. However, there are a few reasons why it's helpful to bundle CSS with React components:

- It's easier to see what CSS applies to a component because the styling is right there in the same file as the component.

- There tends to be a better separation of styling from logic, and as a result, the logic components tend to be a little cleaner.

- The library gives you some protection against style bugs, such as using the wrong CSS class. It also prevents unused CSS from being sent to the page.

- The styled-components library has nice support for global properties.

And there are a few challenges associated with bundling CSS with React components:

- I don't love the syntax, especially for dynamic properties and especially with TypeScript. You'll probably want an editor plugin to help you out.

- It can be a little hard to debug the resulting CSS without additional plugins.

- It can encourage an overreliance on divs that make the layout harder to manage long term.

Overall, though, I think styled-components are pretty interesting and worth considering in your project. Let's add some to our project.

Installing styled-components

With TypeScript, we have to install two packages, and we're going to install an optional third package that will give us slightly better tooling in development:

```
$ yarn add styled-components
$ yarn add @types/styled-components
$ yarn add babel-plugin-styled-components --dev
```

We need to add the Babel plugin to the plugins section of the babel part of our package.json. My babel section now looks like this:

```
"babel": {
  "presets": [
    [
      "./node_modules/@rails/webpacker/package/babel/preset.js"
    ],
```

```
    [
      "@babel/preset-typescript"
    ]
  ],
  "plugins": [
    "babel-plugin-styled-components"
  ]
},
```

Now we can use the styled-components library on the components we added with React.

Creating Our First Styled Component

Let's look at our React components and see how we can use the styled-components library. As we left it back in Chapter 4, React, on page 63, we have four components with display elements on our concert view page: a VenueHeader that adds a header, a VenueBody that controls the grid, a Row that manages a row of seats, and a Seat that actually draws an individual seat.

Our first styled-components change is in VenueHeader. We want to change the styling of the text prompt and manage the spacing a little bit. Otherwise, the functionality is the same: when the option changes, we pass the new value back to the same ticketsToBuyChanged handler, stored in the Venue component and passed to VenueHeader via a prop.

Right at the top of the file we import styled-components. Then the real action comes with our declaration of Header:

chapter_05/07/app/packs/components/venue_header.tsx
```
import * as React from "react"
import styled from "styled-components"

const Header = styled.span`
  font-size: 1.5rem;
  font-weight: bold;
  margin-left: 15px;
  margin-right: 15px;
`
```

We're using the object styled, which comes from the styled-components library, followed by its method span and then a literal string containing CSS syntax, which in this case sets some font and margin properties. We'll talk about what all these bits do in a moment. For now, the structure to remember is styled, followed by an HTML tag, followed by a string of CSS. The return value of all this is a React component, which we are calling Header.

What About Tailwind?

We're using plain CSS in these styled-components rather than using Tailwind utilities because I want to talk about generic CSS here. If you want to use Tailwind along with styled-components, you should look up "Twin" on GitHub.[13]

Later, we can use the Header component in our JSX just like any other component:

```
chapter_05/07/app/packs/components/venue_header.tsx
export const VenueHeader = ({
  seatsPerRow,
  setTicketsToBuyCount,
}: VenueHeaderProps): React.ReactElement => {
  const setTicketsOnChange = (event: React.SyntheticEvent): void => {
    const target = event.target as HTMLSelectElement
    setTicketsToBuyCount(parseInt(target.value, 10))
  }

  return (
    <div>
      <Header>How many tickets would you like?</Header>
      <span className="select">
        <select onChange={setTicketsOnChange}>
          {options(seatsPerRow)}
        </select>
      </span>
    </div>
  )
}

export default VenueHeader
```

And it works. The text inside the call to Header gets passed through as a child and displayed with the new styling.

If you use the browser inspector to look at the resulting HTML, you'll see something like:

```
<span class="venue_header__Header-uae9pq-0 gtmzdP">How many tickets
would you like?</span>
```

The venue_header_Header-uae9pq-0 has no styles attached to it; it's a debugging header. Because we added the Babel plugin, that name includes the file name of the place it came from, venue_header, and the name of the component itself, Header. These names make it easier for us to track the styled code to the resulting HTML. And you'll see that gtmzdP (which will be different in your code), is in the style sheet with the four properties we defined.

---

13. https://github.com/ben-rogerson/twin.macro

What is this code doing? The magic word here is styled, which can be used in one of two ways:

- You can chain styled with an HTML tag name, as we did in this code with span. In this case, the result is a React component where that HTML tag is the top-level tag of the result.

- You can use the name of another React component as an argument to styled. We can even use this to extend our existing component, such as styled(Header).

In either case we end up with a function that directly takes our backtick string (technically called a *tagged template literal*) as an argument. There's some internal JavaScript mechanics going on here, which is why the code is styled.span`css` and not styled.span(`css`), but the details aren't important. What is important is that it's a JavaScript backtick literal, which means we can use ${} interpolations inside the string. (Although it's not the preferred method, you can pass a JavaScript object with key/values rather than a backtick string.)

The resulting value is a regular React component that can be used like any other React component.

Dynamic Styled Components

Next, let's add some additional styling to our actual Seat component. First, though, I see two concerns: our existing Seat uses a lot of Tailwind classes for styling, and we'd like to keep them. Second, we've been adjusting the background color of the seats based on their status, and we need to continue to do that. The styled-components library allows us to do both of these things.

The key point here is that the components that are returned using styled-component are regular React components, which means they can be passed props and you can use those props inside the literal template string to dynamically change the value.

Here's what the Seat looks like with some refactoring to take advantage of styled-components:

chapter_05/07/app/packs/components/seat.tsx
```
import * as React from "react"
import styled from "styled-components"

const stateColor = (status: string): string => {
  if (status === "unsold") {
    return "white"
  } else if (status === "held") {
```

```
      return "green"
    } else {
      return "red"
    }
}

interface SquareProps {
  status: string
  className?: string
}
const buttonClass = "p-4 m-2 border-black border-4 text-lg"

const ButtonSquare = styled.span.attrs({
  className: buttonClass,
})<SquareProps>`
background-color: ${(props) => stateColor(props.status)};
transition: all 1s ease-in-out;

  &:hover {
    background-color: ${(props) =>
      props.status === "unsold" ? "lightblue" : stateColor(props.status)};
  }
`

interface SeatProps {
  seatNumber: number
  status: string
  clickHandler: (seatNumber: number) => void
}
export const Seat = ({
  seatNumber,
  status,
  clickHandler,
}: SeatProps): React.ReactElement => {
  function changeState(): void {
    clickHandler(seatNumber)
  }

  return (
    <td>
      <ButtonSquare status={status} onClick={changeState}>
        {seatNumber + 1}
      </ButtonSquare>
    </td>
  )
}

export default Seat
```

There are a few different things going on here. Let's start by looking at the
definition of ButtonSquare in the middle of the file.

This use of styled-components adds a couple of new features. First, we start with a call to styled.span, but we chain a new method there, resulting in styled.span.attrs({ className: buttonClass }), where buttonClass is a previously defined list of our Tailwind utility classes. The attrs method takes as an argument a JavaScript object and merges that argument into the props as they are passed to the component. In this case, we're passing className as a prop, which React will interpret as a CSS class, so we get the existing styling. If you want to be a little fancier, the attrs method could also take as its argument a function (that function's argument is the props passed to the component and the return value is the attributes to be merged into the props).

Having ensured button styling, we now want to make sure the background color changes. In the previous version, the Seat had a function that converted status into color. In this version, the Seat is passing the status to the ButtonSquare styled component and the styled component is responsible for converting that status into a color.

First, the ButtonSquare is a component getting a prop, so we want to have a TypeScript interface to ensure that the prop has the expected attributes. We define SquareProps to take the status being passed in and the classNames being added in our attrs method. (The styled-attributes library says that if you use className in a props interface, it needs to be optional because of how the library works, so we're using the ?: syntax to mark it as optional.)

Within the template literal for the component, we can use the props by adding functions to be interpolated into the text. We set the background-color to background-color: ${props => stateColor(props.status)};, which sets the color based on the stateColor function defined at the top of the file. The stateColor is the same function as before except that we've moved it out of the Seat component, and we're now returning CSS colors directly, rather than Tailwind class names. We could use Twin, referenced earlier, to give us access to Tailwind class names here, but it's not necessary for this example.

It's a little annoying that you need to define the interpolation as a function, ${props => stateColor(props.status)}, rather than directly, ${stateColor(props.status)}, but it seems like you need the functional version to have the props variable be visible inside the interpolated expression.

We use the props again, this time to help define a hover special status. One nice feature of styled-components is that it has full support for pseudo-elements and nested elements, so we can easily add a hover state. In this case, the hover background color is lightblue if the state is unsold, otherwise, the hover background is the same as the existing background color.

We also added a static transition so that the background colors fade in and out.

Finally, we have to call our new ButtonSquare component, which we do as any other React component:

```
chapter_05/07/app/packs/components/seat.tsx
return (
  <td>
    <ButtonSquare status={status} onClick={changeState}>
      {seatNumber + 1}
    </ButtonSquare>
  </td>
)
```

We pass the props as we would with a regular React component, including the onClick prop, which is handled normally. When the seat's status changes, the prop changes, causing the ButtonSquare to rerender and recompute its background color.

If the styled component is wrapping an HTML element, any known HTML attribute passed as a prop will be transparently passed along to the underlying HTML, even if you use it as a prop in defining the styled component. If the styled component is wrapping another React component, then all props will be passed through to the wrapped component.

There's also a special prop, as, which you'd use if you want the outermost HTML tag to be something other than as defined by styled-components. For example, our ButtonSquare is defined as styled.span, but if we wanted it to be a div, we could call it as <ButtonSquare as="div">.

There's a bit more complexity to styled-components that's outside our scope at the moment. The docs are worth checking out for how to handle more complex cases.[14]

What's Next

In this chapter, we integrated CSS with our Webpacker build and React components. At this point we have the beginnings of a nice little web app going here. If you look ahead to Chapter 9, Talking to the Server, on page 161, we'll talk about moving the application itself forward. But before that, in the next three chapters, we're going to cover some more detailed background about webpack, Webpacker, and TypeScript. We'll be able to use that more detailed background to guide some of the design decisions we'll make in improving the app. First up, TypeScript.

---

14. https://www.styled-components.com/docs

Part II

Going Deeper

With some working code written, we'll take a side trip in this part and talk about the tools in a little more detail. We'll first talk about TypeScript, and then take a look at webpack and Webpacker.

CHAPTER 6

TypeScript

In programming, the *type* of a piece of variable data indicates the set of values that are valid for that data. For example, if I say that a variable is an integer, that means I expect the variable to have a value like 1, -3, or 357 and not a value like banana. If the variable is set to a value that is not of the expected type, we think that something bad will happen. In some languages, the attempt to set data to the wrong value leads to a compiler error; in other languages it leads to incorrect or unspecified behavior at run time.

All high-level programing languages use some concept of type to determine behavior. Which is to say that all of these languages determine behavior by using not just the value of a variable in the system but also information about what kind of value it is.

TypeScript is a superset of JavaScript that optionally allows you to add annotations to the code to specify type information.[1] TypeScript requires a compilation step that enforces type consistency and converts valid TypeScript to JavaScript suitable for browsers. The type system that TypeScript uses makes inferences about types based on the code, even if you do not explicitly provide type information. The goal of using TypeScript is to reduce code errors, first by preventing type mismatches, and as you become more advanced, by making invalid states into compiler-time errors so they are impossible to achieve at run time. TypeScript only enforces type consistency at compile time; it provides no protection against things that might happen at run time.

In this chapter, we'll cover the basics of TypeScript's syntax and semantics and take a glimpse at more advanced features. Throughout the rest of the book, you'll learn about other TypeScript features as they become important in improving the code we will be writing. We've already used some TypeScript

---

1. https://www.typescriptlang.org

features in our concert app to make claims about data types. Now let's go a little deeper on the syntax and see what TypeScript makes possible.

Using TypeScript

We've already installed TypeScript back in Chapter 1, Getting Started with Client-Side Rails, on page 3 by adding the Babel preset-typescript plugin and the webpack fork-ts-checker-webpack-plugin. TypeScript's configuration is managed by a tsconfig.json file, which basically specifies what TypeScript allows and the kind of code that TypeScript emits. (We'll talk about more about the tsconfig.json file in Chapter 14, Validating Code with Advanced TypeScript, on page 269.)

We don't have to explicitly call the TypeScript compiler. With TypeScript in place, whenever webpack processes our code, it will include the TypeScript compilation step. The TypeScript compiler will run, and if all its type checking passes, it will output JavaScript that webpack can package for the browser. If the type checking does not pass, it will return error messages explaining the problem.

The important bit here is that once the code is compiled, TypeScript is done. TypeScript provides no protection at run time if the behavior of your data does not match expectations. This is usually fine as long as all the data is created by your code, but it can be a problem if your code is accepting external data that has not been type checked (for example, incoming JSON data from a server). Client-side TypeScript can guarantee that you are dealing with the data consistently in your code, but it cannot guarantee that the incoming data has the structure you expect.

Understanding Basic TypeScript Types

At its most basic, TypeScript allows you to annotate any variable declaration with a type by using the syntax : <type>, as in let x: number. As we'll see, this can get more complicated, but the starting point is annotating variables with types.

TypeScript defines four basic types:

- boolean: A Boolean value must be either JavaScript's true or false value.

- number: JavaScript only has one numeric type for floating point numbers. TypeScript's number type supports floating point and integer literals, hex literals (0xab32), octal literals (0o1234), and binary literals (0b10010).

- string: TypeScript allows both single and double quotes as string delimiters and supports the backquote (\) syntax for template strings.

- object: TypeScript defines objects as anything that is a value and is not one of the above types, so not just raw objects, but also all instances of classes. Normally, you'd use a more specific type annotation as described below rather than using plain object.

Both null and undefined are also TypeScript types, and you can say something like let z: null = null, though it's not clear why you'd want to.

By default, TypeScript allows the values null and undefined to be assigned to any variable no matter what its declared type is. If you are familiar with other relatively modern static-typed languages like Elm, Rust, or Swift, you may know that those languages force you to explicitly declare when null is a valid value for a given variable. That is not the default case in TypeScript, presumably because forcing explicit null declarations would make dealing with external JavaScript libraries quite complicated. Also, allowing null and undefined values makes it easier to gradually add TypeScript to an existing codebase. However, there is a compiler option, --strictNullChecks, which prohibits assigning null to a value unless explicitly allowed.

Any type in TypeScript can be used as the basis of an array with two different syntaxes that work identically: string[] or Array<string>. The second syntax is an example of a more general TypeScript feature called *generic types*, which allows the same type structure—in this case an Array—to have a different internal type—in this case a string—while still retaining the same behavior no matter the internal type.

Generic types allow you to have type checking in cases where the fact that the type is consistent across a class or function is more important than what specific type is involved.

Data structures are a common use case for generic types. If you have a type that is a list, for example, and you want to write a method that returns the first element of the list, without generics, you might have to write that function signature differently for each potential type of data you might have in the list:

```
function getFirst(list: AStringList): string
function getFirst(list: ANumberList): number
function getFirst(list: AUserList): User
```

and so on. But there is a pattern here: the return value is always the same type as the values that make up the list.

TypeScript allows us to use generics to represent the pattern, like this:

```
function getFirst(list: AList<T>): T
```

The angle brackets here represent the generic type and the T is just an iden-
tifier and could be anything (or at least, anything starting with a capital letter).
Single-letter identifiers are usually used, at least in part, to make a clear
distinction between generics and specific types.

The elements of a TypeScript array need to all be of the same type. If for some
reason you need a linear structure that has multiple types, first you should
think really hard about whether that is what you really want (most likely you
want a class instead). But if you do want something like that, TypeScript calls
that a *tuple*, and the syntax looks like this:

```
let myTuple: [string, number, string] = ["Jennifer", 8, "Lee"]
```

If you access an element of the tuple within the declaration, in this case
myTuple[0], myTuple[1], or myTuple[2], then the return value is inferred to be the
type from that element's tuple declaration. So myTuple[0] is a string and so on.
If for some reason you access an element with a higher index than the elements in the array, please don't do that. TypeScript will let you do this, and
the inferred type of the return value is what TypeScript calls a *union type*,
meaning that the value is a member of one or more basic types.

Static vs. Dynamic Typing

At the most abstract level, there are two different strategies for dealing with
type information in a programing language: *statically* or *dynamically*.

A language with static types requires that each variable be assigned a type
when it is first declared. The language expects to know what the type of a
value is and uses that information to constrain at compile time what values
can be assigned to that variable.

Different static languages have different requirements for how types are
assigned. Some languages, like Java, require the type of every variable to be
explicitly stated when the variable is declared. Other languages, like Type-
Script, allow for *type inference*. In TypeScript, if you assign a variable with a
typical JavaScript assignment like this:

```
let x = "hello"
```

TypeScript infers from the assignment that x is meant to be a string and does
not require further information; you do not have to explicitly declare that x
is a string. Later, if we try to say x = 3, the TypeScript compiler will flag this
as an error because 3 is not a string.

Some static languages also infer that if there's a type like string, there is a type
"array of string," whereas in others you need to explicitly define the existence

of the array. Some languages require you to declare up front whether a value can be null; others don't.

On the other hand, a dynamically typed language, like Ruby or plain Java-Script, assigns types at run time. In a dynamic language, you do not need to ever declare the type of a variable in the code. The language checks type information at run time using the values that are currently set to the variables when language needs to determine behavior—for example, when a method is called on a variable.

Types still have meaning in a dynamic language even if the type is not explicitly assigned. In Ruby, a line of code like 2 + "3" will be an error, but the error will happen at run time rather than compile time. In most dynamic languages the code x + y will have different behavior if x and y are numbers than if they are strings, and this behavior will be determined based on the value of x each time the line of code is executed.

TypeScript turns JavaScript into a statically typed language. Whether or not this is a good change is a surprisingly hard question to answer empirically. Both the general case of static versus dynamic languages and the specific case of TypeScript versus JavaScript are debated endlessly, with actual data difficult to come by. Creating any kind of valid, reproducible, scientific evidence about the general usefulness of programming languages is challenging.

There are a few points that are not disputed *much:*

- A static language will catch errors in compilation that would otherwise potentially remain uncaught.

- Static languages generally are more verbose than dynamic languages, and there is sometimes a time cost to getting the compiler to agree that what you want to do is valid. More modern static languages use type inference to minimize the extra verbosity.

- Dynamic languages are generally more flexible and are usually considered easier to write code in, at least for small programs.

- Static languages provide more information to code analysis tools, so editor and tool support is easier to create. They also provide more meta-information in general, which can be valuable as communication about the code on larger teams.

The idea is that in a good static typing system, the benefits of tool support, communication, and error prevention will outweigh the costs of yelling at the compiler trying to get it to let you do what you want. In the general case of static versus dynamic languages, I think there's a lot of room for debate. In the specific case of TypeScript versus JavaScript, I think there is good reason to think there's some benefit.

Adding Type Annotations to Variables

That last section was a little on the abstract side, so let's talk more concretely.

TypeScript allows you, but does not require you, to annotate your JavaScript code with information about the types of various pieces of data in the code. TypeScript uses this information as a constraint on the values that those pieces of data can contain. If you declare a variable to be a number and then assign it the string value "3", the TypeScript compiler will complain and will not allow the code to be compiled.

If you don't add any explicit type information, however, you don't get the full benefit of using TypeScript. It will still catch some errors, such as assigning two different types of values to the same variable or if you try to send a function the wrong number of arguments. By adding as much type information as you can to your code, you will increase the value of TypeScript's type checking.

You can add type information to TypeScript in a few different ways.

When you assign a value to a variable in TypeScript using let or const (using var is not recommended), TypeScript assumes you intend that variable to be of the literal type of the assigned value.

If you have code that does this:

```
let index = 1
```

TypeScript infers that index is of type number. If you try to assign a different value to index, it will need to be a number. If you pass index to a function, it will only allow it if the expected type of the argument is a number.

In some cases you will know more about the type than TypeScript can infer. For example, I recently wrote the following buggy code:

```
// THIS CODE HAS A BUG
const validValues = this.existingValidValues() + "New"
this.elements().forEach(element => {
  option.hidden = !validValues.includes(element.value)
})
```

The intent of the code was to have existingValidValues return an array of strings, append New to that array, and then check that each element's value was in that array using the includes method.

However, an array + a string does not equal an array in JavaScript (it does in Ruby). Instead, it returns a string:

```
> ["1", "2"] + "3"
"1,23"
```

This caused my includes method to behave incorrectly—it was testing to see if the value was a substring of the resulting string, which is not exactly the same as seeing if the value was an element of the array.

TypeScript did not catch this issue because it assumed that I meant what I said on the first line, and since the expression as I wrote it returns a string, it assumed that I meant validValues to be a string. Which would have been fine under normal circumstances. It would have caught validValues.includes as a type error, but as it happens includes is a method on both string and array in JavaScript, so it didn't notice the type change.

Had I wanted to ensure that the value was of the type I expected, I could have changed that first line to have a type annotation:

```
const validValues: string[] = this.existingValidValues() + "New"
```

The annotation : string[] tells TypeScript that we expect the validValues to be set to an array of strings. We can use type annotations to describe the left-hand side of any variable declaration. Since the expression as written returns a string, the compiler would throw an error. The general use of : followed by a type is going to be the way in which we denote type annotations.

The fix to the code looked like this:

```
let validValues: string[] = this.existingValidValues()
validValues.push("New")
```

The push method updates the array in place and prevents the type issue.

Adding Type Annotations to Functions

Functions also get to participate in the static-typing fun. The parameters and return values can have type annotations, and the function as a whole has its own static type.

Annotating Function Parameters

TypeScript function parameters can have type annotations, with a similar syntax to what we've seen for variable declarations. The annotations work whether the function is a named function, an anonymous function, or a method of a class. All three of these examples have the same typing:

```
function priceOfTicket(row: number, accessType: string) : number { }

let priceOfTicket = function(row: number, accessType: string) : number { }

class Ticket {
  priceOfTicket(row: number, accessType: string) : number { }
}
```

In all three cases, the function priceOfTicket expects two arguments: a number first and a string second. It then returns a number.

Let's talk about the return type first. As currently written, all three of these functions would fail compilation because they claim to return a number, but at the moment they don't return anything. The TypeScript compiler will not compile a function that sets a return type but does not return a value.

If you want to claim explicitly that the function will not return a value, you can use the special type void, which means "no value":

```
function sendAnAlert(message: string) : void { }
```

Now you get the opposite behavior from the compiler—if you try to return a value from a void function, the compiler will complain.

If you don't explicitly specify the return type of the function, you still get TypeScript's best type inference based on the return value, which gives you some type protection:

```
function addThings(a: number, b: number) { return a + b }

let result: string = addThings(2, 3) // this will be a compiler error
```

In this case, TypeScript infers that the return value of the addThings function is a number because the returned value is the sum of two numbers. Later, assigning that value to the result variable, declared to be a string, will cause a compiler error even though the return value of addThings is not explicitly specified.

My recommendation is to be in the habit of explicitly specifying the return type in a function that returns values. Not only is specifying the return type better for communication, if you are relying on type inference, the type system won't catch if you accidentally return the wrong value or forget to return a value at all.

TypeScript function arguments behave differently than regular JavaScript in that the number of arguments to the function—the technical term is the *arity* of the function—is explicitly checked. So the following is valid JavaScript but invalid TypeScript:

```
function addThings(a, b) {
  return a + b
}

const result = addThings(2, 3, 4)
```

The function is declared with two arguments, but we call it with three arguments. TypeScript flags this as a compiler error even though we haven't specified any type information on any of this code. (In plain JavaScript, the third argument would be silently ignored.)

There are several legitimate cases where you might want to send different sets of arguments to the same function, and TypeScript offers a few different features to cover those cases.

First off, you can specify an argument as optional with the ?: syntax, as in:

```
function addThings(a: number, b: number, c?: number) {
  return a + b
}

const result = addThings(2, 3)
```

In this case, we've specified the c argument as optional, meaning that we can call addThings with only two arguments.

However, the optional argument is set to the value undefined if not used, and that might not be the most helpful. So TypeScript allows for a default value for an argument using basically the same syntax as Ruby:

```
function addThings(a: number, b: number, c: number = 0) {
  return a + b + c
}

const result = addThings(2, 3)
```

In this example, we can now safely add all three arguments because if the third argument is not specified, the default value takes over and c is set to 0. If you leave the type annotation off the default argument, function addThings(a: number, b: number, c = 0), then TypeScript uses inference to determine the type.

Optional arguments need to come at the end of the list of arguments, but arguments with default values can come anywhere in the list. Somewhat awkwardly, you can then trigger the default behavior by explicitly passing undefined to that argument.

Sometimes you legitimately want to allow an arbitrary number of arguments to a function, which you can do in TypeScript with the spread operator, ...:

```
function addThings(a: number, ...others: number[]) {
  return a + others.reduce((sum, value) => sum + value)
}

const result = addThings(2, 3, 4, 5, 6)
```

This time, any arguments passed to the method after the first one are accumulated into the others argument, which has an array type. We can then use that array like any other variable.

Annotating Functions as Variables

It's pretty common in JavaScript to pass functions as arguments to other functions or to return functions as the result of a function. And in TypeScript that means we need to be able to specify the types of functions when used as arguments or return values.

This gets a little meta, but the type of a function is based on the type of the arguments and the return value. We've seen small examples of this in our React code as we pass handlers up and down the stack. In the following snippet, the setTicketsToBuy function expects a number argument and returns nothing:

```
interface VenueHeaderProps {
  seatsInRow: number
  setTicketsToBuy: (n: number) => void
}
```

This syntax contains three quirks to be aware of.

First, the type information of the function is carried by the type annotations and not by the names of the arguments. We could specify the type as (newCount: number) => void, and that would be the same declaration.

Second, as far as the type system is concerned, there's no difference between an optional argument denoted with ?: and a default argument denoted with, say, result = 0. From the type system's perspective, both of those forms mean that the method being described has an optional number of parameters.

Third, you can use type inference to put the function type signature on either side of an assignment.

We've already seen this:

```
let priceOfTicket = function(row: number, accessType: string) : number { }
```

This form is equivalent:

```
let priceOfTicket: (row: number, accessType: string) : number =
  function(row, accessType) { /* function body */ }
```

In the second form, the type signature is on the side with the variable, not the side with the value. TypeScript uses that information to infer the types in the actual function.

Adding Type Annotations to Classes

TypeScript takes full advantage of the class features added to JavaScript in ES6. (There are a lot of references for ES6 classes; the basic syntax is available online.)[2] The goal of the TypeScript extensions to class syntax are to allow the TypeScript compiler to treat object attribute references and method calls the way functions and assignments are treated. We want to be able to tell from the class of the instance what attributes exist and the expected type of those attributes.

In TypeScript, any method defined in a class is available to instances of the class. You can annotate arguments and return values of a method just as you would for functions.

The first real change in TypeScript classes compared to JavaScript is the need to explicitly list attributes of the class that would, in plain JavaScript, only be created when assigned. In TypeScript, if you are going to refer to an attribute like this.color = "red", the existence of the color attribute needs to have already been declared.

We've already seen this in our Stimulus controllers, where we explicitly need to specify the properties that Stimulus is going to create so that the TypeScript will let us use them:

```
chapter_05/07/app/packs/controllers/css_controller.ts
import { Controller } from "stimulus"

export default class CssController extends Controller {
  static classes = ["css"]
  cssClass: string
```

---

2.   http://es6-features.org

```
static targets = ["elementToChange"]
elementToChangeTarget: HTMLElement

static values = { status: Boolean }
statusValue: boolean

toggle(): void {
  this.flipState()
}

flipState(): void {
  this.statusValue = !this.statusValue
}

statusValueChanged(): void {
  this.updateCssClass()
}

updateCssClass(): void {
  for (const oneCssClass of this.cssClass.split(" ")) {
    this.elementToChangeTarget.classList.toggle(
      oneCssClass,
      this.statusValue
    )
  }
}
}
```

We are specifying that this class has a property cssClass that is a string, an elementToChangeTarget that is an HTMLElement, and a statusValue that is a boolean. TypeScript uses this information in a couple of ways.

The name CssController can be used as a type just like the basic types we have already covered. You can annotate a variable, function parameter, or return value to be of type CssController and the compiler will require that those instances use only properties that have been explicitly defined by the CssController class.

TypeScript expands upon JavaScript class syntax in that it allows you to avoid repeating a declaration of a property, the naming of the property in the list of constructor parameters, and the assigning of the property.

So instead of:

```
class User {
  firstName: string
  lastName: string

  constructor(firstName, lastName) {
    this.firstName = firstName
    this.lastName = lastName
  }
}
```

you can use a modifier in the constructor parameter list, most commonly private, as shown here:

```
class User {
  constructor(private firstName: string, private lastName: string) {
  }
}
```

The two examples are functionally equivalent. When the constructor is called, TypeScript sets the properties of the instance based on the arguments to the constructor. TypeScript defines private, protected, public, and readonly keywords. A readonly property must either be set literally when it is declared or set in the constructor.

Defining Interfaces

Sometimes the type checking only cares about a subset of the properties of an object, or you have a common set of properties that might be shared by a number of different objects that are otherwise unrelated. It's useful to allow the type checking system to be as specific as possible and to specify that the objects being used are restricted to only the properties that are being used in a specific context.

Alternately, you might have some data in your system, such as the result of a server call that has returned JSON objects, and you'd like to assert in the type system that the certain properties must exist in the data. But you don't necessarily need to declare a class because there might not be any behavior for that data, just a structure you want to use.

You can manage all these issues in TypeScript by using *interfaces*. We've seen this in our React code, where we have been using interfaces to define type information for the props objects passed to each component.

Properties don't have to be just variables; they can also be methods, like onFilterButtonClick(x: Event): void. There are more complex scenarios for some rarer items that we won't get into here. As with functions, you can specify a property is optional by replacing the : with ?:. I recommend doing that rarely, as it weakens the type checking.

Once we have this interface, it's just as much a type as any basic type or class. We can specify the interface as the type of a variable, parameter, or return value, and the TypeScript compiler will enforce that those variables only use the listed properties.

You can also specify that a class implements a particular interface, so we could now say:

```
export default class SeatData implements SeatProps {
  seatNumber: number
  status: string
  clickHandler: (seatNumber: number) => void
  /* and so on */
}
```

Note that we still have to actually declare the properties in the class even though they are already declared in the interface. In practice, what's happening here is that the TypeScript compiler will require the class to declare all the properties of the interface. That's less helpful than you might think.

Interfaces, like classes, can use the extends keyword to mean "everything that other interface has, plus more":

```
interface VipSeatProps extends SeatProps {
  operaGlassesRequested: boolean
}
```

Our new VipSeatData interface still includes the seatNumber and status and clickHandler from the SeatProps interface, but also includes operaGlassesRequested.

Classes and interfaces can extend each other, but I'd recommend trying to keep classes extending other classes and interfaces extending other interfaces to avoid confusion.

Type Checking Classes and Interfaces

The preceding two sections are all leading up to the very important question of what exactly TypeScript checks when it checks a type.

For example, is the following legal?

```
class Hat {
  constructor(private size: number) {}
}
class Shirt {
  constructor(private size: number) {}
}
let x: Hat;
x = new Shirt()
```

In this code we have two classes, Hat and Shirt, that are not related to each other but have the same set of properties, namely an attribute called size, which is a number. Given that setup, can you declare a value of type Hat and then assign it a value of type Shirt?

In many typed languages, this sequence would be an error because the Hat and Shirt classes have no common ancestor. In TypeScript, though, this is legal.

In TypeScript, types are compared only on their list of properties (the TypeScript docs call this "structural typing"). The basic rule is:

Given an assignment, such as left = right, for every property on the left (receiving) side of the assignment, there must be a matching compatible property on the right side of the assignment.

In our earlier example, Hat has one property, a number named size. Shirt has a matching number property named size; therefore, a variable of type Hat can be assigned a value of type Shirt.

This compatibility match does not necessarily go in both directions if the two classes have different property lists. Let's add a property to Shirt:

```
class Hat {
  constructor(private size: number) {}
}
class Shirt {
  constructor(private size: number, private sleeves: string) {}
}
```

Now we've added a second property to shirt. Which of these is now legal?

```
let x: Hat = new Shirt()
let x: Shirt = new Hat()
```

The first line is still legal—Hat only has one property, and Shirt still shares it. But the second line is now a type error because Shirt has a property, sleeves, that is not contained by Hat.

The same basic idea of compatibility holds when you need to determine if two functions are type compatible with each other—meaning whether two functions, as first-class items in the system, can be used in the same place. For every parameter in the function type on the left side of the assignment, there must be a matching parameter (in order) on the right side. The right side can have extra parameters since passing extra parameters to a function and having them be ignored is not at all unusual in JavaScript.

In general, whether a parameter or property is optional or required does not make a difference as far as type compatibility is concerned.

If you are used to Java, or Elm, or some other strictly typed language, the TypeScript rules here may seem odd, and in a way, they are. TypeScript is more permissive than type systems in those languages because they can allow objects of unrelated types to be assigned. In fact, the TypeScript documentation discusses some edge cases where the compiler might allow code that turns out to be unsafe at run time. (We're not going to worry about those cases right here, but if you are curious, check them out on the TypeScript website.)[3]

The stated reason for managing the type system by structure and not relationships is that it turns out to be a good fit for the somewhat free-wheeling approach to types that you see in a typical JavaScript program. In particular, a lot of JavaScript code doesn't make a strong distinction between objects that are just created with object literal syntax and class instances created with new. The TypeScript type system allows you to apply type safety no matter how your objects or functions are created and no matter whether you have a class declaration for them.

A nice side effect of TypeScript's approach to typing is that it allows types to be easily added together to form a combined type. And it turns out that this kind of type composition is also a nice fit for common JavaScript patterns.

Getting Type Knowledge to TypeScript

There will often come a time where you will know more about the type information of data in your code than TypeScript will be able to infer. TypeScript provides a few different ways for you to refine the inferred types so as to allow more accurate typing.

TypeScript allows for typecasting with the keyword any. The any type is the default where TypeScript can't infer a type, and it means that any value is legal there. You can explicitly use any in cases where you think that TypeScript's expected inference is likely to be too constricting.

This is perhaps most helpful when dealing with data from libraries or modules that don't use TypeScript:

```
let externalValue: any = SomeModule.someFunction()
```

The use of any prevents TypeScript from doing any type checking on the externalValue variable, which means that the return value of someFunction won't be used to constrain other code.

In practice, using any allows you to gradually add type checking to existing code by explicitly stating what data is or is not type checked. As you add

---

more type information, often the uses of any can be replaced with more specific types.

Conversely, there are times when you may know the type is more specific than TypeScript assumes rather than more general.

When we know more about the type of the data than the compiler can know, TypeScript provides two ways to send that information to the compiler. The one we'll be using in this book uses the keyword as:

```
let elements: HTMLElement[] = document.querySelectorAll(this.targetSelector)
let inputElements: HTMLInputElement[] = elements as HTMLInputElement[]
```

An alternate syntax, which we won't use because it is confusing in React code, uses angle brackets:

```
let elements: HTMLElement[] = document.querySelectorAll(this.targetSelector)
let inputElements: HTMLInputElement[] = <HTMLInputElement[]>elements
```

An important fact about these type assertions is that they are compile time only—they are only there to give the compiler more information about the properties available on that data. If the data is incorrect at run time, you'll get a run-time error at the time you try to use a nonexistent property, not at the time of this type assertion. There is a way to do run-time type checks in TypeScript, which you'll see how to do in Chapter 14, Validating Code with Advanced TypeScript, on page 269.

There is one other place in which you might have more information than the compiler. If you have functions that return functions, TypeScript may not be able to infer the type of the this parameter in the internal function. To combat that, any TypeScript function definition can define this as the first parameter in an argument list. Defining this explicitly allows you to give this a type but does not affect the parameters that would be used in calling the function.

What's Next

This chapter provided a basic introduction to how TypeScript works. It can get a lot more complicated, though, which you'll see later on in Chapter 14, Validating Code with Advanced TypeScript, on page 269. First, let's talk about how TypeScript gets compiled and sent to the browser using webpack and Webpacker.

webpack

In the beginning, JavaScript was simpler. HTML elements in your markup had attributes with names like onclick, and if you wanted something dynamic to happen, you'd write like one line of code in the onclick attribute. Although this was simple, it was extremely limited. Eventually coders wanted more complex effects in the browser and started placing JavaScript code in files external to the HTML and sending them to the browser via the script tag.

This was still sort of simple but also still sort of limited. As time moved on, JavaScript programs got more and more complicated, and the need to include multiple JavaScript files grew. The dependencies on third-party libraries grew. We added CSS, SASS, CoffeeScript, templates, and on and on. And in addition to just compiling, we added performance-related tasks like minifying code or pruning unused CSS selectors.

There started to be a need to coordinate all of these build tools and make the path from the developers view of the code to the browsers view of the code clearer.

Which brings us, eventually, to webpack,[1] which is far from the first tool to try to take on this mountain of JavaScript build tasks, but is the one that grabbed enough developer mind share that Rails eventually decided to make it the basis of the Rails JavaScript asset management system.

In this chapter, we'll take a look at webpack, which is an external tool adopted by Rails. We'll also take a peek at Yarn and how it manages our dependencies.[2] In the next chapter, we'll add on Webpacker,[3] which is a part

---

1. https://webpack.js.org
2. https://yarnpkg.com
3. https://github.com/rails/webpacker

of Rails that simplifies using webpack within a Rails program. You'll see how we can use both to build our concert app.

Understanding Why webpack Exists

I find it a little hard to get my head around what webpack is actually supposed to be doing, in part because webpack is abstract—it's a mechanism to perform various transformations on your code without making strong claims about what transformations you should do. I don't think it helps much that webpack's official description of itself throws around jargony terms like "static module bundler."

Instead, I find it easier to discuss what problems webpack and its related tools are solving for us. As far as our Rails app is concerned, we're juggling three pieces of software that solve related problems for our client-side code: Yarn, webpack, and Webpacker.

The problem Yarn is designed to solve is: "What version of all my dependent modules does my program rely on?" Yarn is to JavaScript and npm modules what Bundler is for Ruby gems. Yarn's role in life is to make sure we have a manifest of the exact version of all our dependent modules and all their dependent modules and so on. Because JavaScript tends to have more but smaller dependencies than Ruby, managing all of them can be quite a load. Like Bundler, Yarn maintains a lock file with the current versions of all the modules in use. Unlike Bundler, your dependent modules are stored in the application directory, in a subdirectory called node_modules. Also unlike Bundler, if two modules are dependent on different versions of the same underlying module, Yarn will bring in both versions and allow each module to access its own version.

webpack is designed to solve a couple of different problems, such as: "How can my code consistently reference other code, whether it is in another one of my code files or in third-party modules?" and "How can I convert all my disparate front-end assets into something that can be sent to, and managed by, a browser?" webpack has a configuration file (as do many of the tools webpack depends on), which it uses to determine what it should do with the various input files.

Finally, the problem Webpacker is here to solve is: "webpack is really complicated, can you give me some reasonable defaults that work well with a Rails application?" Just as an aside, I find it really confusing that the two tools are named "webpack" and "Webpacker," and even more annoying that webpack's docs don't capitalize "webpack," but Webpacker's docs capitalize "Webpacker."

Where there's any chance of confusion, I'll be specific and refer to Webpacker as "Rails Webpacker." Rails Webpacker provides a default configuration for webpack and quick setup for many popular JavaScript frameworks.

Let's talk about these tools in a little more detail, starting with Yarn. We'll tackle Webpacker in the next chapter.

Managing Dependencies with Yarn

Yarn manages dependencies through a file named package.json—it uses the same format for package.json as Node Package Manager (npm) uses. (I'm not going to go over the fine details of installing Yarn on your system; you can find full documentation on the official website.[4] I'll only say that for the moment, Yarn 2.0 is not fully supported.)

Let's take a look at our code to see what a package.json file looks like at this point:

chapter_05/07/package.json
```
{
  "name": "north-by",
  "private": true,
  "dependencies": {
    "@babel/preset-react": "^7.13.13",
    "@babel/preset-typescript": "^7.12.7",
    "@hotwired/turbo-rails": "^7.0.0-beta.5",
    "@rails/actioncable": "^6.0.0",
    "@rails/activestorage": "^6.0.0",
    "@rails/ujs": "^6.0.0",
    "@rails/webpacker": "6.0.0-beta.6",
    "@tailwindcss/aspect-ratio": "^0.2.0",
    "@tailwindcss/forms": "^0.2.1",
    "@tailwindcss/typography": "^0.3.1",
    "@types/react": "^17.0.3",
    "@types/react-dom": "^17.0.3",
    "@types/styled-components": "^5.1.9",
    "animate.css": "^4.1.1",
    "autoprefixer": "^10.1.0",
    "css-loader": "^5.0.1",
    "css-minimizer-webpack-plugin": "^1.1.5",
    "fork-ts-checker-webpack-plugin": "^6.2.0",
    "mini-css-extract-plugin": "^1.3.3",
    "postcss": "^8.2.1",
    "postcss-flexbugs-fixes": "^5.0.2",
    "postcss-import": "^14.0.0",
    "postcss-loader": "^4.1.0",
    "postcss-preset-env": "^6.7.0",
```

---

4.   https://yarnpkg.com

```
    "react": "^17.0.2",
    "react-dom": "^17.0.2",
    "sass": "^1.30.0",
    "sass-loader": "^10.1.0",
    "stimulus": "^2.0.0",
    "styled-components": "^5.2.3",
    "tailwindcss": "^2.0.2",
    "typescript": "^4.1.3",
    "webpack": "^5.11.0",
    "webpack-cli": "^4.2.0"
  },
  "version": "0.1.0",
  "devDependencies": {
    "@tailwindcss/custom-forms": "^0.2.1",
    "@typescript-eslint/eslint-plugin": "*",
    "@typescript-eslint/parser": "*",
    "@webpack-cli/serve": "^1.3.1",
    "babel-plugin-styled-components": "^1.12.0",
    "eslint": "^7.16.0",
    "eslint-config-prettier": "*",
    "eslint-plugin-prettier": "*",
    "eslint-plugin-react": "^7.23.1",
    "prettier": "^2.2.1",
    "webpack-dev-server": "^3.11.2"
  },
  "babel": {
    "presets": [
      [
        "./node_modules/@rails/webpacker/package/babel/preset.js"
      ],
      [
        "@babel/preset-typescript"
      ]
    ],
    "plugins": [
      "babel-plugin-styled-components"
    ]
  },
  "browserslist": [
    "defaults"
  ],
  "scripts": {
    "eslint": "eslint '*/**/*.{js,ts,tsx}'",
    "eslint_fix": "eslint '*/**/*.{js,ts,tsx}' --fix"
  }
}
```

The package.json file is used to manage dependencies, configure some of those dependent tools, define commands for working with your code, and store information about your code should you choose to publish your code as a node module in its own right. This is different from Ruby gems behavior, where the dependency management is in Gemfile.lock but if you are packaging your code the metadata goes in a .gemspec file and dependency configuration is done separately. We're not going to talk about the metadata that is only used when publishing a module.

A lot of different kinds of information can be placed in a package.json file, but let's start with the information in the file we already have. This file was generated by Rails when we added Webpacker, and we've added a few more modules to it as we've moved forward.

Our package.json file has eight keys:

name

> The name of the module, assuming we are going to package it. Rails Webpacker installation fills this with the name of the application.

version

> The version number as a string. Typically this uses the major version, minor version, and patch version, but I suppose you could put anything in there you want. This is only really relevant if you plan to package the code as a module.

private

> This should be set to true in our case. You'd set it to false if you planned to publish the module.

dependencies

> The dependencies key has a list of packages that this code depends on to run. Our list right now includes (1) Rails-specific packages (the ones prefixed with @rails, and @hotwired); (2) Babel-specific packages that help compile TypeScript and JSX; (3) @types packages, which add type information for other libraries; (4) React and Stimulus packages; and (5) Tailwind and CSS libraries, like postcss and sass.
>
> Each of the package names is the key of a key/value pair, with the version as the value. I sometimes use * for the version in the book's sample code because I'm desperately trying to keep everything current. Mostly, though, you'd specify the version as a string. The version can be an exact match for the version being used by the code, as in "stimulus": "2.0.0",, but often the version number is prefixed with either >, which means any version greater than the listed version is okay, or ^, which means the version being used must match the major and minor version but can have a higher patch version. So "stimulus": "^2.0.0", matches version 2.0.0 and also 2.0.5 but not

2.1.0. If you are familiar with Bundler, this is the way the squiggly arrow operator (~>) works. If you want to match any version, the version string should be either empty, set within quotes (" "), or set as a wildcard character ("*").

You use Yarn to add items to the dependencies list with the command yarn add, as in yarn add typescript. Yarn will add the most recent version of the module, saving the actual code to the node_modules directory, adding the version information to the yarn.lock file and also adding the version to the dependencies list, prefixed by a ^. If you want, you can specify an exact version, as in yarn add typescript@3.3.0. You remove dependencies with yarn remove, as in yarn remove typescript.

devDependencies

Similar to dependencies but for tools that are only used in development, not in execution. Our list currently includes a bunch of linting libraries like eslint and prettier, as well as webpack-dev-server. You use yarn add --dev to add dependencies to this part of the package.json file.

babel

The babel key includes settings for the Babel JavaScript preprocessor.[5] In a Webpacker setup, Babel controls which JavaScript features we use, and also manages TypeScript and React compilation. In our case, we are deferring the Babel presets to a file Webpacker defines, which we'll look at more in Chapter 8, Webpacker, on page 149.

browserslist

The browserslist key includes the configuration settings for Browserslist,[6] a tool used to help the various compilers know what browsers to target and therefore what the compiler can output.

scripts

The scripts key is meant to give you project shortcuts for commonly run JavaScript commands. Something like a simplified version of rake. The key here is the name of the shortcut, and the value is the script to run. I've got two scripts in the package.json file, both related to eslint. You run these scripts with syntax like yarn run eslint, though yarn eslint will also work.

---

5.   https://babeljs.io
6.   https://github.com/browserslist/browserslist

A package.json file may include a lot of other possible parts, but most of them are only necessary if you are publishing a module. If you are interested you can see the whole list online.[7]

Once you have a new or updated package.json file, you can install all the dependencies with the command yarn install or just yarn. Running that command will resolve all the dependencies and the dependencies of the dependencies and so on. It will copy those modules to the node_modules directory of your app, and it will write the exact version information to the yarn.lock file. You'll want to make sure the yarn.lock file is in your source control, but you don't want the node_modules directory there. For one thing, it should be derived on each local machine, and for another, it's huge. (True story—the first time I used Webpacker for a code sample in a book I was writing for the Pragmatic Programmers, I forgot to take the node_modules directory out of the upload, and syncing with the remote source control system took over an hour for a single branch.)

By default, in non-production environments, Rails will leave it up to you to ensure your Yarn dependencies are up to date. You can change this behavior by changing the value of the check_yarn_integrity listen in the webpacker.yml file to true. If the value is true, then if you try to start a Rails server, run a Rake task, or do anything else that starts the Rails environment in a nonproduction environment, Rails will check that the yarn.lock file and the node_modules directory are consistent, and if not, it will stop and ask you to rerun yarn install before proceeding. (Note: Until recently, the default value of this field was true, and you will likely encounter code that does this check automatically.)

When one of your dependent packages releases a new version, to get Yarn to update the yarn.lock file and download the new version, use the command, yarn upgrade <package name>, like yarn upgrade tslint. If you don't include a package name, yarn upgrade will upgrade all the dependencies, at least to match the bounds specified in the package.json file. I can never keep straight that the command here is upgrade and not "update," so just one more time, the Yarn command for getting a new version of a thing is yarn upgrade.

Upgrading Yarn won't change the version string in the package.json file, but it will change the yarn.lock file. Conversely, if you do update the package.json file, you'll still need to run yarn upgrade to download the new version.

If you want to remove a package from the application, the syntax is yarn remove <package name>, as in yarn remove eslint.

---

7.   https://yarnpkg.com/en/docs/package-json

While Yarn helps us manage our dependencies, webpack is what allows us to refer to the dependencies in our code. Let's take a look at webpack next.

Understanding webpack Configuration

It's a little tricky to talk about webpack in the context of our project because webpack's behavior depends on its configuration file, and one of the things Rails Webpacker does is generate that configuration file from different inputs so we don't actually see the real webpack configuration in a file.

However, there's a partial workaround that will allow us to print out the configuration file, or at least most of it, and we're going to use it to guide our way through the way webpack works. We're then going to talk about how Webpacker simplifies webpack.

The workaround to let us actually see our webpack configuration is to go to the file config/webpack/development.js and add the following lines at the end of the script:

```
Object.defineProperty(RegExp.prototype, "toJSON", {
  value: RegExp.prototype.toString
});

console.log(JSON.stringify(module.exports, null, 2))
```

At this point, module.exports is an object containing the webpack config as JSON, so we're just asking to print it to the console with a two-space indent. We're also adding a little bit of extra code so that the regular expressions print properly. This won't get us the full text representation of the webpack config, but I think it's as close as we can easily get.

With that code in place, if you run the command bin/webpack, you'll see the entire webpack configuration in your terminal window.

You won't see the entire thing here in one piece; I'm going to break it down to cover webpack's main concepts. For each section, we'll see the webpack configuration and what it means, and then we'll see how Rails Webpacker uses defaults and convention to generate the configuration.

Mode

I'm going to show all these snippets one by one, but please remember that they are part of the larger configuration file. Also, these snippets may not exactly match the order that your file prints in.

```
{
  "mode": "development",
  "devtool": "cheap-module-source-map",
}
```

Unlike Rails, webpack only cares about two modes: development and production (okay, strictly speaking you can set the mode to none, but please don't do that). This setting sets the NODE_ENV environment variable, and that value is used within the code to manage features. Setting production is typically used to run some optimization plugins that we are not going to detail here.

In Rails, Webpacker sets this variable based on your Rails environment; if you are not in development, you are in production. So, for example, a staging environment gets the production plugins. But, just to be a little confusing, Webpacker allows you to maintain separate configuration files based on your Rails environment. So Webpacker allows you to generate, say, a different environment for testing, but the NODE_ENV environment variable in that configuration will still be set to either development or production by the Webpacker config.

The devtool parameter controls the generation of source maps. A *source map* is a separate file that relates lines in your originally coded file in TypeScript, CoffeeScript, or what have you with the JavaScript file eventually sent to the browser. With a source map, debugging tools in the browser can show you your original file and not the derived file, making the code easier to navigate. The cheap-module-source-map map is a somewhat faster version of a regular source map that has line-to-line fidelity but not column-to-column fidelity. In production, Rails Webpacker sets this parameter to source-map, which generates a separate source map for each file and connects it to the webpack pack so that the browser can find the map.

The use of source-map as a production default is recent in Webpacker—originally it didn't generate production source maps by default. In fact, the webpack documentation specifically says, "You should configure your server to disallow access to the Source Map file for normal users!" in a bright-yellow alert box. But David Heinemeier Hansson and the Basecamp team had a change of heart after reflecting on how the openness and availability of HTML and JavaScript were pretty important in helping people learn the early web, and the default was changed in Rails Webpacker.

If you want to change the behavior back, you can see the options at the webpack documentation.[8] See Customizing Webpacker, on page 155 for an example.

---

8. https://webpack.js.org/configuration/devtool

Entry

Our generated configuration file has an *entry* setting with one entry for each pack. We have defined two packs: the application pack that has the Stimulus code and our CSS, and the venue_display pack that covers the React code:

```
"entry": {
    "application": [
        "/Users/noel/projects/pragmatic/north_by/app/packs/
            entrypoints/application.js",
        "/Users/noel/projects/pragmatic/north_by/app/packs/
            entrypoints/application.scss"
    ],
    "venue_display": "/Users/noel/projects/pragmatic/north_by/app/packs/
        entrypoints/venue_display.tsx"
},
```

The *entry* in a webpack application is a file or files that webpack uses as the starting point for a chunk of code. The expectation is that the entry file will import all the other dependencies in the code (like an asset pipeline manifest file), and webpack will use this information to build a dependency graph—a list of all the dependencies used by the code—so that it can resolve imports and then convert all the code to a browser-friendly file.

By default, a webpack configuration will have one entry point at "main": "./src/index.js". There are two options for the entry syntax. Our application pack, which has two entry files, uses the array syntax. In that syntax, all the entry files are built together.

More commonly, and as our other pack handles it, you can use object syntax, where the key is the name of the pack and the value is the file name that is the entry point for that pack.

You can also specify a function as the value of the entry, which we're not going to do but which you might do if your webpack build depended on a dynamically updated set of files from some external source. Seems like an unusual use case to me, which probably means that I'll see a dozen examples of it next week.

In general, the webpack documents recommend one entry point for each separate HTML page that uses JavaScript components. The entry points can all reference the same underlying code, but by separating a different entry point for each HTML downloaded page, you can focus each page on only the dependencies relevant for that page. This causes a smaller download on each page load to the client at the slight cost of maintaining multiple different pages on the server, where each page likely would have some overlap with the others. This implies that a single-page application would have only one entry point.

Although our configuration doesn't use it, many webpack configurations also have a "context" setting, which gives an absolute path that is used as the base path for all the entry points, preventing you from needing to explicitly specify the entire absolute path for each entry point.

For a Rails app, Webpacker uses a convention to prevent us from having to spell out all the entry points explicitly. Webpacker creates an entry point for each file in the application/packs/entrypoints directory. Our Rails app doesn't need to specify a separate context setting because Webpacker is happy to generate the entire absolute path for each entry point. Webpacker doesn't care how you structure the rest of your files, but it does expect every separate pack you want to generate to have a suitable entry file in that directory.

Output

Our generated configuration has some things to say about the output of webpack's run:

```
"output": {
    "filename": "js/[name]-[contenthash].js",
    "chunkFilename": "js/[name]-[contenthash].chunk.js",
    "hotUpdateChunkFilename": "js/[id]-[hash].hot-update.js",
    "path": "/Users/noel/projects/pragmatic/north_by/public/packs",
    "publicPath": "/packs/"
  },
```

There's a lot here, and all of this has to do with where webpack puts the files that it generates.

Let's start with the path and publicPath options. The path is the absolute internal drive location where you want webpack to place its completed, browser-ready files. The publicPath option is the flip side of that, it's the relative location of the output files when requested by the browser. The public path is made part of any URL that webpack needs to create to refer to assets, so it must be consistent with your server configuration or the browser won't be able to access any resources.

webpack uses the filename property to determine the pattern used to name each individual outputted pack. In this case, the pattern "js/[name]-[contenthash].js" indicates that JavaScript files will go into the js subdirectory. The token [name] will be replaced by the name of the pack and the [contenthash] token will be replaced by a hash digest based on the entire content of the pack being outputted. The hotUpdateChunkFilename is similar, but for, well, hot updates. Hot updates and "chunks" are webpack code optimization features, and we're not going to talk about them here.

All of these outputs are generated by Rails Webpacker based on defaults we can edit. There are a lot of other options for output, but most of them are not relevant to us from our Rails application. A later part of the configuration generated by Webpacker uses plugins to place generated CSS files in "filename": "css/[name].css".

Loaders

The third main webpack concept is *loaders*. A loader is somewhat awkwardly named; it's just a transformation that changes a source file in some way. For example, a Babel loader applies Babel to our code, which is where our Type-Script compiler comes in. Other default loaders handle converting SASS to plain CSS and changing the file name of static file assets. Loaders go into the configuration file as a list inside the module:rules parameter.

Our default configuration includes a few loaders. The configuration for the Babel loader will give you the general idea:

```
{
  "test": "/\\.(js|jsx|mjs|ts|tsx|coffee)?(\\.erb)?$/",
  "include": [
    "/Users/noel/projects/pragmatic/north_by/app/packs"
  ],
  "exclude": "/node_modules/",
    "use": [
      {
        "loader": "/Users/noel/projects/pragmatic/north_by/node_modules/
            babel-loader/lib/index.js",
      "options": {
        "cacheDirectory": true,
        "cacheCompression": false,
        "compact": false
      }
    }
  ]
}
```

There are two parts here: the *test* and the *use*. In our case, the test provides a regular expression. If a file matches that regular expression, the rule for that loader is invoked (there are other test options that are less commonly used). The regular expression here matches any file that ends with .js, jsx, mjs, .ts, .tsx, coffee, and any of that list with the additional suffix of .erb—the erb files can be configured to be parsed by ERB before TypeScript, though I don't think we are currently so configured.

The use option specifies what to do if the file passes the test. In this case, it specifies a loader to pass the file to and a set of options to pass to the loader. Multiple loaders can be specified, in which case they are all applied to the file.

Rails Webpacker includes a loader for static images, several loaders for CSS or SASS, and Babel for processing JavaScript files. Other loaders can be added manually.

Resolve

You'll see that our webpack configuration file has sections called resolve and resolveLoader. These sections manage how code in our app can address code that is not in the same file.

The resolve section starts with a list of extensions:

```
"extensions": [
  ".js",
  ".jsx",
  ".mjs",
  ".ts",
  ".tsx",
  ".coffee",
  ".css"
],
```

This list of extensions has a small but important part to play in module resolution. When you import a file without its extension, as in import * as ActiveStorage from "@rails/activestorage", webpack searches for a file with one of these extensions—in order—to determine which file to actually import. If you want to explicitly include the extension of the file in the import statement, you must have a wildcard ("*") entry in the list.

Another important entry in this part of the configuration is the list of modules:

```
"modules": [
  "/Users/noel/projects/pragmatic/north_by/app/packs",
  "node_modules"
],
```

This list is the complete list of where webpack should look to find modules, in our case, we look in our app files first, and then in the node_modules directory for third-party modules.

The resolveLoader section is only used to find webpack's own loaders. In our case, the configuration is:

```
"modules": [
  "node_modules"
],
"plugins": [
  {}
]
```

which means loaders are only searched for in the node_modules directory.

Plugins

Plugins are small bits of code that can have arbitrary effects on the webpack process. webpack itself splits a lot of its features into plugins so they can be added only to projects that use them. You can see a list of official plugins online,[9] and there are a lot of third-party ones as well.

As for what plugins our application uses, Rails Webpacker adds four of them to the default configuration, but our little pretty-printer for the environment fails on plugins because they are typically JavaScript objects in their own right and aren't converted to JSON usefully. So this isn't exactly what you see in the printout, but it is what our configuration resolves to:

```
"plugins": [
  {
    "keys": [ // LOTS OF STUFF ],
    "defaultValues": { // LOTS OF STUFF }
  }
]
```

What do all of these do?

The keys and defaultValues are courtesy of the EnvironmentPlugin, which is provided by webpack and makes your entire list of environment variables visible to webpack in case you want to refer to them in your code.

CaseSenstivePathsPlugin is a third-party module that prevents conflicts between developers using MacOS and other operating systems. For example, in MacOS, files that have the same name but different case, like test.js and Test.js, are considered the same file, whereas other systems would consider them different files. Because of this, a developer on a Mac might reference a file using the wrong case; it'll work for the Mac but then error for other machines. This plugin avoids that by causing a build error if an import statement doesn't match the actual case of the file on disk.

---

9.   https://webpack.js.org/plugins

The MiniCssExtractPlugin is the plugin that pulls CSS files that we import into a separate CSS file on disk, and the WebpackAssetsManifest is what generates the hash and chunkhash part of the output file so that saved files have a format like application-8f20d660421d3ae59057.js.

Dev Server

Our development configuration has a lot of options for configuring the webpack-dev-server program. We can use webpack-dev-server to live reload webpack assets while in development. This is a great lead-in to Rails Webpacker, and how to leverage it during development.

What's Next

In this chapter, we saw how webpack lets us write files in the structure we want and still convert them to files that are manageable for a browser. Our Rails app uses webpack through the wrapper of Webpacker. In the next chapter, we'll take a look at how Webpacker works to make webpack integrate more easily with Rails.

CHAPTER 8

Webpacker

As Rails 6 developers, our primary interaction with webpack is going to be through the Webpacker tool provided by Rails. In this chapter, we'll take a look at using Webpacker in development and how to customize it when you want additional features.

As I write this, the current version of Webpacker is 6.0 beta 6. I expect there to be some changes before 6.0 goes final.

Installing Webpacker

 The Webpacker gem is a default part of a new Rails 6 installation, which means Webpacker goes in the Gemfile. And by default, the webpack:install task is run when the app is created. You can skip Webpacker entirely with rails new . --skip-webpack-install. After the app is created, you can add Webpacker to an existing app with the rake task rails webpacker:install.

Webpacker Basics

Webpacker is a wrapper around webpack, designed to make webpack easier to manage within a Rails application.[1] The main thing Webpacker does is generate a webpack configuration using a set of inputs that is hopefully simpler to deal with than a full webpack configuration. It uses a YAML file, config/webpacker.yml, to specify a lot of webpack values, and specific environment overrides are in the config/webpack directory.

That basic configuration gives you the following features:

- Any file in app/packs/entrypoints with a known extension (usually a JavaScript or CSS extension) is the entry point of a new *pack*. The name of the pack

---

1.   https://github.com/rails/webpacker

is the base name of the file. If there are multiple files with the same base name but different extensions, they are combined into the same pack.

- Any file in app/packs can include any other file in app/packs relative to app/packs. Any file in node_modules can also be included.

- Resources in a pack can be added to a page by using the helper method javascript_pack_tag.

- CSS in a pack can be added to a page by using the helper method stylesheet_pack_tag.

- Static images can be used in a link or img tag with the asset_pack_path helper method.

- In development, Rails automatically calls webpack to compile code on a page load if the webpack files have changed. You can trigger this compilation manually by running a script named bin/webpack.

- A development server, bin/webpack-dev-server, can be run. This compiles webpack on page save, and live reloads the page if possible. When using webpack-dev-server, webpack assets aren't saved to disk; they are served by the dev server.

- When deploying, the webpack compiler can be invoked to put your static files in the public directory where they can be read.

That's a lot of things! Let's, well, unpack them.

Writing Code Using Webpacker

In development, we mostly worry about three things: writing our code, getting our code on to the page, and being able to recompile the code quickly and easily.

Somewhat uncharacteristically for Rails, Webpacker does not suggest any structure for your code beyond having the entry point be in app/packs/entrypoints. The important feature is that you can import files relative to either app/packs (for your own code) or node_modules (for third-party code).

That said, some suggestions:

- Keep as little code as possible in your actual entry point; it should mostly just import things.

- Where possible, having multiple modular small pack files is probably better than having a single one. (There's a webpack optimization that makes this optimal from a download standpoint.)

- If you import a directory, rather than a file, the module system will automatically import the index.js (or index.ts) file in that directory. We've already seen this in our boilerplate code: the pack imports controllers, and controllers/index.js handles the autoload of controller modules. You can use this to modularize your imports somewhat and make it easy to share common imports across pack files.

- Your framework of choice may have some community standards for how code is structured. If so, you should follow them.

- I wouldn't put anything other than entry point files in the entrypoints directory, and I wouldn't create any subdirectories there either. But I wouldn't use those subdirectories for regular source code.

- It's tempting, but avoid creating a top-level app/packs/src directory on the ground that anything in the app/packs directory is source of some kind or other. Try to be more specific about top level names.

- I would, though, try to separate out CSS into app/packs/stylesheets.

To use a pack in your Rails code, you use the helpers javascript_pack_tag or stylesheet_pack_tag. These use webpack "chunks" by default. In webpack, a chunk is a way to extract common dependencies so that if you are importing multiple packs, shared dependencies are only downloaded to the browser once.

Both of the helpers work the same way. The arguments are a list of pack names and an optional set of options. The helper creates a script tag (for JavaScript) or a link tag (for CSS) for each pack name in the list. Both methods just defer to the existing Rails helpers javascript_include_tag and stylesheet_include_tag, and any options are just passed right through; although in practice, most of the options to the existing Rails helpers have to do with modifying the eventual URL and aren't really relevant to packs.

There's a little bit of tension between the classic Rails structure of just putting the javascript_include_tag in the header for all pages and what is probably a more webpack-idiomatic structure of having a lot of small packs and only loading the ones you need for each page. Therefore, if your setup is at all complicated, I recommend you use the Rails content_for feature to customize the header on a per-page basis.

To do this, in the HTML header where you might otherwise have the call to javascript_pack_tag, try this instead:

```
<%= yield(:packs) %>
```

Then in any page that uses packs, do something like this:

```
<% content_for :packs do %>
  <%= javascript_pack_tag(:application) %>
<% end %>
```

The yield/content_for construct allows you to customize the webpack output on a page-by-page basis and has the side benefit of making the available Java-Script visible on the individual page itself, which can make it a little easier to figure out what's going on.

Integrating Webpacker with Frameworks

Once upon a time, when this book was young and Hotwire was just a gleam in DHH's eye, Webpacker included installation scripts for many different frameworks and tools. The Webpacker team has abandoned that approach, presumably on the grounds that keeping up to date with nearly a dozen different JavaScript tools can be exhausting. (I can relate.) Also, most tools provide webpack instructions now, and those can be used directly.

However, there are some special cases:

CoffeeScript

> If you install the correct loader, yarn add coffeescript coffee-loader, Webpacker will compile .coffee files using the CoffeeScript compiler.[2]

CSS

> You need to install several packages for CSS support: yarn add css-loader mini-css-extract-plugin css-minimizer-webpack-plugin. There's an optional change to the config/webpack/base.js file for easier file resolving. Also, you can optionally add support for PostCSS (yarn add postcss-loader), Sass (yarn add sass sass-loader), Less (yarn add less less-loader), or Stylus (yarn add stylus stylus-loader). Files with the correct extension will be processed by that tool:

```
const { webpackConfig, merge } = require("@rails/webpacker")
const customConfig = {
  resolve: {
    extensions: [".css"],
  },
}
module.exports = merge(webpackConfig, customConfig)
```

ERB

> With the rails-erb-loader installed, any webpack file can have an .erb extension, which causes the file to be parsed by ERB before any other processing.[3]

---

2.   https://coffeescript.org
3.   https://github.com/usabilityhub/rails-erb-loader

React

> Installing yarn add react react-dom @babel/preset-react causes the Babel preset to adjust to compile .jsx files (and .tsx files if you are using TypeScript).[4]

TypeScript

> Installing yarn add typescript @babel/preset-typescript makes Babel aware of .ts files, and yarn add fork-ts-checker-webpack-plugin adds the actual type checking to the compiler. You also need a tsconfig.json file, which we'll talk about in Chapter 14, Validating Code with Advanced TypeScript, on page 269.[5]

Stylesheets and Assets

With Webpacker, you can include CSS files and external modules into your JavaScript in the same way you would a JavaScript module. In fact, many of the CSS frameworks package themselves as npm modules for easy installation (though in some cases you need your own SCSS file to import them). But even if you have written a CSS or SCSS file, you would still include it using the same import syntax you would use for a JavaScript file.

Once included, Webpacker uses the mini-css-extract-plugin to create a separate pack for the CSS information that you then load. Alternately, you can use a css or scss file with the same name as the js pack to create a Stylesheet pack.

Often, third-party Node modules will have CSS imports as well as JavaScript imports (for example, enhanced form tools like Chosen[6]). The CSS file is just included in the entry point along with the JavaScript file.

If you have included PostCSS,[7] you also need to create a postcss.config.js file, which you can use if you want PostCSS behavior and which involves many different kinds of processing on CSS and SCSS files.

If you want to access static files served by webpack, Webpacker provides a few helper files. Images require a little bit of special treatment. The image_pack_path and image_pack_tag helpers mimic the default Rails image_path and image_tag helpers and assume that image paths are relative to app/packs/images. So our previous example uses image_pack_tag("chevron-right.svg") to find a file that is at app/packs/images/chevron-right.svg. For images that are not in the app/packs/images directory, prepend your file with media, as in image_pack_tag("media/static/file.gif"). Webpacker also provides a favicon_pack_tag and a generic asset_pack_path helper.

---

4. https://reactjs.org
5. https://www.typescriptlang.org
6. https://harvesthq.github.io/chosen
7. https://postcss.org

Running webpack

Rails offers three ways to compile your webpack packs:

- Running bin/webpack from the command line
- Compiling automatically from the Rails development server
- Running bin/webpack-dev-server to automatically compile when files are changed

Rails provides bin/webpack, which is just a command-line interface to running the webpack compiler. You can run this at any time, and webpack will output files to (by default) /public/packs.

Rerunning webpack manually all the time is something of a pain, so Rails will do it for you in development. By default, if Rails encounters a pack_tag helper and there are changed files in the pack, Rails will automatically rerun webpack before rendering the page. That works, but it can be slow, especially if you are compiling a lot of files.

The alternative is webpack-dev-server, which is a server that manages compilation and delivery of your webpack files in development. To run it, you need to start a new terminal session, go to your application directory, and invoke this command:

```
$ bin/webpack-dev-server
```

You'll see some output from the compilation of your webpack assets and then the server will wait. When you save a file that is part of a pack, the dev server will recompile, and will also live reload a browser page if you have one open. If the compilation fails, the reloaded browser page will get an error message. This is usually more convenient in development than just allowing Rails to compile on page hit.

A Note or Two from Experience

webpack-dev-server recompiles and reloads when the JavaScript changes. It does not recompile and reload when you change your Rails view file. So staring at the browser waiting for your changes to show up does not work if you've only touched the view file.

Also, if you are working on multiple Rails apps at once, make sure you close webpack-dev-server on the apps you aren't working on or you'll get weird results if your running webpack-dev-server doesn't match your running application.

You can configure the dev server—the default configuration is stored in the config/webpack.xml file, and those values are passed right through to the webpack config. I've never needed to touch these values. The configuration does let you change the port and host that the server listens on, and I can see where that would be useful if you had multiple apps running at once or if you had a non-standard development environment (for example, you might need to change the host if you are using Docker).

Deploying Webpacker in Production

Deploying Webpacker to production or staging is similar to deploying previous Rails asset tools. Webpacker creates a Rake task, webpacker:compile, which is made part of the existing Rake task assets:precompile and which is likely part of your existing deployment script. If you are starting a new project without an existing asset pipeline, you can still use assets:precompile for compatibility with older build tools. It's essentially an alias to webpacker:compile. The compilation uses the RAILS_ENV value to determine which version of the Webpacker configuration to load.

Customizing Webpacker

Webpacker provides great defaults for webpack, but defaults aren't always enough; you may still need to customize.

One way to customize Webpacker is to change the settings in the config/webpacker.yml file. You can't add new settings to this file, but you can change the defaults that are already there, including the input and output paths, webpack-dev-server settings, and extensions to look for.

More elaborate customizations involve changes to the configuration files in the config/webpack directory. This directory contains four files by default: an environment.js and then a development.js, production.js, and test.js file. The way this works is that Webpacker chooses which file to load based on the Rails environment and each of these files sets the NODE_ENV value (the test.js uses the Node environment of "development"). The files then require in the environment.js file, do any environment-specific tweaks, and then export the resulting webpack configuration.

By default there are no environment-specific tweaks, but you can add some. The idea here is that the generated webpack configuration is loaded into a variable called environment. The value of environment is the webpack configuration as a JavaScript object. To make changes, you need to add keys or change the values of keys in accordance with webpack's configuration.

For example, I talked earlier about how Webpacker enables source maps in production. If you'd like to override that choice, you can add the following lines to the config/webpack/production.js file after the environment variable is created but before it is exported:

```
environment.config.merge({ devtool: 'none' })
```

Adding plugins is a little different; you need to prepend them to the environment.plugins array. The exact syntax is going to depend on the plugin, so check the documentation.[8] Here is an example that uses the ProvidePlugin to automatically load jQuery and attach it to the global identifiers most often used to invoke it.[9] The prepend method here is defined by Rails Webpacker's ConfigList and takes a name for the plugin and inserts it at the beginning of the configuration list.

```
environment.plugins.prepend(
  "Provide",
  new webpack.ProvidePlugin({
    $: "jquery",
    jQuery: "jquery",
    jquery: "jquery",
    "window.jQuery": "jquery",
  })
)
```

If you need the plugin to be invoked in a particular order, usually because you are adding a plugin that requires or is required by another plugin, you can use the insert method, which takes the same first two arguments and then a third argument, which is an object of the form {before: key} or {after: key}. So if you wanted the jQuery plugin to be loaded before some other plugin named, it might look like this:

```
environment.plugins.insert(
  "Provide",
  new webpack.ProvidePlugin({
    $: "jquery",
    jQuery: "jquery",
    jquery: "jquery",
    "window.jQuery": "jquery",
  }, {before: "Dependent"})
)
```

---

8.   https://webpack.js.org/plugins
9.   https://webpack.js.org/plugins/provide-plugin

Similarly, you can add your own loaders. Webpacker already provides an example here for TypeScript. The Rails configuration has it split over two files, but combined, it would look like this:

```
environment.loaders.prepend('typescript', {
  test: /\.(ts|tsx)?(\.erb)?$/,
  use: [
    {
      loader: 'ts-loader',
      options: PnpWebpackPlugin.tsLoaderOptions()
    }
  ]
})
```

Again, you have the option of using prepend or insert to specify the order.

In the case of a loader, if the loader is working with a file type that is not already in your configuration, you also need to update the config/webpacker.xml file to add your new extension to the existing list. If you look at that file now, you'll see that the extensions key has had .ts and .tsx added to it.

What's Next

With our build system explained, we're ready to add more complex features to the code. In the next part, we'll talk about communicating with the server, managing state, and how we can manage communications both with our server and across our client pages as part of our Stimulus and React code.

Part III

Managing Servers and State

In this part, we'll look at communicating with the server and managing the state of the data in your client-side application. We'll discuss a common JavaScript pattern called a reducer, and we will apply it in Stimulus and React. Then we'll talk about Redux, a library that implements the reducer pattern and is commonly used with React.

Talking to the Server

Communicating with the server is an important task of client-side apps. The server is usually the source of data truth, and it has information the client needs. For example, server information may have changed, and we may need updated data to draw a new part of the client application. The server also often needs to be informed of actions taken on the client.

In a Hotwire environment, you can use Turbo Frames and Turbo Streams to manage a lot of server interactivity through regular HTTP requests to the server, which then returns regular HTML responses. However, sometimes you may want to manage server communication as part of your Stimulus and React code.

In this chapter, we'll look at using Stimulus to mediate a form submission in our sample application to get information from the server about which concerts are sold out. Then, we'll discuss what to do when you have to contact a server that returns data rather than HTML. We'll also look at how to get React components to receive API data and incorporate it into their state by sending and receiving data about which seats in the concert have already been held.

Using Stimulus to Manage Forms

Turbo is designed to allow regular form submissions to trigger interactive changes on a page without having to reload the entire page. Sometimes, though, you need a little more client-side zest. You might want the form to be submitted on a user action other than clicking a Submit button. Or you might want to gather data from elsewhere on the page. In either case, you can use Stimulus to mediate your form submission.

If you look at the schedule page of our application, it has a search bar that currently does nothing except maybe offer typing practice. What we'd like it to do is return search results on typing. Specifically we want the following functionality:

- Typing in the box triggers a form submission with search results.

- Receiving search results uses Turbo Frames to place those results in a modal that overlays our page.

- Clearing the search field clears the modal.

- Clicking outside the modal window clears the modal.

For those of you who use the Hey email app,[1] this functionality is based on Hey's search functionality, though this is a simplified version of it.

To make this work, we need a polyfill. Generically, a *polyfill* is code that allows you to use a feature even if that feature has not been implemented on all browsers. Typically, the polyfill checks to see if the feature exists, and if it doesn't, the polyfill implements the feature (or a stripped-down version of it) on the browser so that code can be more easily shared between different browsers.

There's a slight difference in browser APIs as I write this, in that Apple's Safari browser does not implement a method we need to handle form submissions correctly. To rectify that, we need to install this polyfill package:

```
$ yarn add form-request-submit-polyfill
```

The method we need is requestSubmit. (I'll explain why in a moment.)

Now, some logistics. To get this to work, we need a functional server-side search. This isn't a book about server-side search optimization, so we'll go with something simple:

```
chapter_09/01/app/models/concert.rb
def self.search(query)
  joins(:bands)
    .where("concerts.name ILIKE ?", "%#{query}%")
    .or(Concert.where("concerts.genre_tags ILIKE ? ", "%#{query}%"))
    .or(Concert.joins(:bands).where("bands.name ILIKE ?", "%#{query}%"))
    .uniq
end
```

Our concerts all contain data randomly generated via our seed file. In this code, we're using SQL like statements to return any concert where the concert name, a band's name, or the list of genres contains the query string as a substring. We're throwing a uniq on the end because otherwise we'll get

---

1. http://hey.com

duplicate entries if multiple band names match. This is in no way complex enough to be a full production-level search, but it's fine for now.

We need to create a regular Rails endpoint for this search, and the natural place for it is the index method of the ConcertsController:

chapter_09/01/app/controllers/concerts_controller.rb
```ruby
def index
  @query = params[:query]
  @concerts = Concert.search(@query)
end
```

We also need a view for this. Here's the outer part:

chapter_09/01/app/views/concerts/index.html.erb
```erb
<%= turbo_frame_tag("search-results") do %>
  <article class="fixed bg-gray-300 z-10
                  rounded-3xl ring-4 ring-gray-800
                  max-w-screen-lg w-full
                  mr-20 ml-32 px-6 py-2 mt-2
                  overflow-y-auto overscroll-contain"
           data-search-target="results">
    <div class="text-3xl font-bold text-center">Search Results</div>
    <% @concerts.each do |concert| %>
      <%= render(
            "concerts/search_result",
            concert: concert,
            query: @query
          ) %>
    <% end %>
  </article>
<% end %>
<%= link_to "New Concert", new_concert_path %>
```

This is a reasonably standard Rails view. It is surrounded by a Turbo Frame called search-results (aptly named because it's going to contain search results). We've also got a little Stimulus nugget in there, data-search-target="results", which will make more sense in a moment. And we've got an outer article tag with a big pile of Tailwind CSS that translates, roughly, to: "Put this element in a fixed position with a z index so that it will display over the underlying display like a modal, and give it a light gray background color, rounded corners, and an outline ring. Position it appropriately (that's the third and fourth line starting with max-w-screen and ending with mt-2), and make sure overflow text is scrollable." The Tailwind is a little more succinct. Effectively we get some HTML that will look like a modal box on top of our existing schedule.

In addition, we also have an internal partial inside the @concerts.each loop—added because I wanted the display to be visually distinct from the existing display. There's not much logic to it, but for the sake of completeness, here it is:

chapter_09/01/app/views/concerts/_search_result.html.erb
```erb
<article class="my-6 max-w-screen-lg">
  <div>
    <%= concert.start_time.by_example("Jan 2 @3:04 PM") %>
    <div class="font-bold text-xl">
      <%= link_to(concert, data: {"turbo-frame": "_top"}) do %>
        <%= highlight(concert.name, /#{query}/i) %>
      <% end %>
      <div class="float-right">
        <% if concert.sold_out? %>
          Sold out
        <% else %>
          <%= pluralize(concert.unsold_ticket_count, "Tickets") %>
          Remaining
        <% end %>
      </div>
    </div>
    <div>
      <%= highlight(concert.bands.map(&:name).join(", "), /#{query}/i) %>
    </div>
    <div><%= concert.genre_tags.split(",").to_sentence %></div>
    <div><%= concert.venue.name %></div>
  </div>
</article>
```

I want to point out here that we have what is more or less a functional Rails search. If you go to localhost:3000/concerts, you'll see an index page. If you go to localhost:3000/concerts?query=bruce, you'll see search results. They'll look a little odd because we've styled them for a modal display, but they're not that bad. My point is that we can think about this as a progressive enhancement. We might have started with search being on a completely different page, but we've decided to make it part of the existing page for a better user experience.

Let's make that work. First, we need to put a working form into the schedule display page. As currently written, we have a text_field_tag on that page that is surrounded by a couple of divs. That's our form. I'm going to pull out that entire div, currently, the one that is class="flex justify-center" and put it in its own partial:

chapter_09/01/app/views/schedules/_search_form.html.erb
```erb
<%= turbo_frame_tag("search-form") do %>
  <div data-controller="search">
    <%= form_with(
        url: concerts_url,
        method: "get",
        data: {
```

```erb
        "turbo-frame": "search-results",
        "search-target": "form",
        action: "input->search#submit"
      }
    ) do %>
  <div class="flex justify-center">
    <div class="w-4/5">
      <%= text_field_tag(
          "query", "",
          placeholder: "Search concerts",
          type: "search",
          id: "search_query",
          "data-search-target": "input",
          class: "w-full px-3 py-2
                  border border-gray-400 rounded-lg"
        ) %>
    </div>
  </div>
  <% end %>
  <%= turbo_frame_tag("search-results") %>
  </div>
<% end %>
```

A few things are going on here.

We've surrounded the whole thing with a Turbo Frame named search-form, which is there solely to ensure that the form submit is inside a Turbo Frame so that its submission will be considered a Turbo request. We've also got a div with a data-controller named search that declares the Stimulus controller we're going to write.

The actual text field is now surrounded by a normal Rails form_with form that submits a GET request to concerts_url, which Rails will interpret as ConcertsController with an index action—exactly the controller action for search that we just wrote.

The form has three data attributes, all of which are of interest to the Hotwire world. We declare data-turbo-frame as search-results, meaning that when the form is submitted, the response HTML should have a search-results frame that replaces the existing search-results frame, which you can see is at the end of the partial. We declare data-search-target, marking this element as the form target of the search controller. And we declare a Stimulus data-action so that when the form receives an input event, the submit method of the search controller is invoked.

The text field itself only changes to declare itself the input target of the search controller, and as mentioned, we end the snippet with an empty Turbo Frame named search-results.

Now all we need is the Stimulus controller to manage this. We haven't put a Submit button on the page—instead, we want the form to submit and display results whenever anything is typed in the text field.

Our first pass at the search controller is quite short:

```
chapter_09/01/app/packs/controllers/search_controller.ts
import { Controller } from "stimulus"
import "form-request-submit-polyfill"

export default class SearchController extends Controller {
  static targets = ["form", "input"]
  formTarget: HTMLFormElement

  submit(): void {
    this.formTarget.requestSubmit()
  }
}
```

What happens here is that typing in the text field triggers an input event in the text field, which then propagates up to the form. The form has declared a Stimulus action input#search->submit so when it receives the event, the submit method of this controller is invoked. All that method does is requestSubmit on the form, which submits the form and does so with the event Turbo Frames is looking for. (The Safari method for submitting forms doesn't send the event Turbo needs; it doesn't have this method, which is why we have to import the polyfill.)

And this works. Run it, type in the text box, and you'll get search results. Thanks to the Rails highlight helper, you'll even get the matching part of each string highlighted.

What's happening here is that we are using JavaScript to submit a regular form request, and then Turbo is parsing the results. Because the form tag specifies data-turbo-frame=search-results, Turbo is parsing out the search-results Turbo Frame from the HTML response and inserting it in the page where we have already placed a blank Turbo Frame with the search-results ID.

A few niceties are still worth adding. Right now there's no way to get rid of the modal once it pops up. Also, the search can get tangled up if the user types too fast. We can fix both of those problems with a little more Stimulus.

Adding JavaScript Actions to Search

What would be nice is for the modal to be reset when we delete all the characters in the search bar as well as when we click outside the window. However, the latter might be a bit tricky. To get the "outside the window" part to work, by definition we need to capture click events outside the scope of our Stimulus controller. Luckily, Stimulus has a way to do that.

First, we need to add an action to our search results object:

```
chapter_09/02/app/views/concerts/index.html.erb
<article class="fixed bg-gray-300 z-10
                rounded-3xl ring-4 ring-gray-800
                max-w-screen-lg w-full
                mr-20 ml-32 px-6 py-2 mt-2
                overflow-y-auto overscroll-contain"
         data-search-target="results"
         data-action="click@window->search#resetOnOutsideClick">
```

The new line here is data-action="click@window->search#resetOnOutsideClick". Stimulus allows you to attach global event listeners by appending your event name with @window to add listeners for the entire window, or @document for listeners on the global document. In this case, a click anywhere in the window will go to the SearchController's resetOnOutsideClick method, so we'd better write that (this functionality is based on similar code from Hey.com):

```
chapter_09/02/app/packs/controllers/search_controller.ts
resetOnOutsideClick(event: Event): void {
  if (!this.element.contains(event.target as HTMLElement)) {
    this.reset()
  }
}

reset(): void {
  this.resultsTarget.classList.add("hidden")
  this.resultsTarget.innerText = ""
  this.inputTarget.value = ""
}
```

Hey, I Can See Your JavaScript

One of the reasons I'm able to use Hey.com as a great source of how to use Hotwire to build a website is that the Hey team has decided not to hide or obfuscate their run-time JavaScript. If you are running Hey.com, you can see the JavaScript in the browser inspector source tab. Being able to read a site's client code used to be common, but as obfuscation tools became available, most sites decided to hide their code. DHH explains on Signal v. Noise how Hey decided to give back to the web by allowing their source to be viewable.[2]

---

2.   https://m.signalvnoise.com/paying-tribute-to-the-web-with-view-source.

What our resetOnOutsideClick method is doing is taking the event.target, which is the item being clicked, and this.element, which is the DOM event of the controller, and calling reset if the target is not in the element. That is to say, any click outside the search form or result element will close the element. The reset method hides the result element, sets its text to blank (so that it doesn't show past results when redisplayed), and sets the input target—the text field itself—to blank.

Debouncing User Input

With that feature, we can now change our submit to reset if the input is blank, and close the window. We can also take care of the networking problem, using a procedure often called *debouncing*. Take a look at this code:

```
chapter_09/02/app/packs/controllers/search_controller.ts
basicSubmit(): void {
  if (this.inputTarget.value === "") {
    this.reset()
  } else {
    this.formTarget.requestSubmit()
  }
}

submit(): void {
  this.debounce(this.basicSubmit.bind(this))()
}

debounce(functionToDebounce, wait = 300) {
  let timeoutId = null

  return (...args) => {
    clearTimeout(timeoutId)
    timeoutId = setTimeout(() => {
      timeoutId = null
      functionToDebounce(...args)
    }, wait)
  }
}
```

Our actual submit logic is in the basicSubmit method. If the input field is blank, we reset; otherwise, we submit the form. The actual submit method that is invoked by the form action, wraps that basicSubmit inside a call to debounce.

The debounce function is a little confusing because it's treating functions as variables. The basic idea here is that we take a function—functionToDebounce in the code—and put it on a delay so that it waits a certain amount of time before that function is actually called. However, we also set the timer up so that if debounce is invoked again during the delay time, the first delay is canceled and we start again with a new delay. The upshot is that the functionToDebounce is only invoked after debounce has not been triggered for whatever the time delay is.

The debounce function takes a function as an argument and returns a new function that wraps the argument in a debouncing timer. That returned function does two things when called: it clears the existing timeout and it sets up a new timeout. JavaScript's setTimeout function takes a callback argument, which is invoked after the delay time. Inside the callback, we clear the timeoutId and call the original argument function. However, if the returned function is called again, it calls clearTimeout, which cancels the existing timer and starts a new one. Again, the result is that the original argument function is only called after the event is not invoked for a set amount of time.

And that gives us some form behavior in Hotwire with Turbo and Stimulus. You can augment this by using Stimulus to manage other data you might add to the form before submission.

Now, let's take a look at what to do when you have to contact a server that returns data rather than HTML.

Stimulus and Ajax

Even though "the Hotwire way" is all about sending and receiving HTML between the client and the server, you may still need to receive plain data sometimes. For example, you may have a legacy API section of your code, or it may be useful to call a third-party API from your client. Let's look at how we would make those API calls in our Stimulus code.

The simplest mechanism for making Ajax calls in modern JavaScript is with the fetch function and the async/await syntax for handling asynchronous behavior. (The Rails UJS library provides an ajax method, but the fetch function is easier to integrate with more modern JavaScript because the Rails ajax method does not use JavaScript promises. And Rails UJS might get deprecated any day now.)

The fetch method takes two arguments: the URL to contact, and an object containing optional arguments, like method for HTTP method, body, and so on.

The return value for fetch is a Response object wrapped in a JavaScript promise. A *promise* is a JavaScript object that represents an asynchronous process that will be executed eventually and might return data when it is done. Calling a method named then on the promise object allows a function to be invoked only when the process has ended successfully.

If you've written JavaScript code in the last few years, you might be familiar with this pattern, where multiple asynchronous actions result in promises that nest one after the other:

```
updateData() {
  fetch("/sold_out_concerts").then (response) => {
          response.text().then (text) => {
            // do something with tex
    }
  }
}
```

In these cases where multiple asynchronous events need to happen, the sequence of then calls on the various promises can get complicated. The async and await keywords were introduced to simplify using asynchronous processes:

```
asnyc updateData() {
  const response = await fetch("/sold_out_concerts")
  const text = await response.text()
  // do something with text
}
```

The async keyword marks the updateData function as having asynchronous calls within it, and therefore, able to handle the await keywords inside it. Within an async function, the await keyword expects a promise as its argument, and the code waits there until the promise resolves. In this case, a successful fetch returns a response wrapped in a promise, and by using await, the code sits in place until the response is received. Similarly, response.text also returns a promise, and we again await the response before the code flows forward.

Using Data in Stimulus

With async, await, and fetch in our toolbox, we can get our Stimulus controller to contact the server to get data about which concerts are sold out. We could also do this with Turbo Streams, but for the moment let's assume we're locked into an existing API for the sold-out data. Let's also assume for the moment that we need to get continuous data and we're choosing to do this by polling the server continuously for updates. (Later, we'll look at how to use ActionCable for server push.)

On the Rails side, I'd like to set this up as its own route by adding a new singular resource to the routes.rb file:

```
chapter_09/03/config/routes.rb
Rails.application.routes.draw do
  resources(:favorites)
  resource(:schedule)
  resources(:shopping_carts)
  resources(:ticket_orders)
  resources(:tickets)
  resources(:gigs)
  resources(:concerts)
  resources(:bands)
  resources(:venues)
➤ resource(:sold_out_concerts, only: :show)
  devise_for(:users)
  root(to: "schedules#show")
end
```

This lets us put the API code in a new controller, which is good both from a conceptual standpoint—it's a completely different kind of request—and from a practical standpoint—as its own route, it might be easier to separate into a designated service later on.

Here's what that API controller looks like:

```
chapter_09/03/app/controllers/sold_out_concerts_controller.rb
class SoldOutConcertsController < ApplicationController
  def show
    concerts = Concert.includes(:venue, gigs: :band).all
    sold_out_concert_ids = concerts.select(&:sold_out?).map(&:id)
    render(json: {sold_out_concert_ids: sold_out_concert_ids})
  end
end
```

Here, we're returning a JSON file to be parsed on the client with the IDs of all the sold-out shows. (We could also send an updated list of tickets remaining, but we'll do that a different way using ActionCable in Chapter 10, Immediate Communication with ActionCable, on page 187.) The JSON file has only one field, sold_out_concert_ids, which is an array of numbers.

When designing the client side, we have an immediate scaling issue to deal with. We could make each of our individual concerts a separate Stimulus controller that would each try to get this information. That might be fine if they were checking a global variable, but we probably don't want all of them making separate API calls to determine individual on-sale status. That's a lot of redundant calls to the sever.

This problem can be solved in a few different ways. What we're going to do here is create a Stimulus controller whose job it is to poll the server globally. That object will then change data attributes in the DOM, and we'll use Stimulus to pick up those data changes and update the display accordingly.

Our centralized object uses async/await to fetch our data:

```
chapter_09/03/app/packs/controllers/sold_out_data_controller.ts
import { Controller } from "stimulus"

export default class SoldOutDataController extends Controller {
  static targets = ["concert"]
  concertTargets: Array<HTMLElement>

  connect(): void {
    setInterval(() => this.updateData(), 1000 * 60)
  }

  async updateData(): Promise<void> {
    const response = await fetch("/sold_out_concerts")
    const jsonString = await response.text()
    const jsonObject = JSON.parse(jsonString)
    const soldOutConcertIds = jsonObject["sold_out_concert_ids"].map((id) =>
      id.toString()
    )
    this.concertTargets.forEach((concertElement: HTMLElement) => {
      concertElement.dataset.concertSoldOutValue = soldOutConcertIds.includes(
        concertElement.dataset.concertIdValue
      )
    })
  }
}
```

This is a regular Stimulus controller that, when it is connected the DOM, uses setInterval to call the updateData method every 60 seconds (1000 milliseconds x 60). The updateData method calls fetch, awaits a response, and then parses the JSON.

The Stimulus controller sets up an arbitrary number of targets named concert, and when it receives data, it loops through those targets using the concertTargets plural property generated by Stimulus. Inside the loop, it checks the data attributes of the target for a concertIdValue, which it compares to the list of sold-out IDs. It then sets a data attribute called concertSoldOutValue to true if the ID is in the JSON data, and false otherwise.

How does that help us? Looking at the fact that both the attributes start with concert and end in Value suggests that they are meant to be value data in a Stimulus ConcertController, which is in fact the case.

Let's take a look at how we set up the Stimulus controllers in our HTML. We want one version of the SoldOutDataController, so we declare that at the top of our schedule show page:

```
chapter_09/03/app/views/schedules/show.html.erb
<section data-controller="sold-out-data">
```

Then, in our concert display partial view, we declare the concert controller and we declare each concert as a target of the SoldOutDataController:

```
chapter_09/03/app/views/concerts/_concert.html.erb
<article
  class="my-4"
  data-sold-out-data-target="concert"
  data-controller="concert"
  data-concert-id-value="<%= concert.id %>"
  data-concert-sold-out-value="<%= concert.sold_out? ? "true" : "false" %>"
  data-concert-tickets-remaining-value="<%= concert.unsold_ticket_count %>">
```

We have five relevant data attributes in this code block. First, we use data-sold-out-data-target to declare the element a concert target of the SoldOutDataController, then we declare the element to have a data-controller of its own: concert. Then we declare three values for the concert controller: an ID, a true or false for sold out, and a "tickets remaining" value. We populate all of these server side with their correct initial values.

It's probably worth mentioning that as simple as this is, by setting the SoldOutDataController outside of this partial, we're creating a dependency where using this partial expects there to be a SoldOutDataController defined elsewhere in the view. That's fine for our purposes right now—we're only using the view in a case where we have such a controller—but it's something to keep an eye on in your own Stimulus applications.

Later in the same file, we replace the entire HTML tag that had the count of remaining tickets with a blank tag that is a target of the concert controller:

```
chapter_09/03/app/views/concerts/_concert.html.erb
<span data-concert-target="tickets"></span>
```

And now, the big reveal that ties it all together: the ConcertController:

```
chapter_09/03/app/packs/controllers/concert_controller.ts
import { Controller } from "stimulus"

export default class ConcertController extends Controller {
  static targets = ["tickets"]
  ticketsTarget: HTMLElement
```

```
static values = { id: Number, soldOut: Boolean, ticketsRemaining: Number }
soldOutValue: boolean
ticketsRemainingValue: number

soldOutValueChanged(): void {
  if (this.soldOutValue) {
    this.ticketsTarget.innerText = "Sold Out"
  } else {
    const ticketsRemaining = `${this.ticketsRemainingValue} Tickets Remaining`
    this.ticketsTarget.innerText = ticketsRemaining
  }
}
}
```

It's really only a couple of lines of code after we're through declaring the targets and values, but the key is the name of the method: soldOutValueChanged. It's a method hook called by Stimulus when the soldOutValue changes, or when the associated data attribute, data-concert-sold-out-value, changes. And, if you look back at the SoldOutDataController, that's exactly what we do.

Again, you could argue that we're creating a dependency between the two controllers by hard-coding the name of the data attribute of one controller in another. I'm not very bothered by that since the naming pattern is consistent and enforced by Stimulus. You could make the name of the attribute to change another data attribute, but that seemed needlessly confusing here.

Anyway, this works. The SoldOutDataController calls the server, returns its JSON, and changes the correct data attributes. The ConcertController detects the change, the soldOutValueChanged method is invoked, and the text on the page is updated automatically.

You can prove this works by invoking the Rake task rails north_by:sell_out_shows, which is in the chapter_09/03 version of the code that sells out three shows at random. If the Rails server is running and the schedule page is open, sometime over the next minute the page will poll for new data and the page will change in response.

Acquiring Data in React with useState

Now we are going to get our React page to also interact by making API calls to server. When last we left our React page in Dynamic Styled Components, on page 109, it was displaying the seating information for one specific concert. What we'd like it to do now is get that seating information from the server and update it if it changes. This will use the fetch method we've already seen, as well as a new React hook called useEffect.

Updating the seating information involves adding the following features to the page:

- When the React components load, they need to get the current seating status from the server.

- That status needs to get passed down from the Venue component to the seat component that uses the status to display. In this chapter, we're going to keep the status in our component; in Chapter 12, Managing State in React, on page 227, we'll look at how we can keep the status in a central global repository.

- We need to make sure a user can't adjust a seat that is already sold. (This is a UI bit we didn't do when we were working on this page earlier.)

- When the user does click on a seat, adding it to the shopping cart, we want the page to update the server so that any other user looking at the page sees the updated status.

That's a lot, but most of it is similar to React features we've already used. Note that we don't need to explicitly handle authentication, since our React code is not a single-page app; the Rails server is handling it and will handle it in the Rails session on our API calls.

Let's look at the new React parts first. Once that's done, we need to add a couple of new Rails controller actions, but we'll talk about them after we see how the React code works. We have a hierarchy of components here—Venue to VenueBody to Row to Seat—and they all change at least a little bit.

We start with a small change to the top-level call in our pack entry point, just changing it so the setup data is being passed in the props.

First we need to change the concert show page to send some props:

chapter_09/04/app/views/concerts/show.html.erb
```
<div id="react-element"
    data-row-count="<%= @concert.venue.rows %>"
    data-seats-per-row="<%= @concert.venue.seats_per_row %>"
    data-concert-id="<%= @concert.id %>"></div>
```

chapter_09/04/app/packs/entrypoints/venue_display.tsx
```
import * as React from "react"
import * as ReactDOM from "react-dom"
import Venue from "components/venue"

document.addEventListener("turbo:load", () => {
  const element = document.getElementById("react-element")
  if (element) {
    ReactDOM.render(
```

```
      <Venue
        rowCount={parseInt(element.dataset.rowCount, 10)}
        seatsPerRow={parseInt(element.dataset.seatsPerRow, 10)}
        concertId={parseInt(element.dataset.concertId, 10)}
      />,
      document.getElementById("react-element")
    )
  }
})
```

Now, we need to update the Venue to use that data.

The Venue Component

The Venue component fetches the data from the server so that each individual
Seat component isn't making its own data request. To acquire this data when
the component renders, we need something analogous to the Stimulus connect
method, which is automatically invoked when the component is added. We
can do that in React using a hook called useEffect.

Here's the entire Venue component:

chapter_09/04/app/packs/components/venue.tsx
```
import * as React from "react"
import VenueBody from "components/venue_body"
import VenueHeader from "components/venue_header"

interface VenueProps {
  concertId: number
  rowCount: number
  seatsPerRow: number
}

export interface TicketData {
  id: number
  row: number
  number: number
  status: string
}
export type RowData = TicketData[]
export type VenueData = RowData[]

const Venue = ({
  concertId,
  rowCount,
  seatsPerRow,
}: VenueProps): React.ReactElement => {
  const [ticketsToBuyCount, setTicketsToBuyCount] = React.useState(1)
  const [venueData, setVenueData] = React.useState<VenueData>([])

  React.useEffect(() => {
    const fetchData = async () => {
```

```
    const response = await fetch(`/tickets.json?concert_id=${concertId}`)
    const json = await response.json()
    setVenueData(json)
  }

  fetchData()
  const interval = setInterval(() => fetchData(), 1000 * 60)
  return () => clearInterval(interval)
}, [])

return (
  <>
    <VenueHeader
      seatsPerRow={seatsPerRow}
      setTicketsToBuyCount={setTicketsToBuyCount}
    />
    <VenueBody
      concertId={concertId}
      seatsPerRow={seatsPerRow}
      rowCount={rowCount}
      ticketsToBuyCount={ticketsToBuyCount}
      venueData={venueData}
    />
  </>
)
}

export default Venue
```

Let's start with the familiar. We added a concertId to the VenueProps. We'll wind up passing this all the way down to the Seat so that we can identify the page when we communicate with the server.

We also added some new types: TicketData, which represents a single ticket and is an id, row, seat, and status. Then we used the TypeScripts type command to define RowData as an array of TicketData objects and VenueData as an array of RowData, which makes VenueData a two-dimensional array of tickets. (These aliases are really only there for readability.)

We added the concertId to the props list in the parameter, and we added a new useState hook for what will be the incoming VenueData. At the end of the component, we are now passing the venue data and concert id to the VenueBody child component.

Using useEffect

The Venue component uses a new hook called useEffect. The useEffect hook allows a React component to trigger behavior when the component renders and to allow that behavior to have a side effect.

In general, React tries to be a functional representation of the world, which means a React component wants to convert state directly into DOM elements without having any other effect on the system. However, we often need to do things that are not purely functional. We might need to log output. We might need to send events to other items or register to receive events from other items. In our case we want to retrieve the seating data from the server, which is updating our state based on an external source. Collectively, the things you might do that aren't directly converting state to DOM elements are called *side effects.*

React very much wants you to avoid side effects in the part of the code that renders output and provides the useState hook as a place to have non-functional interactions with the rest of the world. A component can have multiple useEffect hooks, and in fact, the React core teams' recommendation is to have many small effect hooks rather than one large one.

At its simplest, the useEffect hook takes just one argument. This argument is a function that presumably performs a side effect. This function is, by default, invoked after rendering, every time the component renders.

If you look at the useEffect method in the Venue component, you'll see that it's a little more involved than a simple function—there's actually an internal function called fetchData that is declared as async. Inside the fetchData function, we call our Rails server, await the response, and then use the setVenueData function from our useState hook to update the state of the component. The body of the useEffect argument calls that internal fetchData function and embeds it in a setInterval call so that it will be reinvoked every minute.

The reason for this rigmarole around the internal method is that you are not allowed to declare the argument to useEffect to be async in its own right. (To be clear, TypeScript won't let you make the argument async; you can get away with it in plain JavaScript, but it's considered a bad idea.) Hence, we use the workaround here to give us an asynchronous effect. There are also third-party add-ons that have written custom asynchronous versions of useEffect.[3]

Here's what happens now when the Venue component is rendered:

- The component renders with the venueData set to its initial value, an empty array.

- The function argument to useEffect is called, triggering a call to the server and eventually updating the value of the venue data.

---

3. https://github.com/rauldeheer/use-async-effect

- The updated venue data value triggers a rerender of the Venue component.

By default, that rerender would trigger another invocation of the argument to useEffect, which we don't want. We want to be more in control of the calls to the server, and we definitely don't want that setInterval to be invoked multiple times.

The second argument to useEffect, which is optional, allows us more control over when the useEffect function is invoked. There are three possible values for that second argument:

- If the second argument is not present, the effect is invoked every time the component renders.

- If the second argument is an empty array, the effect is only invoked the first time the component renders and never again.

- If the second argument is an array containing values, those values are typically values from the props array. (In our case, we might have something like [rows, concertId].) If that array contains values, the effect is only invoked on rendering if one of the values in the array changed. Under most circumstances, if you have props referenced in the useEffect, then every props value so referenced should be part of this array.

You can use this second argument for performance purposes to minimize calls to the external effect, and it can also be used as we're using it here, to prevent an infinite cascade of changing values and rerenders.

You might also need to perform cleanup between renders or when the component unmounts. This can be done with the useEffect hook, but the syntax is convoluted. If useEffect has a return value, then that return value is itself a function. The returned function is meant to be a cleanup and is invoked before the next render of the component begins and again when the component unmounts from the React component tree. The cleanup only happens when useEffect is invoked, so if you are using the second argument to useEffect to only trigger the effect when certain props change, then the cleanup is only performed before the next useEffect.

In our case, the return value () => clearInterval(interval) is invoked when the component unmounts to prevent the code from hitting the server once a minute until the end of time. Since we have a second argument of [], the useEffect hook is never retriggered, and the cleanup only happens when the component unmounts.

Passing Data Through Our React Code

Following our change through, the VenueBody component doesn't change much, it just takes in the extra values and passes them along, giving each row its corresponding RowData:

```
chapter_09/04/app/packs/components/venue_body.tsx
import * as React from "react"
import Row from "components/row"
import { VenueData } from "components/venue"

interface VenueBodyProps {
  concertId: number
  rowCount: number
  seatsPerRow: number
  ticketsToBuyCount: number
  venueData: VenueData
}

const rowItems = ({
  concertId,
  rowCount,
  seatsPerRow,
  ticketsToBuyCount,
  venueData,
}) => {
  const rowNumbers = Array.from(Array(rowCount).keys())
  return rowNumbers.map((rowNumber: number) => (
    <Row
      concertId={concertId}
      key={rowNumber}
      rowData={venueData[rowNumber]}
      rowNumber={rowNumber}
      seatsPerRow={seatsPerRow}
      ticketsToBuyCount={ticketsToBuyCount}
    />
  ))
}

export const VenueBody = (props: VenueBodyProps): React.ReactElement => {
  return (
    <table className="table">
      <tbody>{rowItems(props)}</tbody>
    </table>
  )
}

export default VenueBody
```

The Row component carries a lot of load here. It maintains a client-side status of each seat, which is based on its ticket status and also the number of tickets the user is looking to buy, so as to prevent buying tickets so close to an already sold ticket that you can't buy an entire block. It also has the click handler invoked when a user clicks on a seat.

Here's the new version of the row:

chapter_09/04/app/packs/components/row.tsx
```tsx
import * as React from "react"
import Rails from "@rails/ujs"
import Seat from "components/seat"
import { RowData, TicketData } from "components/venue"

interface RowProps {
  concertId: number
  rowData: RowData
  rowNumber: number
  seatsPerRow: number
  ticketsToBuyCount: number
}
const Row = (props: RowProps): React.ReactElement => {
  const [seatStatuses, setSeatStatuses] = React.useState(
    Array.from(Array(props.seatsPerRow).keys()).map(() => "unsold")
  )

  React.useEffect(() => {
    if (props.rowData) {
      setSeatStatuses(
        props.rowData.map((ticketData: TicketData) => ticketData.status)
      )
    }
  }, [props.rowData])

  function isSeatValid(seatNumber): boolean {
    if (seatNumber + props.ticketsToBuyCount > props.seatsPerRow) {
      return false
    }
    for (let i = 1; i < props.ticketsToBuyCount; i++) {
      const seatStatus = seatStatuses[seatNumber + i]
      if (seatStatus === "held" || seatStatus === "purchased") {
        return false
      }
    }
    return true
  }

  function validSeatStatus(seatNumber): string {
    const seatStatus = seatStatuses[seatNumber]
    if (seatStatus === "held" || seatStatus === "purchased") {
      return seatStatus
    } else {
      return isSeatValid(seatNumber) ? "unsold" : "invalid"
    }
  }
}
```

```
function newState(oldStatus: string): string {
  if (oldStatus === "unsold") {
    return "held"
  } else if (oldStatus === "held") {
    return "unsold"
  } else {
    return "invalid"
  }
}

function updateSeatStatus(seatNumber: number): string[] {
  return seatStatuses.map((status: string, index: number) => {
    if (
      index >= seatNumber &&
      index < seatNumber + props.ticketsToBuyCount
    ) {
      return newState(seatStatuses[seatNumber])
    } else {
      return status
    }
  })
}

function onSeatChange(seatNumber: number): void {
  const validStatus = validSeatStatus(seatNumber)
  if (validStatus === "invalid" || validStatus === "purchased") {
    return
  }
  const newSeatStatuses = updateSeatStatus(seatNumber)
  setSeatStatuses(newSeatStatuses)
  fetch(`/shopping_carts`, {
    method: "POST",
    headers: {
      "X-CSRF-Token": Rails.csrfToken(),
      "Content-Type": "application/json",
    },
    body: JSON.stringify({
      concertId: props.concertId,
      row: props.rowNumber + 1,
      seatNumber: seatNumber + 1,
      status: newSeatStatuses[seatNumber],
      ticketsToBuyCount: props.ticketsToBuyCount,
    }),
  })
}

const seatItems = Array.from(Array(props.seatsPerRow).keys()).map(
  (seatNumber: number) => {
    return (
      <Seat
        clickHandler={onSeatChange}
        key={seatNumber}
```

```
          seatNumber={seatNumber}
          status={validSeatStatus(seatNumber)}
        />
      )
    }
  )

  return <tr className="h-20">{seatItems}</tr>
}

export default Row
```

There are some small changes here because we are passing concertId and row-Data into the props. There are a few bigger changes as well.

First, we have a useEffect hook here to manage the seat status. Each row maintains a local status of seats based on the ticket data, which is updated by a local click. The useEffect hook here regenerates that local status when the row data changes. So, to continue the workflow, if the Venue gets a new set of row data, it will get passed through to this component, and the effect hook will fire and update the status of the seats to reflect the new data.

There are a few relatively minor changes to deal with the new "purchased" status and then another big change in the onSeatChange click handler.

We've updated this method to make a fetch call back to the server to update data there. We're specifying a new endpoint, /shopping_carts, and that the call is a POST.

We're also adding two headers. The X-CSRF-Token header is used by Rails to verify that the form actually comes from the application itself and to prevent a cross-site scripting attack. The value Rails.csrfToken() is defined for us by the @rails/ujs package. Setting the content type to JSON lets us send the body as JSON, which we then do, setting a JSON object with the concertId, the row and seatNumber, the new status, and the number of tickets to buy. The endpoint will update ticket values, and subsequent calls to query for ticket status will show these tickets as held.

Finally, the Seat itself mostly just changes by adding the new data and adding a status color for "purchased." Because we're managing the status here, we no longer have to pass TicketData to the Seat.

```
chapter_09/04/app/packs/components/seat.tsx
import * as React from "react"
import styled from "styled-components"

const stateColor = (status: string): string => {
  if (status === "unsold") {
    return "white"
```

```
    } else if (status === "held") {
      return "green"
    } else if (status === "purchased") {
      return "red"
    } else {
      return "yellow"
    }
}

interface SquareProps {
  status: string
  className?: string
}
const buttonClass = "p-4 m-2 border-black border-4 text-lg"

const ButtonSquare = styled.span.attrs({
  className: buttonClass,
})<SquareProps>`
  background-color: ${(props) => stateColor(props.status)};
  transition: all 1s ease-in-out;

  &:hover {
    background-color: ${(props) =>
      props.status === "unsold" ? "lightblue" : stateColor(props.status)};
  }
`

interface SeatProps {
  clickHandler: (seatNumber: number) => void
  seatNumber: number
  status: string
}

export const Seat = ({
  seatNumber,
  status,
  clickHandler,
}: SeatProps): React.ReactElement => {
  function changeState(): void {
    clickHandler(seatNumber)
  }

  return (
    <td>
      <ButtonSquare status={status} onClick={changeState}>
        {seatNumber + 1}
      </ButtonSquare>
    </td>
  )
}

export default Seat
```

Adding Rails Endpoints

To make this React code work, we need to add a couple of endpoints to the Rails code: one to return ticket data and one to update shopping cart status.

The ticket status is just an update to the index method of the TicketsController to let it respond to .json requests:

chapter_09/04/app/controllers/tickets_controller.rb
```ruby
def index
  @tickets = if params[:concert_id]
    Ticket.where(concert_id: params[:concert_id])
      .order(row: :asc, number: :asc)
      .all
      .reject(&:refunded?)
  else
    Ticket.all
  end
  respond_to do |format|
    format.html
    format.json do
      render(
        json: @tickets.map(&:to_concert_h).group_by { |t| t[:row] }.values
      )
    end
  end
end
```

The to_concert_h method is new and is just a simple serializer of ticket information:

chapter_09/04/app/models/ticket.rb
```ruby
def to_concert_h
  {id: id, row: row, number: number, status: status}
end
```

The other is a separate controller that takes a concert ID, a seat number, and a number of tickets, and updates the status of the whole ticket batch:

chapter_09/04/app/controllers/shopping_carts_controller.rb
```ruby
class ShoppingCartsController < ApplicationController
  def create
    seat_number = params[:seatNumber]
    seat_range = seat_number...seat_number + params[:ticketsToBuyCount]
    tickets = Ticket.where(
      concert_id: params[:concertId],
      row: params[:row],
      number: seat_range
```

```
    ).all
    tickets.update(
      status: params[:status],
      user: params[status] == "held" ? current_user.id : nil
    )
    render(json: tickets.map(&:to_concert_h))
  end
end
```

And with that, the React code should work. You can verify this by opening the same concert page in two different browser windows. Click on one to purchase some tickets, and in the fullness of time, the other will update and display those changes.

What's Next

Being able to communicate with the server via polling is nice, but we still have a delay between when the change is made and when the server is polled. We could have a more direct update if the server were able to update the client when a change happens. A way to do that on the web is using the WebSocket protocol, and Rails provides ActionCable as a library for making WebSocket connections and broadcasting updates to clients. We'll take a look at both ActionCable and WebSockets in the next chapter.

CHAPTER 10

Immediate Communication with ActionCable

In the last chapter, we talked about communicating with the server using regular HTTP requests and receiving either HTML or JSON in response. One feature of our server interactions in both Stimulus and React is that we are simulating a real-time connection with the server by polling the server repeatedly. Polling this way has a couple of potential drawbacks. There's some extra overhead to make all the HTTP calls locally, and pestering the server often can have bad performance implications.

An alternative for client-server communications is to use the WebSocket protocol. The WebSocket protocol allows a client and a server to communicate over a single long-lived connection. A common analogy is that regular HTTP connections perform like walkie-talkies in that only one of the two parties can broadcast at a time. A WebSocket is like a phone, where both parties can talk at once. A WebSocket is effectively a stream in both directions, where both client and server can perform actions when new data is received.

Rails provides a library called ActionCable,[1] which is a wrapper around WebSockets that makes it easy to use a WebSocket on both the client and the server end. Beyond that, Hotwire and Turbo provide utilities that allow us to combine ActionCable and Turbo Streams to provide ActionCable functionality without writing any new JavaScript.

In this chapter, we're going to take a look at the Turbo Streams methods that allow us to send Turbo Stream data with ActionCable and then how to use

---

1. https://guides.rubyonrails.org/action_cable_overview.html

ActionCable with Stimulus controllers. We'll also adapt our React components to receive ActionCable messages. But first, let's get ActionCable set up.

Installing ActionCable

Installing ActionCable has already been done as part of our generic Rails setup. The Ruby gem is part of our Gemfile, and the JavaScript package is already in our package.json file. I did install the package @types/actioncable with yarn add @types/actioncable, which contains TypeScript definitions for ActionCable client-side code, allowing us to use TypeScript with ActionCable.

ActionCable has some configuration that you can see in the config/cable.yml file:

```
chapter_10/01/config/cable.yml
development:
  adapter: redis
  url: redis://localhost:6379/1

test:
  adapter: test

production:
  adapter: redis
  url: <%= ENV.fetch("REDIS_URL") { "redis://localhost:6379/1" } %>
  channel_prefix: north_by_production
```

ActionCable typically runs in the background, out of band from the user's HTTP requests, so that ActionCable broadcasts don't delay the server responses. Hotwire changes the ActionCable default so that the development environment uses Redis, an in-memory data storage tool, to manage background processing.[2]

The easiest way to install Redis in your development environment is via Docker. If you are comfortable with Docker, you can just run the following command: docker run --rm -it -p 6379:6379 redis:latest, and it will run a standard Redis image that communicates on the expected port and will work for our development purposes.

If you don't want to use Docker for Redis, you can change the development environment to adapter: redis and delete the url line. The async adapter simulates background tasks without actually using a background queue, which is fine for our development, but the default production environment still expects Redis to be installed to store ActionCable data in-memory.

---

2.   https://redis.io

Turbo Streams and ActionCable

The turbo-rails gem, which we added when we installed Hotwire and Turbo in Chapter 1, Getting Started with Client-Side Rails, on page 3, provides a set of helpers for managing ActionCable connections. Those helpers allow Rails to automatically send Turbo Stream HTML over the ActionCable connections and then enable the Turbo Stream actions to be executed on the client when the message is received.

Very broadly, these helpers allow us to do three things:

- Connect a view to an ActionCable channel via a helper method in the view itself

- Broadcast a Turbo Stream to an ActionCable channel as part of the response to a controller request

- Broadcast a Turbo Stream to an ActionCable channel automatically as a callback when an ActiveRecord is modified

The helpers provided by the turbo-rails gem used for communicating via ActionCable differ in how much default behavior they assume and how much you can specify. At one end, you can just send arbitrary content over an ActionCable channel managed by Turbo Streams. Or you can send content, and turbo-rails can wrap it in a Turbo Stream HTML structure. Or you can take advantage of the defaults and have the default partial for your model sent to a stream with a default name. Which option you choose depends on how closely your need can be modeled by Rails conventions and also how comfortable you are defining channel behavior in your ActiveRecord model.

Preparing Our Views

ActionCable is particularly useful in allowing us to keep multiple browser sessions in sync, whether that means different devices for the same user, or multiple users looking at the same information. In this section, we're going to make it so that declaring a concert a favorite in one browser instantly updates any other browsers that may be open for that user.

Before we start, we can do some refactoring of our views to make it much easier to incorporate the turbo-rails ActionCable helpers. We have a problem that is a general problem in a lot of applications and will probably be similar to issues you might have.

To make sense of the problem, I think it will help to back up a step and look at how our data flow is changing.

In the code as it exists, when we click the Make Favorite button to turn a concert into a favorite, we send a form request to our server, and it sends back a response made up of Turbo Stream flavored-HTML, which Turbo on the client side uses to update the DOM.

In the version we are about to write, we still click the Make Favorite button and still get an HTML request, but after the new Favorite object is created on the server side, the server queues up—and eventually sends—a Turbo Stream message back to the client via ActionCable. Then Turbo again updates the DOM based on the Turbo stream. (We're sending the message using turbo-rails commands that attach to the model, but the general problem still holds even if we sent the message via ActionCable from the controller or from some extra service object.)

What's important to understand about the ActionCable response is that it happens outside the regular Rails request/response cycle. Because of that, the ActionCable broadcast does not have access to global variables or session variables based on the request because it no longer takes place inside the session. Specifically, for our purposes, many of our view partials we've been using to display the schedule depend on the current_user global variable to determine whether the concert is a favorite and whether to display the Edit button.

We need to change the code so that any partials that will be called by ActionCable have the user passed to them rather than calling current_user inside the partial.

The concert display partial at app/views/concert/_concert.html.erb uses current_user four times. Replacing those usages with user is easy enough, but we also need to go after calls to that view. Specially, the ConcertController needs to change its references:

chapter_10/01/app/controllers/concerts_controller.rb
```ruby
def show
  if params[:inline]
    render(@concert, user: current_user)
  end
end
```

chapter_10/01/app/controllers/concerts_controller.rb
```ruby
def update
  respond_to do |format|
    if @concert.update(concert_params)
      format.html do
        redirect_to(@concert, user: current_user)
      end
```

```ruby
      format.json { render(:show, status: :ok, location: @concert) }
    else
      format.html { render(:edit) }

      format.json do
        render(json: @concert.errors, status: :unprocessable_entity)
      end
    end
  end
end
```

A similar change needs to be made in app/views/schedule_day/_schedule_day.html.erb to add user: current_user to the call to render individual concerts, and to app/favorites/create.turbo_stream.erb and app/favorites/destroy.turbo_stream.erb — the chapter_10/01 code directory has all the changes.

Broadcasting with Turbo Streams

Now with our view code suitably cleaned up, it's time to start broadcasting. ActionCable works in terms of *channels*. The client specifies that it wants to subscribe to a channel by name, the server then sends messages to that channel, and Rails knows to direct those messages across the correct Web-Sockets. When using Turbo, the turbo-rails gem does a lot of the behind-the-scenes work with a Turbo::StreamsChannel class and a lot of helper methods that access that class.

On our client side, we need to register that our view wants to receive messages in a channel—our schedule page wants to receive messages that a concert has been moved to or from the current user's favorite status. There's a helper for that:

```
chapter_10/01/app/views/schedules/show.html.erb
<%= turbo_stream_from(current_user, :favorites) %>
```

The helper is turbo_stream_from, and it takes as an argument an arbitrary list of items that are put together to create the name of the stream being listened to. Each of these calls connects you to one stream—multiple arguments mean the name of the stream has compound parts. To listen to multiple streams, you need to call turbo_stream_from multiple times.

In our case, we have two parts to the stream name: the current_user and the symbol :favorites. The turbo-rails gem basically concatenates all the bits together, but if the object defines something meaningful for to_gid_param or to_param, it uses that value. The most common use case is to use an ActiveRecord object in the stream name and use the object's ID to differentiate it from other objects. For example, for current_user, that value will be something like user:5, giving us a full name of user:5:favorite, based on the user ID. This means that if you log in as another user and open a browser as that user, the two ActionCables will be distinct as far as the server is concerned.

There's one more part to the stream name, which is that turbo-rails digitally signs the names so that the user ID number isn't actually leaked to the browser in plain text, making the names harder to spoof. A side effect of this name signing is that on the server side, we need to use turbo-rails helpers to interact with the ActionCable because they will automatically do the same name signing; otherwise, the names of the streams won't match and the message won't be broadcast where you expect it to go.

That's the client side. On the server side, we need to make sure that whenever a Favorite object is created or destroyed, we send the appropriate message down the appropriate ActionCable.

Perhaps surprisingly, we make that declaration in the Favorite model object. I say *surprisingly* because sending something over an ActionCable is a view responsibility and not typically seen as a responsibility of the model. On the other hand, the turbo-rails development team has gone to some trouble to make it not only possible but also relatively uncomplicated to allow you to connect the ActionCable via the model. (Strictly speaking, you don't have to connect via the model, but more on that in a second.)

Let's look at the code and then discuss the architecture implications. Here's what our Favorite ActiveRecord class looks like with the Turbo Stream support enabled:

```
chapter_10/01/app/models/favorite.rb
class Favorite < ApplicationRecord
  belongs_to :user
  belongs_to :concert

  after_create_commit -> do
    broadcast_append_later_to(user, :favorites, target: "favorite-concerts")
  end

  after_destroy_commit -> { broadcast_remove_to(user, :favorites) }
end
```

The code here uses ActiveRecord callbacks to trigger messages to the Active-Cable channel. *ActiveRecord callbacks* are hooks that are invoked by Rails at various times in the life cycle of the object.[3] The callbacks typically take a method name or a Ruby lambda method as an argument.

---

3. https://guides.rubyonrails.org/active_record_callbacks.html

Let's take this one callback at a time. The first callback is after_create_commit. It is triggered after a newly created active record object is saved to the database. Inside the block that is invoked when the callback is triggered, we call a method named broadcast_append_later_to.

The method broadcast_append_later_to is one of a family of methods defined in a module called Broadcastable, which turbo-rails mixes into every ActiveRecord class. Every part of that name is important and also suggests the other methods in the module. Let's break it down:

- broadcast: All the methods in the broadcastable module start with broadcast. All of these methods render something and then wrap the rendered text inside a turbo-stream tag.

- append: This is the action of the resulting Turbo Stream response. There are also methods for all the other Turbo Stream actions (replace, update, prepend, remove) and a generic broadcast_action family of methods that takes the action as an argument.

- later: This ensures the method performs the ActionCable broadcast asynchronously using ActiveJob. If you leave off later in the method name, the broadcast is performed in-band as part of the database save. Generally, it's best to avoid doing the render in-band as it might be slow and would delay whatever is waiting on the database save.

- to: This signifies that the first set of arguments to the method is the name of the ActionCable channel. If to is left off (as in broadcast_append_later), the name of the ActionCable channel is inferred from the identity of the object in question.

So we are rendering an action, wrapping it in an append Turbo Stream action, and then broadcasting it in the background to an ActionCable channel. The non-keyword arguments to the method are the name of the channel, user, and :favorites. The block is evaluated via instance_eval, so user, in this context, is self.user—the user attached to the favorite object that has just been created. The method takes a keyword argument called target, and the value of that argument is the DOM ID that will be the target of the resulting Turbo Stream, meaning it is the DOM ID to which the HTML will be appended (the default value is the pluralized name of the model class). Any further arguments—we don't have any here—are evaluated as though they were being passed to render, partial:, locals:, and whatever else. If no render path is provided, we use the default Rails partial class for the path, which in our case is app/views/favorites/_favorite. The locals array always has self merged into it as the class name, so even though we don't specify a locals array, the partial is called with {favorite: self}.

That's a lot for one line of code.

We can now also parse the method that goes with the final call-back—after_destroy_commit—and is executed when an ActiveRecord object is deleted from the database: broadcast_remove_to. So: broadcast, then the remove action, to the named stream, which is still user, :favorites. The broadcast_remove_to method assumes that the target DOM ID is dom_id(self), or for us, favorite_<ID>. This is good because that's what we used. We don't need to do the removal in the background because there's no render step, so the ActionCable broadcast won't noticeably delay the original action.

With this code in place, our cable *almost* works. Open two browsers and log in as the same user—with Redis running if you have the app configured to use Redis. Make one of the concerts a favorite. You'll notice that the other browser gets the concert sliding in to the favorites with the same CSS anima-tion, and the original browser gets the concert sliding in—twice. It gets the append from the Turbo Stream from the original form response and then it also gets the append from the ActionCable broadcast.

Fixing that is easy enough. We can change the app/views/favorites/create.tur-bo_stream.erb file to remove the turbo_stream.append call, since we know that the append will happen via the ActionCable route. While it may be easy to make this change, it can be tough to keep track of all the changes when some changes come from a form submission and others come via ActionCable. It might be easier to have everything happen via ActionCable.

That's a good thought, because even if we make that change, we still have a problem, which is that the *other* Turbo Stream calls in app/views/favorites/create.tur-bo_stream.erb happen in the browser that originates the action via the form response, but not in the browser that receives the action via the ActionCable response.

This issue can be fixed in a couple of different ways. One way is to split each of the individual bits of the existing Turbo Stream response into its own partial and create a different callback for each one. However, because we already have a file that has all our Turbo Stream responses together, it seems easier to just adapt that and only have one callback. The most straightforward way to do this is to adapt our existing create and destroy responses to be partial views that expect favorite to be a local variable, like this:

```
chapter_10/02/app/views/favorites/_create.turbo_stream.erb
<%= turbo_stream.append("favorite-concerts-list", favorite) %>
<%= turbo_stream.replace(dom_id(favorite.concert)) do %>
  <%= render(favorite.concert, user: user) %>
<% end %>
<%= turbo_stream.update("no-favorites") do %>
   
<% end %>
<%= turbo_stream.update(
    "favorites-count",
    plain: user.favorites.count
  ) %>
```

```
chapter_10/02/app/views/favorites/_destroy.turbo_stream.erb
<%= turbo_stream.remove(dom_id(favorite)) %>
<%= turbo_stream.replace(dom_id(favorite.concert)) do %>
  <%= render(favorite.concert, user: user) %>
<% end %>
<% if user.favorites.empty? %>
  <%= turbo_stream.update("no-favorites") do %>
    No favorite concerts yet
  <% end %>
<% end %>
<%= turbo_stream.update(
    "favorites-count",
    plain: user.favorites.count
  ) %>
```

In both cases the instance variable @favorite has been replaced with the local variable favorite, and current_user has been replaced by user.

Then we can trigger those partials from the ActionCable callbacks. The Broadcastable helper methods don't quite do what we want here, specifically because those helper methods expect a single payload and wrap the response in a turbo-stream tag and because our partials already have multiple Turbo Stream calls. So we can do this:

```
chapter_10/02/app/models/favorite.rb
class Favorite < ApplicationRecord
  belongs_to :user
  belongs_to :concert

  after_create_commit -> do
    Turbo::StreamsChannel.broadcast_stream_to(
      user, :favorites,
      content: ApplicationController.render(
        :turbo_stream,
        partial: "favorites/create",
        locals: {favorite: self, user: user}
      )
    )
```

```ruby
  end
  after_destroy_commit -> do
    Turbo::StreamsChannel.broadcast_stream_to(
      user, :favorites,
      content: ApplicationController.render(
        :turbo_stream,
        partial: "favorites/destroy",
        locals: {favorite: self, user: user}
      )
    )
  end
end
```

Here we're now backing up and calling a method that Turbo provides in its more general ActionCable implementation, Turbo::StreamsChannel.broadcast_stream_to. The arguments are the name of the channel—still user, :favorites—and the content to be sent, which we're generating by calling ApplicationController.render directly. The first argument is the format, and the remaining arguments describe the rendering.

One other thing: we no longer want the form response to have any content because all the changes will be broadcast via the ActionCable. In the FavoritesController, both respond_to lines need to be changed to format.turbo_stream { head(:ok) }.

And with that, we're working again. The favorites list, the concert display, and the navigation count all update in both browsers. We have the same functionality, but we're broadcasting to an arbitrary number of clients logged in to the same page.

In cases when you want to send a message to the same stream to execute the create, update, and destroy actions, turbo-rails provides the shortest shortcut of all. The method, broadcasts_to takes a symbol as an argument and calls that symbol to determine the name of the stream. So where our existing broadcast_stream_to takes user as an argument, you would use the symbol form broadcasts_to(:user), and turbo-rails calls self.user at run time to determine the stream name.

By using broadcasts_to, you generate three callbacks: an append turbo stream when a record is created, a replace turbo stream when a record is updated, and a remove turbo stream when a record is destroyed. All three have slightly different defaults, but they all use the dom_id of the record where they can.

For example, in our Favorites class, if we wrote broadcasts_to(:user), our destroy action would remove an element with dom_id(self) based on the record being removed, and the update action would similarly expect to update dom_id(self).

The create callback is different because you would not expect an element with the dom_id of a new record to exist already. For create, there is a default that an append action is sent targeting an element with an ID of the plural name of the record, which in our case is favorites. Also remember that you can override those defaults. For example, you can change the append action to a prepend action by passing action: prepend to the broadcasts_to method. You can change the target of the append action by either passing a target: argument or by overriding a class method named broadcast_target_default.

Finally, if you are extremely keyed in to the Rails defaults, there is a method simply named broadcast that takes the same arguments as broadcasts_to but assumes that the name of the ActiveRecord channel is based on self.

Stimulus and ActionCable

The Turbo ActionCable helpers are great, but they don't cover every use case for ActionCable we might have. You may need to use ActionCable by using custom JavaScript on the client, either because there is an already existing endpoint or because your task doesn't quite fit with the Turbo patterns. In this section, we're going to use ActionCable to rebuild the "sold out" feature we previously built using polling in Chapter 9, Talking to the Server, on page 161.

To use ActionCable directly, we need to create objects on the client and on the server. On the server, we have *channels* and *connections*. An ActionCable channel is roughly analogous to a Rails controller. The channel is where you put the code that responds to data the server receives over the socket and where you set up the structure of the data being sent to the client. Turbo created a generic channel for us to use; here we're going to build a custom one.

The connection class is a little more abstract. It's used by the channel and typically handles authorization. In setting up our project, Rails created the two top-level classes, ApplicationCable::Connection and ApplicationCable::Channel, that we can use as base classes. On the client side, we'll call a method called createConsumer, which returns a data object that we can use to subscribe to a specific server-side channel, and then specify what we want to happen in response to received data.

Let's look at an example of using ActionCable to broadcast sold-out concert data to our schedule page. We'll need to write some server-side code and some client-side code. On the server side, we need to create a channel and also set up the place where data is sent to that channel. On the client side, we need to respond to data when it's sent.

We've set up this functionality to be the most basic ActionCable as possible—the data only flows one way from the server to the client, and the identical broadcast goes to all subscribers. The schedule is the same for everybody.

We can start by asking Rails to generate some boilerplate:

```
% rails generate channel ScheduleChannel
```

This will generate the following files: a server-side file, app/channels/schedule_channel.rb; a test file in spec/channels/schedule_channel_spec.rb (since we have RSpec installed); and a client-side file, app/packs/channels/schedule_channel.js.

I'm terribly sorry about this, but as I write this there's still a mismatch between Rails and Webpacker 6, and Rails may try to create the JavaScript files in a different directory (app/javascript). If so, you'll need to move all of them to app/packs.

If this is your first ActionCable Rails generation, Rails will also create an index.js file for app/packs/channels. Like the similar file created for Stimulus controllers, this will automatically load any file in that directory ending in _channel.js. Rails will also create a file at app/packs/channels/consumer.js, which frankly, is just a shortcut for calling the ActionCable method createConsumer. (It will make more sense in a minute when we talk about our client-side code.) We are going to ignore these boilerplate files and integrate ActionCable ourselves.

The first thing we need to do server side is define the channel. The channel does not do very much here:

```
chapter_10/03/app/channels/schedule_channel.rb
class ScheduleChannel < ApplicationCable::Channel
  def subscribed
    stream_from("schedule")
  end

  def unsubscribed
    # Any cleanup needed when channel is unsubscribed
  end
end
```

The two methods, subscribed and unsubscribed, are automatically called by ActionCable when a new connection subscribes to the channel and when that connection explicitly unsubscribes. A more complex channel might have some logic in those methods. In our case, all we need to do is use the subscribed method to attach the new subscriber to a stream using the stream_from method. The argument to stream_from is the name of the stream, which we'll use to guide future broadcasts. In our case, the name schedule is a static literal; however, in other cases, the name might dynamically depend on an incoming parameter when the subscription is made. (Our next example from our concert show page, for instance, will need to specify which concert is being subscribed to.) Not all channel classes are this small; channels that expect to receive data from the client will add methods to respond to those requests.

We can send data to this stream from anywhere in our Rails program by calling the method ActionCable.server.broadcast with the first argument being the name of the stream to broadcast to and the second argument being the data to send.

Because you can add that broadcast statement anywhere, we now need to decide where to add it. If this sample code were a real program, what we'd likely do is after every ticket purchase check to see if the purchase results in a newly sold-out concert and, if so, broadcast the message. However, this sample code isn't a real program, and we don't really have ticket sales built in. So for the moment, we're going to repurpose the SoldOutConcertsController that we used earlier to send JSON data:

```
chapter_10/03/app/controllers/sold_out_concerts_controller.rb
class SoldOutConcertsController < ApplicationController
  def show
    concerts = Concert.includes(:venue, gigs: :band).all
    sold_out_concert_ids = concerts.select(&:sold_out?).map(&:id)
➤   ActionCable.server.broadcast(
➤     "schedule",
➤     {soldOutConcertIds: sold_out_concert_ids}
➤   )
    render(json: {soldOutConcertIds: sold_out_concert_ids})
  end
end
```

The key line here is ActionCable.server.broadcast("schedule", soldOutConcertIds: sold_out_concert_ids), which triggers our ActionCable broadcast with a hash of data that is identical to the data we would also send out as a normal render. Again, that's just sample coding here. Normally the ActionCable broadcast would not always be in the same place as the regular render command.

By default, the subscription sends the data right down to the client without further processing. If you'd like further processing, you can do a couple of things when you declare the stream in the channel using stream_from. The stream_from method takes an optional keyword argument that can have one value: coder: ActiveSupport::JSON. With that argument set, all incoming messages are decoded as JSON before passing on. Alternately, you can pass a block to stream_from; the messages are passed to the block and the result of the block is what is sent to the client.

Now we need to catch the data on our client side. From our previous example, we have our class SoldOutDataController that was polling the server to get new data about the list of sold-out concerts. We just need to repurpose that class to set up an ActionCable subscription:

```
chapter_10/03/app/packs/controllers/sold_out_data_controller.ts
import { Controller } from "stimulus"
import { createConsumer, Channel } from "@rails/actioncable"

export default class SoldOutDataController extends Controller {
  static targets = ["concert"]
  concertTargets: Array<HTMLElement>
  channel: Channel
  started: boolean

  connect(): void {
    if (this.channel) {
      return
    }
    this.started = true
    this.channel = this.createChannel(this)
  }

  createChannel(source: SoldOutDataController): Channel {
    return createConsumer().subscriptions.create("ScheduleChannel", {
      received({ soldOutConcertIds }) {
        source.updateData(soldOutConcertIds)
      },
    })
  }

  updateData(soldOutConcertIds: number[]): void {
    this.concertTargets.forEach((concertElement: HTMLElement) => {
      concertElement.dataset.concertSoldOutValue = soldOutConcertIds
        .includes(parseInt(concertElement.dataset.concertIdValue, 10))
        .toString()
    })
  }
}
```

This class has changed somewhat to support receiving from ActionCable. In the first line, we import createConsumer and Channel from the @rails/actioncable library. In our connect method, we check to see if the channel has been created, and if not, we create it.

The createChannel method is what actually connects our client to the server via a WebSocket. We call the method createConsumer().subscriptions.create. The first part of this createConsumer() returns a Cable class, which knows about subscriptions, and we can call the create method to create a new subscription. The call to create takes two arguments. The first is the name of the channel class on the server (not the name of the stream). The second argument is a JavaScript object that defines methods that are automatically called when various events happen. The method we are concerned with is received, which is called when new data is received. The other two that you can have here are connected and disconnected.

The received method is a callback invoked when data is passed, and it's doing the same thing with the data that we were doing before, just in a slightly different order. It decodes the data and passes it to updateData, which does the same Stimulus dataset updates as this code did before. We have a couple of type issues, and decoding this way keeps the concert IDs as integers rather than strings, so we need to do an integer comparison rather than a string.

You can see that this works by first calling the rake task, rails north_by:sell_out_shows and then opening up a second browser window and hitting http://localhost:3000/sold_out_concerts. The new window will display a list of sold-out concerts. Simultaneously, the schedule page you already have open will have the newly updated concert displays change to "Sold Out." Please note that this example is slightly faked; ideally we'd update the concert display every time a ticket was sold, which we'll get to in a moment. In a real application, we'd set the sold-out state as we know it in the Rails view, and the ActionCable workflow would show updates.

Here's the full workflow:

- The web request is routed to the show method of the SoldOutConcertSource. (We happen to have a broadcast method call there; it could be anywhere.)

- The broadcast call causes ActionCable to send data to any web browser that has subscribed to that stream. (Our client in the original browser happens to be such a subscriber and receives that data.)

- The callback method that we defined under the name received when we subscribed is invoked with the new data.

- That callback method does whatever it does. In our case, it signals to interested client code that the list of sold-out concerts has changed, and one bit of interested client code changes the browser DOM in response.

That's actually kind of a lot of interaction that we got with only a handful of lines of code.

Now let's build some ActionCable into our React page and make it interactive in both directions.

React and ActionCable

Currently, our concert show page makes a fetch call to the server to determine the current status of the seats on the page, and it makes a POST call to put a seat on hold after you click on it. We can replace both of these calls with a single ActionCable subscription—granting, of course, that this is an absurdly minimalist implementation since we're not doing a full security setup or complicated state transitions or anything like that.

ConcertChannel on the Server

Server side, we need to create a new ActionCable channel. This one will have the same subscribe method as our previous channel, but we need to add a method for our client side to call to actually reserve a ticket:

```ruby
chapter_10/04/app/channels/concert_channel.rb
class ConcertChannel < ApplicationCable::Channel
  def subscribed
    stream_from("concert_#{params[:concertId]}")
  end

  def unsubscribed
    # Any cleanup needed when channel is unsubscribed
  end

  def added_to_cart(data)
    cart = ShoppingCart.find_or_create_by(user_id: data["userId"])
    cart.add_tickets(
      concert_id: data["concertId"],
      row: data["row"],
      seat_number: data["seatNumber"],
      tickets_to_buy_count: data["ticketsToBuyCount"],
      status: data["status"]
    )
    result = Ticket.grouped_for_concert(data["concertId"])
    ActionCable.server.broadcast("concert_#{data["concertId"]}", result)
  end
end
```

This is a little more complicated than our earlier channel. In the subscribed method, our stream_from name is now a dynamic string: concert_#{params[:concert_id]}". This suggests two things. First, it means that different concerts will have different streams, so we don't have to worry on the client about seeing messages not meant for the page we are on. It also means that the client will need to pass the concert ID as a parameter when it subscribes.

And you probably noticed the added_to_cart method. This method is called when the client sends a message that tickets are to be added to the cart. It combines

the functionality we had put in the ShoppingCartsController to update tickets and
the functionality we had in TicketsController to return a data structure of all the
tickets sorted by row. I've refactored that functionality into the Shopping Cart
and Ticket classes, as shown here:

chapter_10/04/app/models/shopping_cart.rb
```ruby
class ShoppingCart < ApplicationRecord
  belongs_to :user

  def add_tickets(
    concert_id:, row:, seat_number:, tickets_to_buy_count:, status:
  )
    seat_range = seat_number...seat_number + tickets_to_buy_count
    tickets = Ticket.where(
      concert_id: concert_id, row: row, number: seat_range
    ).all
    tickets.update(status: status, user: user)
  end
end
```

chapter_10/04/app/models/ticket.rb
```ruby
def self.for_concert(concert_id)
  return Ticket.all unless concert_id
  Ticket.where(concert_id: concert_id)
    .order(row: :asc, number: :asc)
    .all
    .reject(&:refunded?)
end

def self.grouped_for_concert(concert_id)
  return [] unless concert_id
  for_concert(concert_id).map(&:to_concert_h).group_by { |t| t[:row] }.values
end
```

For our purposes, this means our channel expects a message that tells it to
invoke the add_to_cart method with the same data that was passed to the original fetch endpoint, and it uses ActionCable.server.broadcast to send the same
complete list of seat setup data back over the channel. This broadcast will go
to all the clients subscribed to the channel, crucially including the client that
sent the message in the first place.

On the client side, we need to subscribe to the channel. We also need to send
a message to it when we click on a seat, and we need to respond to the
resulting data. Mostly this involves a slight restructuring of the existing code.

In the Venue component, since we still need to do our data fetch in the useEffect
hook but don't want to poll the server anymore and instead want to subscribe
to an ActionCable channel, we need to add a call to create the subscription:

chapter_10/04/app/packs/components/venue.tsx

```tsx
import * as React from "react"
import VenueBody from "components/venue_body"
import VenueHeader from "components/venue_header"
import { createConsumer, Subscription } from "@rails/actioncable"

interface VenueProps {
  concertId: number
  rowCount: number
  seatsPerRow: number
}

export interface TicketData {
  id: number
  row: number
  number: number
  status: string
}
export type RowData = TicketData[]
export type VenueData = RowData[]

let subscription: Subscription

const Venue = ({
  concertId,
  rowCount,
  seatsPerRow,
}: VenueProps): React.ReactElement => {
  const [ticketsToBuyCount, setTicketsToBuyCount] = React.useState(1)
  const [venueData, setVenueData] = React.useState<VenueData>([])

  React.useEffect(() => {
    const fetchData = async () => {
      const response = await fetch(`/tickets.json?concert_id=${concertId}`)
      const json = await response.json()
      setVenueData(json)
    }
    fetchData()
  }, [])

  if (subscription === undefined) {
    subscription = createConsumer().subscriptions.create(
      { channel: "ConcertChannel", concertId: concertId },
      {
        received(data) {
          setVenueData(data)
        },
      }
    )
  }

  return (
    <>
```

```
      <VenueHeader
        seatsPerRow={seatsPerRow}
        setTicketsToBuyCount={setTicketsToBuyCount}
      />
      <VenueBody
        concertId={concertId}
        seatsPerRow={seatsPerRow}
        rowCount={rowCount}
        ticketsToBuyCount={ticketsToBuyCount}
        venueData={venueData}
        subscription={subscription}
      />
    </>
  )
}
```

export default Venue

We've taken this call to create the subscription out of useEffect for kind of quirky logistical reasons—useEffect happens after the component loads, whereas we want this subscription to be created before the rest of the component loads so that it can be passed down the React component tree. However, we don't want the subscription to be created more than once, so we create a variable outside the component definition to store the subscription and then only create the subscription if it does not already exist.

The actual creation of the subscription is only slightly different from what we did in the Stimulus ActionCable example. Rather than have the first argument to create be the name of the channel, the first argument is a JavaScript object that has a channel attribute. That attribute determines which channel we are connecting to; every other attribute gets passed to the subscribed method as part of the params hash. As we saw earlier in our definition of the server-side channel, we need to pass the concert ID so that we can specify the name of the channel. In response to the data, in the received part of the code we call the same setVenueData method we were already calling in response to this data when it was coming from an HTTP request.

The place where the client side sends data back to the ActionCable channel happens in the Row component, so we need to pass the subscription to the parameters of the VenueBody and then to the Row. The VenueBody only changes to accommodate importing ActionCable, receiving the subscription as a parameter, and passing it along to each row.

The Row component changes to receive the parameter and then there's a change to the onSeatChange method as well:

```
chapter_10/04/app/packs/components/row.tsx
function onSeatChange(seatNumber: number): void {
  const validStatus = validSeatStatus(seatNumber)
  if (validStatus === "invalid" || validStatus === "purchased") {
    return
  }
  const newSeatStatuses = updateSeatStatus(seatNumber)
  setSeatStatuses(newSeatStatuses)
  props.subscription.perform("added_to_cart", {
    concertId: props.concertId,
    row: props.rowNumber + 1,
    seatNumber: seatNumber + 1,
    status: newSeatStatuses[seatNumber],
    ticketsToBuyCount: props.ticketsToBuyCount,
  })
}
```

The subscription object is passed through as props.subscription and then we call the perform method on it. The first argument to perform is the name of the method to be invoked on the receiving channel, and the second argument is a JavaScript object that is received as the data argument to the method being invoked. In this case, we're passing all the same data that we would have been passing to the AJAX POST call.

And that is that. If you open two browsers side by side to the same concert page and click on a seat in one of them, the other browser will change to reflect that action almost immediately.

There is one other thing we can do, which is send the new ticket purchase back to our schedule page to adjust the number of tickets remaining to reflect the change. We have a couple of options here, depending on how much we want to upend the work we've already done in this channel. We could change the "sold out" messages we're sending to the JSON channel to update the amount of tickets available and tweak our existing Stimulus code to handle that. Or we could use a Turbo Stream helper to automatically send a message when a Ticket is updated.

Both of these are viable options, but since we already have a Schedule channel to receive the data, we'll use that. However, later in Appendix 1, Framework Swap, on page 321, when we rewrite the React page in Stimulus, we'll try it the other way.

We get this new feature with only a few small changes. First, our ConcertChannel needs to add a second broadcast when something is added to the cart:

chapter_10/05/app/channels/concert_channel.rb

```ruby
class ConcertChannel < ApplicationCable::Channel
  def subscribed
    stream_from("concert_#{params[:concertId]}")
  end

  def unsubscribed
    # Any cleanup needed when channel is unsubscribed
  end

  def added_to_cart(data)
    cart = ShoppingCart.find_or_create_by(user_id: data["userId"])
    cart.add_tickets(
      concert_id: data["concertId"],
      row: data["row"],
      seat_number: data["seatNumber"],
      tickets_to_buy_count: data["ticketsToBuyCount"],
      status: data["status"]
    )
    result = Ticket.grouped_for_concert(data["concertId"])
    ActionCable.server.broadcast("concert_#{data["concertId"]}", result)
    concert = Concert.find(data["concertId"])
    ActionCable.server.broadcast(
      "schedule",
      {
        concerts: [
          {
            concertId: data["concertId"],
            ticketsRemaining: concert.tickets.unsold.count
          }
        ]
      }
    )
  end
end
```

Here we have a second broadcast to the schedule channel. The data format has changed; it's now an array called concerts, where each element in the array is an object with the properties concertId and ticketsRemaning. In this particular use case, the array will only have one element, but you could imagine a case where we need to refresh multiple concerts at once.

On the client side, we need to update the SoldOutDataController that receives the broadcast:

chapter_10/05/app/packs/controllers/sold_out_data_controller.ts

```typescript
import { Controller } from "stimulus"
import { createConsumer, Channel } from "@rails/actioncable"

interface ConcertRemainingData {
```

```typescript
    concertId: number
    ticketsRemaining: number
}

export default class SoldOutDataController extends Controller {
  static targets = ["concert"]
  concertTargets: Array<HTMLElement>
  channel: Channel
  started: boolean

  connect(): void {
    if (this.channel) {
      return
    }
    this.started = true
    this.channel = this.createChannel(this)
  }

  createChannel(source: SoldOutDataController): Channel {
    return createConsumer().subscriptions.create("ScheduleChannel", {
      received({ concerts }) {
        source.updateData(concerts)
      },
    })
  }

  updateData(concerts: ConcertRemainingData[]): void {
    concerts.forEach(({ concertId, ticketsRemaining }) => {
      this.concertTargets.forEach((e) => {
        if (e.dataset.concertIdValue === concertId.toString()) {
          e.dataset.concertTicketsRemainingValue = ticketsRemaining.toString()
          e.dataset.concertSoldOutValue = (
            ticketsRemaining === 0
          ).toString()
        }
      })
    })
  }
}
```

Three changes were made here. First, at the top of the file, there's a new interface ConcertRemainingData that contains the concertId and the ticketsRemaining. Strictly speaking, this isn't necessary, but TypeScript likes to know this information, and we do have it. Second, the createChannel changes slightly to expect concerts as the top-level key in the incoming JSON when data is received. And third, the updateData method changes too. For each entry in the data, it checks all the concert targets, and if the IDs match, it updates the tickets remaining and sold-out information in the element dataset. (For performance reasons, you'd probably want the concertTargets to already be indexed to avoid the inner loop, but it's not a significant problem yet.)

And we have one more small change to make to ensure the display actually updates. To do this, we need to change the name of the method in the Concert-Controller to watch the tickets remaining value, like this:

```
chapter_10/05/app/packs/controllers/concert_controller.ts
import { Controller } from "stimulus"

export default class ConcertController extends Controller {
  static targets = ["tickets"]
  ticketsTarget: HTMLElement

  static values = { id: Number, soldOut: Boolean, ticketsRemaining: Number }
  soldOutValue: boolean
  ticketsRemainingValue: number

  ticketsRemainingValueChanged(): void {
    if (this.ticketsRemainingValue === 0) {
      this.ticketsTarget.innerText = "Sold Out"
    } else {
      const ticketsRemaining = `${this.ticketsRemainingValue} Tickets Remaining`
      this.ticketsTarget.innerText = ticketsRemaining
    }
  }
}
```

And this works. Now if you open a browser to the schedule page and a different browser to a concert page, selecting seats in the concert page will update the tickets remaining list on the schedule page.

What's Next

In this chapter, we used ActionCable to create a live data stream that both the client and server could use to send data and commands. If you are like me, the amount of state being passed around on the page is getting annoying. On the React side, we have code that is just shuttling data up and down the tree, and on the Stimulus side, we haven't fully implemented the filters because we have no easy way for multiple controllers to share global state. In the chapters that follow, we address these issues.

Managing State in Stimulus Code

As we've been building our sample concert application in this book, we've spent a lot of time worrying about managing state. By *state*, I mean the set of values the front end needs in order to draw the correct information to the screen and properly manage user interaction. In the Hotwire and Stimulus universe, state and data are largely managed by adjusting the dataset of various DOM elements and using the browser and Stimulus controllers to work with that information. While a Hotwire and Stimulus application may use external classes to manage client-only abstractions, you probably don't need a separate class beyond the DOM just to manage the state of the application.

In this chapter, we'll build out our calendar filter to the schedule page using the DOM to hold our client-side state. We'll also look at how to use the MutationObserver API to detect DOM changes that might indicate client-side state updates. Later, we'll see that a complex React app often does use separate classes to hold state values that Stimulus tries to keep in the DOM.

Using Data Values for Logic

Let's go back to our schedule page. At the top of the page is a run of calendar dates and the Show All button. Earlier, in Chapter 3, Stimulus, on page 37, we added the CssController to make it so that these dates show and hide a red border to indicate which one is active. What we didn't do at the time was wire that state up to allow those dates to act as a filter on the schedule display.

The functionality we want is as follows:

- If none of the date buttons are active, all dates are shown.

- If any of the date buttons are active, only the dates with active buttons are shown.

- The Show All button returns all buttons to the inactive state, making all dates visible.

Two factors make this feature slightly more difficult than the previous Stimulus example. Whether an item displays is dependent on not just the state of that item, but also on the state of the group as a whole. Also, the buttons affect a part of the page that is outside their own subtree of the DOM.

You can manage this in Stimulus in a few different ways. Here's the base HTML for the solution I picked (it's in the schedule show page, surrounding the calendar header code):

```erb
chapter_11/01/app/views/schedules/show.html.erb
<div class="grid grid-cols-7 gap-0 mb-6"
     data-controller="calendar">
  <% @schedule.schedule_days.each do |schedule_day| %>
    <% date_string = schedule_day.day.by_example("2006-01-02") %>
    <div class="text-center border-b-2 border-transparent"
         id="calendar-day-<%= schedule_day.day_string %>"
         data-controller="css"
         data-css-css-class="border-red-700"
         data-css-status-value="false"
         data-css-target="elementToChange"
         data-calendar-target="calendarDay"
         data-schedule-id="day-body-<%= schedule_day.day_string %>"
         data-action="click->css#toggle click->calendar#filter">
      <%= schedule_day.day.by_example("Jan 2") %>
    </div>
  <% end %>
  <div data-action="click->calendar#showAll">
    Show All
  </div>
</div>
```

Here's my rationale behind these choices.

There's a new Stimulus controller, calendar, which is defined such that it contains all the calendar dates and the Show All button but does not contain the schedule displays for each date, which are lower on the page. I see two competing possibilities for the scope of the calendar controller: I could have chosen to make it bigger such that it incorporated basically the entire page, including both the date displays at the top and the schedule page at the bottom. Or I could have made the scope of the controller smaller such that each individual calendar date got its own controller instance.

I think that even if both the date and the schedule were inside the controller, I still would need logic tying each date to its schedule part, so it's not clear to me what advantage I get from making the controller bigger. At the same time, having all the dates inside the same controller makes the logic for determining status based on the state of the group as a whole somewhat easier, so making the controller smaller seems like it would result in more complex code.

For each date inside the loop, this code adds two Stimulus attributes: data-calendar-target="calendarDay" to identify the date as a target of the calendar controller and data-schedule-id to link the element to the DOM ID of the schedule part displaying the same day. A second action, click->calendar#filter, was also added to the element. Remember, Stimulus guarantees that the second action won't be fired until the first one is complete, so we know that the data-css-status-value targeted by the first action will have already flipped when we evaluate the second action.

Lower in the view, the "Show All" display is annotated to a different action, cleverly named click->calendar#showAll.

We need to add the expected DOM ID to the schedule day display in app/views/schedule_days/_schedule_day.html.erb:

```
chapter_11/01/app/views/schedule_days/_schedule_day.html.erb
<section id="day-body-<%= schedule_day.day_string %>"
         data-controller="css"
         data-css-css-class="hidden"
         data-css-status-value="false">
```

And here's the Stimulus controller that connects all those pieces:

```
chapter_11/01/app/packs/controllers/calendar_controller.ts
import { Controller } from "stimulus"

export default class CalendarController extends Controller {
  static targets = ["calendarDay"]
  calendarDayTargets: HTMLElement[]

  everyDayUnselected(): boolean {
    return this.calendarDayTargets.every((target: HTMLElement) => {
      return target.dataset.cssStatusValue === "false"
    })
  }

  filter(): void {
    const everyDayUnselected = this.everyDayUnselected()
    this.calendarDayTargets.forEach((target: HTMLElement) => {
      const show =
        everyDayUnselected || target.dataset.cssStatusValue === "true"
      const schedule = document.getElementById(target.dataset.scheduleId)
      schedule.classList.toggle("hidden", !show)
    })
  }
```

```
  showAll(): void {
    this.calendarDayTargets.forEach((target: HTMLElement) => {
      target.dataset.cssStatusValue = "false"
      const schedule = document.getElementById(target.dataset.scheduleId)
      schedule.classList.toggle("hidden", false)
    })
  }
}
```

The filter action is the more complicated of the two actions. We start by using the DOM data attributes to determine the state of the system in the everyDayUn-selected method. The everyDayUnselected method returns true if and only if the cssStatusValue for every one of the targets is "false". Unfortunately, we have to check against the string version of "false" because the value is part of a different controller; otherwise, we'd be able to use the Stimulus Values API to define the value as a Boolean and have Stimulus typecast it for us.

For each of our calendarDayTargets, meaning for each of the date displays, we determine if the corresponding schedule item should be shown. The answer is yes if the cssStatusValue is "true" or if every day is unselected. Then we use the regular DOM getElementById method to determine our matching schedule element and set a hidden class on that element. This works because we know that the click->css#toggle action has already happened, so we know that the cssStatusValue has already changed to its new value.

The showAll method similarly loops over all our calendar day targets. But instead of using the filter logic, it just sets the cssStatusValue of all of them to false. Doing so triggers the cssStatusValueChanged method of the CssController, which removes the border class we set. It doesn't also automatically reset the corresponding schedule item, so we need to do that manually.

And this works, showing how we can use the DOM to store the data we need for more complex client-side effects.

Observing and Responding to DOM Changes

If we want to use the DOM as a place to hold on to the state of the client-side system, it's helpful to be able to know when that state changes. In a Hotwire system, where new HTML text might be added to the DOM as a result of a form submission or an ActionCable text receipt, being able to detect that HTML change and perform an action based on it allows for a lot of cool behavior, even while keeping the drawing logic on the server side.

We can do this by using the MutationObserver API, which is a standard part of every recent browser. Stimulus itself is powered by MutationObserver calls, so any browser that can run Stimulus can manage MutationObservers. Browsers that are older than, say, Internet Explorer 11, need the @stimulus/polyfill package to run.

For our purposes here, we're going to use a MutationObserver object to solve a minor problem in our schedule page. When we list favorite concerts, it'd be nice if that list were sorted by the date of the concert. The problem is that even if we sort the initial server-side list, as new favorites come in via Turbo Stream, we can only append them. What we want is to have them go into the list in their correctly sorted place. To do this, we're going to use the MutationObserver API to build a generic Stimulus controller that will sort its internal targets whenever a new target is added. (This code is a somewhat simplified version of what Hey.com uses to sort email when they are added back into the "already seen" list.)

The logic here is:

1. Detect when a new item has been added to the list, and then
2. Ensure the item list is properly sorted.

To make this work, we need to make a couple of minor changes in the ERB file for the favorite list. Specifically, we need to make some changes to the actual list of favorites:

```erb
chapter_11/02/app/views/favorites/_list.html.erb
<div id="favorite-concerts-list"
     data-controller="sort">
  <% current_user.favorites.sort_by(&:sort_date).each do |favorite| %>
    <%= render(favorite, animate_in: false) %>
  <% end %>
</div>
```

That div element also has a new Stimulus data-controller named sort. And the loop over the list now has a sort_by(&:sort_date), which ensures that the initial server-side rendering of the list is sorted by date. We also added an animate_in: false local to the actual render call, which we will use to keep the initial page load from animating but still allow new favorites to animate in.

The sort_date feature is just a convenience method on Favorite that grabs the start time of the associated concert:

```ruby
chapter_11/02/app/models/favorite.rb
def sort_date
  concert.start_time.to_i
end
```

And we need to make a minor change in the _create_turbo_stream partial to ensure our appended favorites are animated:

chapter_11/02/app/views/favorites/_create.turbo_stream.erb

```
➤ <%= turbo_stream.append("favorite-concerts-list") do %>
➤   <%= render(favorite, animate_in: true) %>
➤ <% end %>
<%= turbo_stream.replace(dom_id(favorite.concert)) do %>
  <%= render(favorite.concert, user: user) %>
<% end %>
<%= turbo_stream.update("no-favorites") do %>
   
<% end %>
<%= turbo_stream.update(
    "favorites-count",
    plain: user.favorites.count
  ) %>
```

Here we changed the one line in the first partial call to have its arguments include animate_in: true.

We need to do one more bit of view management before we can get to the Stimulus controller. The actual _favorite partial needs to declare a couple of things right up front:

chapter_11/02/app/views/favorites/_favorite.html.erb

```
<%- animate_in ||= false %>
<article class="my-6
        <%= animate_in ? "animate__animated animate__slideInRight" : "" %>"
        id="<%= dom_id(favorite) %>"
        data-animate-out="animate__slideOutRight"
        data-sort-target="sortElement"
        data-sort-value="<%= favorite.sort_date %>">
```

We made a few changes here. We added two new Stimulus-related attributes to the outer article tag: data-sort-target and data-sort-value. We set up the article element as a target of the sort controller, which we haven't seen yet, and we dropped the value it's being sorted on in the data-sort-value attribute. We've also made the animate in CSS classes dependent on an animate_in local being passed with a true value.

And with all that, we can now write a generic sort controller in Stimulus:

chapter_11/02/app/packs/controllers/sort_controller.ts

```
import { Controller } from "stimulus"

export default class SortController extends Controller {
  static targets = ["sortElement"]
  sortElementTargets: HTMLElement[]

  initialize(): void {
```

```
      const target = this.element
      const observer = new MutationObserver((mutations: MutationRecord[]) => {
        observer.disconnect()
        Promise.resolve().then(start)
        this.sortTargets()
      })
      function start() {
        observer.observe(target, { childList: true, subtree: true })
      }
      start()
    }

    sortTargets(): void {
      if (this.targetsAlreadySorted()) {
        return
      }
      this.sortElementTargets
        .sort((a: HTMLElement, b: HTMLElement) => {
          return this.sortValue(a) - this.sortValue(b)
        })
        .forEach((element: HTMLElement) => this.element.append(element))
    }

    targetsAlreadySorted(): boolean {
      let [first, ...rest] = this.sortElementTargets
      for (const next of rest) {
        if (this.sortValue(first) > this.sortValue(next)) {
          return false
        }
        first = next
      }
      return true
    }

    sortValue(element: HTMLElement): number {
      return parseInt(element.dataset.sortValue, 10)
    }
  }
}
```

The first important part of our sort controller happens in the initialize method, which is called immediately when the controller is loaded, as opposed to create, which is called when an instance of the controller is detected in the DOM. Right away the method creates a new MutationObserver object. The constructor for MutationObserver takes one argument, a callback function that is invoked when the observer is both active and detects a change.

In our case, the main part callback is to call the sortTargets method of the controller. The arguments to the callback are a list of mutation records that store information about each change and the newly created mutation observer itself, though in our case, we don't actually need information about the changes. Around the call to sortTargets, we are disconnecting and then reconnecting the observer to prevent an infinite loop of changes triggering changes.

The mutation change records specify the type of the change (either attributes, characterData, or childList) and the target, which is the actual DOM element being mutated. It then specifies other information about the change itself in attributes named addedNodes, removedNodes, and attributeName. (A full list of mutation types can be found online.[1])

By itself, creating the MutationObserver object does nothing. You need to also tell it to observe something, which we do in the next line with observer.observe(this.element, { childList: true, subtree: true }). The observe method takes two arguments. The first is the target element to be observed, in this case this.element, which is the element that the controller is defined on. The observer looks for changes within that target element. The second argument is an options object, which is a collection of true/false flags that tell you what kinds of mutations should trigger the callback.

Possible options, and therefore mutation types, are as follows (all values default to false):

- attributes: If true, the MutationObserver triggers the callback if the value of an attribute on the element changes. If the option, attributeOldValue is also true, the previous value of the attribute is passed to the callback at mutation-Record.oldValue. If attributeFilter is passed as an option, it's a string list of attribute names that are the only attributes whose changes we care about.

- characterData: If true, the MutationObserver triggers the callback if the text inside the element changes. If characterDataOldValue is also true, the old value is also added to the MutationRecord at mutationRecord.oldValue.

- childlist: If true, the MutationObserver triggers the callback if a new child is added to the target element or an existing child is removed.

- subtree: If true, the MutationObserver also looks at changes recursively down the DOM tree of the target element; otherwise, only changes to the target element apply.

In many cases, your callback function would switch on the type of the change or take advantage of the mutation record data, but in our case, we don't really need that information. All we care about here is that the childList has changed.

---

1. https://developer.mozilla.org/en-US/docs/Web/API/MutationRecord

Our sortTargets method takes the list of the elements that are sortElementTargets and, well, sorts them, using the value of their data-sort-value attribute for comparison. Once it has a sorted list, it reappends them in order back to the parent, which has the effect of having all the children display in order. We also have a guard clause where nothing happens if the targets are already sorted, which also should prevent the MutationObserver from looping endlessly since the changes to the element from appending objects also qualify as mutations.

This SortController is pretty generic, and we could use it almost anywhere to keep a list of items sorted without any further JavaScript.

And this works. What's nice is that the timing is such that the sorting happens before the display so that our incoming element only appears to enter the DOM once in the correct location (rather than appearing at the bottom and then moving to the correct location), and the animation still fires, giving the new object the appearance of entering from the right in the correctly sorted location.

There's one little problem, which is that as written, the animation happens too often. When a new favorite is added, all the favorites with animate_in as true reanimate and slide in because the animation class is still in the element's class list and the element is getting removed and reinserted, triggering the animation again. What we want is to have the animate__slideInRight class removed after the element slides in once.

While we could do this with another custom controller or by modifying the sort controller, we can actually also do it without writing any new JavaScript with our existing CssController, which also manages whether a CSS class is in or out of an element based on its status. Here's what I did:

```erb
chapter_11/03/app/views/favorites/_favorite.html.erb
<%- animate_in ||= false %>
<article class="my-6 animate__animated"
         id="<%= dom_id(favorite) %>"
         data-animate-out="animate__slideOutRight"
         data-sort-target="sortElement"
         data-sort-value="<%= favorite.sort_date %>"
         data-controller="css"
         data-css-target="elementToChange"
         data-css-css-class="animate__slideInRight"
         data-css-status-value="<%= animate_in ? "true" : "false" %>"
         data-action="animationend->css#toggle">
```

This code adds the CssController to the same article element with a few data attributes. The data-controller=css attribute establishes that the controller is there, and we also set the element up as its own target with data-css-target="ele-mentToChange". The next attribute, data-css-css-class="animate_slideInRight" says that the CSS controller cares about whether that animation class is in or out of the class list based on the status value. The status value is set with data-css-status-value="<%= animate_in ? "true" : "false" %>"—in other words, the starting status is true if we want the element to animate; otherwise, not. Finally, the data-action="animationend->css#toggle" sets a different data action. Our past uses of the CssController have been toggled by click; this time, we're toggling when the animation ends.

If we start this partial with animate_in set to true, then the data-css-status-value is true. When Stimulus connects the CSS controller, it calls statusValueChanged, and since the status value is true, it adds the CSS class, animate_slideInRight to the class list. The element then animates in. When the animation ends, the animationend event is fired, causing Stimulus to call toggle on the controller, setting the status value to false, and removing the animate_slideInRight class. Now if you add a second favorite, the existing class no longer has an animation CSS attached and doesn't animate again.

I realize that you might look at all this HTML and think it's verbose. All I can say is it made me genuinely happy, in real time as I wrote this—this was not a planned digression, but a bug I found while writing the example and fixed quickly without writing any new JavaScript.

Rendering CSS with Data Attributes

To show how generic our SortController is, I'm going to use it to fix a different problem with our schedule page. Right now, if you edit a concert on the page and change its start time, the concert page does not re-sort to insert the concert based on its new time.

This is admittedly a small problem, even by the standards of this sample app, but I want to show this solution because I think it's neat, and I think it shows a technique for leveraging Turbo and Stimulus that you may not have thought of. (This is also based on something Hey.com does.)

A Couple of Cautions

This technique does re-sort the concerts without writing new JavaScript, but it does require some CSS that is a little bit "out there," and it does break our calendar filters, which requires a line or two of JavaScript to fix. We also lose our show/hide buttons for each day, but you could get them back if you really wanted to.

Currently, the concerts are displayed in a nested loop—we have a list of days, we loop over each day, and then loop the concerts in that day to display the page. We're going to replace that behavior with just a simple list of the concerts sorted by start time. Our sort controller can then handle the concert list. However, the problem with displaying the concerts in a single list is that we lose our headers at the beginning of each day. We're going to get them back by using plain old CSS.

First, we need to solve one housekeeping problem. As currently written, each concert is wrapped in a Turbo Frame. When the Edit button is pressed, Turbo Frames changes the inner HTML of the frame to display the form, and then when the form is submitted, it changes the inner HTML again to display the edited concert.

Our problem is how updating the inner HTML of the form submission will interact with our sort. As with the favorites example, our sort controller will be sorting based on the outermost part of each concert's HTML display, which is the turbo-frame tag. We're going to need to put the start date as a sort value on that tag, just like we did for the favorites. But the new favorites were being created with Turbo Streams as brand-new DOM elements all the way through. However, the form submissions are using Turbo Frames and only changing the text inside the turbo-frame, meaning that if we change the date of the concert in the form, any change to the sort value attribute on the outer turbo-frame itself won't get picked up and the concert won't get re-sorted.

A solution is to make the form response a Turbo Stream with a replace action rather than a Turbo Frame response. By doing so, the entire turbo-frame tag is replaced, including the outer frame itself, which means that any sort value attributes we place on the turbo-frame will also change.

To do this, we need to add one line of code to the controller method to specify a response for turbo_stream formats, much the way we did for the FavoritesController back in Chapter 2, Hotwire and Turbo, on page 19:

chapter_11/04/app/controllers/concerts_controller.rb
```ruby
def update
  respond_to do |format|
    if @concert.update(concert_params)
      format.turbo_stream {}
      format.html do
        redirect_to(@concert, user: current_user)
      end

      format.json { render(:show, status: :ok, location: @concert) }
    else
      format.html { render(:edit) }
```

```
      format.json do
        render(json: @concert.errors, status: :unprocessable_entity)
      end
    end
  end
end
```

And we need to move our partial render to the associated view file:

chapter_11/04/app/views/concerts/update.turbo_stream.erb
```erb
<%= turbo_stream.replace(dom_id(@concert)) do %>
  <%= render(@concert, user: current_user) %>
<% end %>
```

This renders the same partial we were rendering before but as a Turbo Stream replace action.

Now we need to make the schedule show page display a list of concerts rather than a nested loop of days:

chapter_11/04/app/views/schedules/show.html.erb
```erb
<section data-controller="sort">
  <% @concerts.sort_by(&:start_time).each do |concert| %>
    <%= render(concert, user: current_user) %>
  <% end %>
</section>
```

We replaced the previous loop with just a loop over all the concerts sorted by start time so we start with a correct list (@concerts was already being produced by the controller). And we made the surrounding section tag declare a Stimulus SortController with data-controller="sort".

Inside the _concert partial, we need to make a couple of changes to support the SortController. Specifically, the outer turbo_frame-tag needs some attributes:

chapter_11/04/app/views/concerts/_concert.html.erb
```erb
<%= turbo_frame_tag(
    dom_id(concert),
    class: "concert",
    "data-sort-target": "sortElement",
    "data-sort-value": concert.start_time.to_i,
    "data-#{concert.start_time.by_example("2006-01-02")}": true
  ) do %>
```

Here we added a data-sort-target="sortElement" to make this visible to the SortController and a data-sort-value with the concert start time so the SortController has a value to use. We also added a DOM class, concert, and a dynamic data attribute. The dynamic data attribute is data-#{concert.start_time.by_example("2006-01-02")}, which means it will look like data-2021-02-15=true. Both of these attributes will be used by our new CSS.

At this point, the sorting works. But we don't have headers on each of the dates. This is where our CSS comes in.

Without going into a full CSS description, a few useful features of CSS will help us out here:

- The ::before selector allows us to insert content before a matching element.

- The [attribute] selector syntax allows us to match CSS on the existence of a specific attribute in an element.

- The first-child selector allows us to limit matches to elements that are the first child of our parent.

- The :not selector allows us to match elements that don't have a particular attribute.

- The + selector allows us to match on an element based on its previous sibling element.

All of these are enough to give us the CSS we need with one additional complication: because all of our text and data attribute names are based on the date of the concert, we only know them at run time, so we need to generate the CSS dynamically using ERB as part of the view file.

This is, to be fair, probably not recommended as a general thing to do, but again, it's here as an example of what you can do with CSS and minimal JavaScript.

Here's what I did. The following code is placed at the top of the show file for schedules, though I think it might be more proper to put it in a Rails content_for block so it could be in the HTML header. This works, though:

chapter_11/04/app/views/schedules/show.html.erb
```erb
<style>
  <% @schedule.schedule_days.each do |schedule_day| %>
    <% today = "data-#{schedule_day.day.by_example("2006-01-02")}" %>
    .concert[<%= today %>]:first-child::before,
    .concert:not([<%= today %>]) + [<%= today %>]::before
    {
        content: "<%= schedule_day.day.by_example("Monday, January 2, 2006") %>";
        font-size: 1.875rem;
        line-height: 2.25rem;
        font-weight: 700;
    }
  <% end %>
</style>
```

What this code is doing is looping through the list of days and dynamically generating a CSS selector for each day. Here's what one path through the loop looks like:

```
.concert[data-2021-01-20]:first-child::before,
.concert:not([data-2021-01-20]) + [data-2021-01-20]::before
{
  content: "Wednesday, January 20, 2021";
  font-size: 1.875rem;
  line-height: 2.25rem;
  font-weight: 700;
}
```

Translating this from CSS into English, we have a set of styles that describe a big, bold font and the date as our content. This is our header text.

These styles match two separate conditions separated by a comma, both of which specify ::before, which means the header text will go before a matched element. The first condition is any element that has a CSS class of concert, a data-attribute of data-2021-01-20, and is the first child of its parent. This catches the first concert in our list and puts a header in front of it.

The second condition is more complicated. It matches an element if the element has the data-attribute, data-2021-01-20 and its previous sibling element does not. In other words, it catches boundaries between days, and inserts a header before the first element of any new day. Therefore, if we have two elements in a row, the first with data-2021-01-19 and the second with data-2021-01-20, this selector will match the second element.

And this works. If you change the time or date of a concert, the Stimulus controller will re-sort it, and the CSS selectors will automatically put the headers in the correct places.

Now, for our calendar filters at the top to still work, we need to make a small change because the headers that they were making visible or invisible no longer exist:

chapter_11/04/app/packs/controllers/calendar_controller.ts
```
import { Controller } from "stimulus"

export default class CalendarController extends Controller {
  static targets = ["calendarDay"]
  calendarDayTargets: HTMLElement[]

  everyDayUnselected(): boolean {
    return this.calendarDayTargets.every((target: HTMLElement) => {
      return target.dataset.cssStatusValue === "false"
    })
  }
```

```
filter(): void {
  const everyDayUnselected = this.everyDayUnselected()
  this.calendarDayTargets.forEach((target: HTMLElement) => {
    const show =
      everyDayUnselected || target.dataset.cssStatusValue === "true"
    this.toggleAssociatedConcerts(target.dataset.scheduleAttribute, !show)
  })
}
showAll(): void {
  this.calendarDayTargets.forEach((target: HTMLElement) => {
    target.dataset.cssStatusValue = "false"
    this.toggleAssociatedConcerts(target.dataset.scheduleAttribute, false)
  })
}
toggleAssociatedConcerts(
  attributeName: string,
  toggleValue: boolean
): void {
  document
    .querySelectorAll(`.concert[${attributeName}]`)
    .forEach((element) => {
      element.classList.toggle("hidden", toggleValue)
    })
}
}
```

All this does is have both the filter and showAll methods defer to a toggleAssociat-edConcerts method that looks for all the matching concerts and makes them visible or invisible as required. The CSS headers will update automatically to match.

But there's one problem here. This CSS will only work as written if you change the concert date to one of the already existing dates. Changing to a date outside the list of CSS-generated dates will not match any of the selectors and you won't get a date header. There are a few ways around this problem (limiting the set of dates or generating more CSS, for example), though I suspect a full generic solution would require more custom JavaScript.

That said, I think this technique of using the CSS selectors directly is interesting. We've had a few cases where Stimulus changed a data attribute and as a result added CSS classes to an element. The possibility of having the styling depend directly on the data attribute itself is another way of adding data flexibility without writing JavaScript.

What's Next

In this chapter, we managed state in our Stimulus page using the DOM to hold our state. React works differently—it uses a JavaScript pattern called a *reducer*. In the next chapter, we'll look at how React manages state to use React's internal reducer pattern.

Managing State in React

As we've built up the React page in our app, we've been passing properties and handlers up and down the DOM tree to allow our data to be shared between components. This is somewhat complicated and error prone. We can use a global data store to keep us from having to do all this property passing—all we'll need to do is make sure each component subscribes to the global store and sends actions to it to change state. React comes with built-in features to support this kind of global data sharing, and it contains hook methods that we can use in our functional components to access this data.

To see how global data can help, in this chapter we're going to add a new feature to our concert page that builds up a price subtotal based on the number of tickets the user has on hold and allows the user to clear all tickets from the subtotal section. As currently implemented, this would involve even more passing of data up and down the DOM tree, but we can use contexts and reducers to centralize the data.

Using Reducers

Global data have different problems than local data. In particular, we need to make sure that changes to the global data store happen consistently for all users so that different parts of the application all have access to data in the same state.

We're going to solve our global data problem by refactoring our data using a JavaScript pattern called a *reducer* and a related structure called a *store*.

A *reducer* is a JavaScript function that takes two arguments. The first argument is an object representing a state. The second argument represents an action to take. The return value is a new state object representing the state of the data after the action is performed. The action is meant to describe the state change in terms of application logic, while the reducer converts that to changes in data.

Let's look at a simple example in which we will count American coins. The state of the world is the total number of coins and the total value of the coins. A reducer to partially handle this task might look like this:

```
const initialState = {count: 0, value: 0}

const reducer = (state, action) {
  switch (action.type) {
        case "AddPenny": {
            return { count: state.count + 1, value: state.value + 1 }
    }
    case "AddNickel": {
            return { count: state.count + 1, value: state.value + 5 }
    }
    // and so on...
  }
}
```

Then you'd call this method with something like:

```
const withAPenny = reducer(initialState, {type: "AddPenny"})
const pennyAndNickel = reducer(withAPenny, {type: "AddNickel"})
```

The idea is that you only change state via the reducer function, which—JavaScript being JavaScript—is a constraint you have to enforce yourself. Each call to the reducer function returns a new instance of the state object that is separate from all the other instances.

This is somewhat more verbose than, you know, not doing this kind of change with a reducer, which obviously raises the question, Why use this structure at all? To be perfectly honest, this is a case where my own taste in software structures clashes a little bit. I find this pattern, as typically implemented in JavaScript, to be verbose. That said, the basic idea of making the central state immutable and only accessible via specific methods is still a good one, and we'll stick with talking about the pattern, as you are most likely to see it in other JavaScript code.

One problem with a reducer on its own is the possibility that different callers to the reducer might get out of sync. A solution to that is to also maintain a store. For our purposes here, a *store* is a centralized object that manages access to both a single source of central data and a related reducer. For our coin example, a store might look like this:

```
export class CoinStore {
  static state = {count: 0, value: 0}
  static getState(): { return state }
  static dispatch(action) {
    CoinStore.state = reducer(CoinStore.state, action)
    return CoinStore.state
  }
}
```

Again, we're holding off on TypeScript annotations. This code sets up a store with a single point of access:

```
CoinStore.dispatch({type: "AddPenny"})
CoinStore.dispatch({type: "AddNickel"})
const finalState = CoinStore.getState()
```

In this case, you know that your return value from dispatch is the current state, but typically you only ask for the state explicitly, otherwise you act on it only through actions.

Using Context to Share State

For our app, we're going to use two React hooks to help us share state. The first hook we're going to use is useContext, which lets us use a feature of React called a *context*. In React, contexts allow us to share global data among components without passing that data via props.

To use a context, we surround our code with a special JSX component called a *context provider*. The context provider is initialized with a value, and then any component inside that provider, no matter how many levels down, can use the useContext hook to give that component inside access to the data in the context.

The specific data we want to share in our context is a reducer function that will provide our common state and a dispatch function to allow us to update that state. We'll also use a React hook called useReducer, which takes as an argument a function that implements the reducer pattern and provides some ease of use for accessing the reducer.

Changing our code to use a context and a reducer ends up being a significant refactoring of our React code, so let's outline what the data flow looks like:

- Our existing data model sets a bunch of data at the Venue level, which is passed down to each Row.

- Each Row maintains a list of the statuses of its component seats and passes that information to each Seat.

- The Seat status is held in the Row because the status depends on the status of neighboring seats and the Row is where all that data is stored.

- When we click on a Seat, that data is passed back up to the Row, which updates the status and passes the status back down to the Seat.

If we add the subtotal calculator, which would be a sibling component to the rows, the situation gets even more complicated. The click event on a Seat would need to be passed all the way back up to the Venue and then down to the subtotal calculator. Similarly, a click on the "Clear All" button would need to be passed up to the Venue and down to all the rows to clear all of the user's seats.

Here's a diagram:

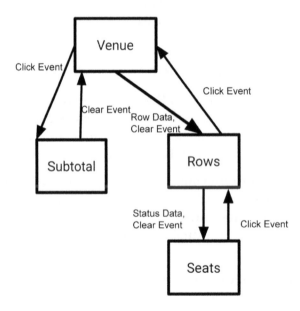

This promises to be a huge pain—and is exactly the kind of thing that has caused me to avoid React sometimes. But the combination of contexts and reducers allows us to avoid much of this rigmarole. We can store the reducer inside the context and get safe global data.

The context allows us to set the initial state globally when the page loads, and then each individual Seat component can query the context to determine its own status without having to deal with passing props around. Using a reducer inside the context guarantees that the global data will remain consistent. The result is that not only do we have less data being passed through the system but display logic can also end up situated closer to the actual display element. In this case, we specifically wind up moving a lot of display code from the Row component to the Seat component.

The code looks more like this:

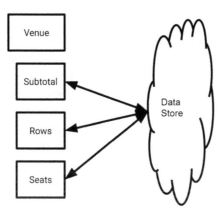

Let's look at how our React page changes with contexts. Creating a context and reducer in React involves a few steps:

1. Create the context.
2. Declare the reducer with a default state.
3. Optionally fetch starting data.
4. Place the context in your JSX as a parent component.

The context then is visible to all the child components inside the JSX context element.

Declaring the Context

In this section, we're going to recreate all the existing page logic plus the subtotal calculator, except for the part that communicates with the server via ActionCable. (ActionCable's asynchronous behavior adds complications, so we'll talk about those issues after we get the basic logic done.)

To make all this work, we're going to wrap our Venue component inside a new top-level App that will hold the context. Not only is this a little more consistent with common React style, but also it allows us to separate the application logic of the Venue component from the React logistics of the application.

The code changes to make this work start all the way back in our ERB file for the concert show page. We need to remove more HTML out of the ERB file that will go in our subtotal calculation. We've got three div elements in app/views/concerts/show.html.erb that need to be removed—the line that says, "Current Tickets Purchased"; the one that says, "Current Tickets Cost"; and the "Clear Tickets" button. We'll put them back in the React components in a moment.

Authentication

It may seem a little weird that we haven't discussed authentication much. I do realize that most of your apps will involve authentication and that handling authentication can be a challenge. Here's the thing, though. We're not doing a single-page application, and for what we are doing, existing Rails authentication works fine. ActionCable calls from controllers track the Rails user session, as do any server calls we've been making from our Stimulus and React code to the Rails server. So, for these apps, handle authentication in any server-side-Rails way you want. Let Rails manage the session, and it'll be fine.

I'm going to describe the code changes top-down, starting from the pack entry point and going down to the seat. After we see all the changes in the components that use the context and reducer, then we'll look at the code in the actual context and reducer.

First we need to use the as-yet-unbuilt App component as the top-level component in our Webpacker entry point, instead of Venue; this just swaps out the names:

```
chapter_12/01/app/packs/entrypoints/venue_display.tsx
import * as React from "react"
import * as ReactDOM from "react-dom"
import App from "components/app"

document.addEventListener("turbo:load", () => {
  const element = document.getElementById("react-element")
  if (element) {
    ReactDOM.render(
      <App
        rowCount={parseInt(element.dataset.rowCount, 10)}
        seatsPerRow={parseInt(element.dataset.seatsPerRow, 10)}
        concertId={parseInt(element.dataset.concertId, 10)}
      />,
      element
    )
  }
})
```

Now we need to create and use a React context.

Placing the Context

Here's the `App` component, which both creates and uses the context and reducer:

```
chapter_12/01/app/packs/components/app.tsx
import * as React from "react"
import Venue from "components/venue"
import { venueReducer, initialState } from "contexts/venue_context"
import { VenueAction, VenueState } from "contexts/venue_types"

export interface AppProps {
  concertId: number
  rowCount: number
  seatsPerRow: number
}

export interface IsVenueContext {
  state: VenueState
  dispatch: React.Dispatch<VenueAction>
}

export const VenueContext = React.createContext<IsVenueContext>(null)

export const App = (props: AppProps): React.ReactElement => {
  const [state, dispatch] = React.useReducer(
    venueReducer,
    initialState(props)
  )
  React.useEffect(() => {
    const fetchData = async () => {
      const response = await fetch(
        `/tickets.json?concert_id=${props.concertId}`
      )
      const tickets = await response.json()
      dispatch({ type: "setTickets", tickets: tickets })
    }
    fetchData()
  }, [])

  return (
    <VenueContext.Provider value={{ state, dispatch }}>
      <Venue />
    </VenueContext.Provider>
  )
}

export default App
```

The file starts with some declarations. We start by importing React, then importing our `Venue` component and a few names from new files called venue_context and venue_types that we'll talk about in a moment. Then we declare two TypeScript interfaces, one for the AppProps and one that will be used for the context called IsVenueContext. The AppProps interface describes the data we just passed to this component as props: the concert ID, the number of rows, and the number of seats in a row.

The IsVenueContext has two elements: a state element of type VenueState, which is defined in the context file, and a dispatch element of type React.Dispatch<VenueAction>. Could this be related to the state and dispatch we just talked about for reducers and stores? Oh, the suspense…

The context is created next, outside the actual component function:

```
export const VenueContext = React.createContext<IsVenueContext>(null)
```

The React.createContext function here creates a React context. The TypeScript generic notation IsVenueContext tells us the expected type of the data in the context, and the argument to the method is a default starting value. We don't have a useful default, yet our starting value is coming from the reducer a few lines down, so we can start with null.

After making createContext call, our context is now available for use. First, though, we're going to set up and populate the reducer to put in the context.

React has a hook method called useReducer that is similar to useState and is meant for when you are using the reducer pattern in your React app. Like useState, the useReducer hook causes React to update components when the reducer changes.

The useReducer hook can take two or three arguments. The first argument is always a function that is a reducer, meaning it matches the reducer pattern of taking state and action arguments and returning a state. If you have two arguments, the second argument is the initial state of the reducer. If you pass the hook three arguments, the third argument is a function that returns the initial state of the reducer and takes the second argument to the hook as its argument.

That's a little confusing, so let me put it this way—the following two calls are roughly identical:

```
useReducer(reducer, initialState(arg))
useReducer(reducer, arg, initialState)
```

The difference is that in the first line, initialState is called before the useReducer hook is invoked, and in the second line, initialState is called lazily after the hook is invoked.

In our call to useReducer, we pass it two variables, venueReducer, which is the reducer function we have not seen yet that is defined in the venue_context file, and initialState(props), also defined in the venue_context, which sets up our basic data.

The useReducer hook returns an array of two values: state and dispatch. The state returns the current state of the reducer, and dispatch is a function that takes an action object, very similar to how we used dispatch when calling a store in our coin example.

The only thing we are using the reducer for right now is to put the state and dispatch values into the context. This makes the reducer state and reducer dispatch function available to any component within the context.

Fetching Initial Data

Immediately after we call useReducer, we use the useEffect hook to fetch initial data from the server. I'd honestly rather have this fetch call be part of the reducer itself, but it's tricky to do asynchronous calls in a reducer; we'll see one solution to this problem in Chapter 13, Using Redux to Manage State, on page 253. This code is similar to the useEffect call that we had in the Venue component and uses the same indirection to allow the asynchronous behavior. Instead of passing the resulting data to a useState setter, we're calling dispatch({ type: "setTickets", tickets: tickets }) to pass the data to the reducer—it's the same dispatch that was the return value from useReducer.

The server side changes slightly here to return the data as a list of ticket objects rather than a 2D array of them. We'll now handle conversion to the array client side. Here's the TicketController#index method that receives the API call:

chapter_12/01/app/controllers/tickets_controller.rb
```ruby
def index
  @tickets = Ticket.data_for_concert(params[:concert_id])
  respond_to do |format|
    format.html
    format.json do
      render(json: @tickets)
    end
  end
end
```

And here's the method in the Ticket model that actually generates the data:

chapter_12/01/app/models/ticket.rb
```ruby
def self.data_for_concert(concert_id)
  for_concert(concert_id).select(&:unavailable?).map(&:to_concert_h)
end
```

```
def unavailable?
  held? || purchased?
end
```

Now we need to make the context available to the rest of the app.

Using the Context

In React, you use a context by making a JSX element called a *provider*. You can see our provider in the returned JSX at the end of the file. We create a JSX element called VenueContext.Provider and place our existing Venue component inside it. We pass one prop to the provider, called value, which is an object with {state, dispatch}. That object syntax defines an object where the key and value have the same name, in other words, the object being passed to the prop is {state: state, dispatch: dispatch}.

As keys, state and dispatch are defined by the IsVenueContext interface. The state and dispatch values, however, came from the previous line's call to the useReducer hook, const [state, dispatch] = React.useReducer(venueReducer, fetchState(props)).

Let's walk through our app to see how the components change now that the data is managed by the context.

Venue

The Venue component no longer needs to take properties in just to pass them along. Without having to pass properties or handle data, the Venue component gets a lot simpler:

```
chapter_12/01/app/packs/components/venue.tsx
import * as React from "react"
import Subtotal from "components/subtotal"
import VenueBody from "components/venue_body"
import VenueHeader from "components/venue_header"

export const Venue = (): React.ReactElement => {
  return (
    <>
      <Subtotal />
      <VenueHeader />
      <VenueBody />
    </>
  )
}

export default Venue
```

This component is just calling three other components: the VenueHeader and VenueBody we already had, and our new one, Subtotal.

VenueHeader

VenueHeader is our first example how to use the context and the reducer from a component that is inside the context provider:

```
chapter_12/01/app/packs/components/venue_header.tsx
import * as React from "react"
import styled from "styled-components"
import { IsVenueContext, VenueContext } from "components/app"

const Header = styled.span`
  font-size: 1.5rem;
  font-weight: bold;
  margin-left: 15px;
  margin-right: 15px;
`

const options = (seatsPerRow) => {
  const arrayOfNumbers = Array.from(Array(seatsPerRow).keys())
  return arrayOfNumbers.map((i) => (
    <option key={i + 1} value={i + 1}>
      {i + 1}
    </option>
  ))
}

export const VenueHeader = (): React.ReactElement => {
  const context = React.useContext<IsVenueContext>(VenueContext)
  const setTicketsOnChange = (event: React.SyntheticEvent): void => {
    const target = event.target as HTMLSelectElement
    context.dispatch({
      type: "setTicketsToBuy",
      amount: parseInt(target.value, 10),
    })
  }

  return (
    <div>
      <Header>How many tickets would you like?</Header>
      <span className="select">
        <select onChange={setTicketsOnChange}>
          {options(context.state.seatsPerRow)}
        </select>
      </span>
    </div>
  )
}

export default VenueHeader
```

This component has changed some. It takes no props, for one. The first thing we do in the component function itself is call a new hook called useContext: const context = React.useContext<IsVenueContext>(VenueContext).

The argument to useContext is the name of a context whose provider has this component in scope. The return value is the context itself. By using this hook we guarantee that the component will be refreshed if the context changes—just as if the data in the context had been passed as props, but without the complexity of actually passing them.

The rest of the component has changed slightly. When we pass the number of seats in a row to generate the list of options, we now take that number from context.state.seatsInRow rather than from the props. The setTicketsOnChange handler triggers a call to the reducer using context.dispatch. The dispatch call changes the state, which means the context has changed and which triggers a redrawing of all the components that use the context.

VenueBody

The VenueBody component still largely creates a bunch of rows but now also uses the context to determine how many rows to create. One thing we need to deal with here is that the arrays being created by our Array.from trick start at zero, but the actual ticket data has both row and seats starting at 1. For this code, we're converting both row and seat to the 1-based array as soon as we can:

```
chapter_12/01/app/packs/components/venue_body.tsx
import * as React from "react"
import Row from "components/row"
import { IsVenueContext, VenueContext } from "components/app"

const rowItems = (rowCount) => {
  const rowNumbers = Array.from(Array(rowCount).keys())
  return rowNumbers.map((rowNumber) => (
    <Row key={rowNumber + 1} rowNumber={rowNumber + 1} />
  ))
}

export const VenueBody = (): React.ReactElement => {
  const context = React.useContext<IsVenueContext>(VenueContext)
  return (
    <table className="table">
      <tbody>{rowItems(context.state.rowCount)}</tbody>
    </table>
  )
}

export default VenueBody
```

The Row component is no longer tracking the state of its seats, so it can be much simpler:

```
chapter_12/01/app/packs/components/row.tsx
import * as React from "react"
import Seat from "components/seat"
import { IsVenueContext, VenueContext } from "components/app"

interface RowProps {
  rowNumber: number
}

const Row = ({ rowNumber }: RowProps): React.ReactElement => {
  const context = React.useContext<IsVenueContext>(VenueContext)

  const seatItems = Array.from(Array(context.state.seatsPerRow).keys()).map(
    (seatNumber) => {
      return (
        <Seat
          key={seatNumber + 1}
          seatNumber={seatNumber + 1}
          rowNumber={rowNumber}
        />
      )
    }
  )

  return <tr className="h-20">{seatItems}</tr>
}

export default Row
```

Note that we haven't totally abandoned the use of props—the row number of each individual row isn't a part of the global state, so we pass it to that row as a prop. Similarly, each Seat component will get its row and seat number as props.

The Seat component takes on all the application logic for seat status, so it picks up some of the complexity that the other components have lost:

```
chapter_12/01/app/packs/components/seat.tsx
import * as React from "react"
import styled from "styled-components"
import { TicketData } from "contexts/venue_types"
import { IsVenueContext, VenueContext } from "components/app"

const stateColor = (status: string): string => {
  if (status === "unsold") {
    return "white"
  } else if (status === "held") {
    return "green"
  } else if (status === "purchased") {
    return "red"
```

```
    } else {
      return "yellow"
    }
}

interface SquareProps {
  status: string
  className?: string
}
const buttonClass = "p-4 m-2 my-10 border-black border-4 text-lg"

const ButtonSquare = styled.span.attrs({
  className: buttonClass,
})<SquareProps>`
  background-color: ${(props) => stateColor(props.status)};
  transition: all 1s ease-in-out;

  &:hover {
    background-color: ${(props) =>
      props.status === "unsold" ? "lightblue" : stateColor(props.status)};
  }
`

interface SeatProps {
  seatNumber: number
  rowNumber: number
}

export const Seat = ({
  seatNumber,
  rowNumber,
}: SeatProps): React.ReactElement => {
  const context = React.useContext<IsVenueContext>(VenueContext)
  const seatMatch = (ticketList: TicketData[], exact = false): boolean => {
    for (const heldTicket of ticketList) {
      const rowMatch = heldTicket.row == rowNumber
      const seatDiff = heldTicket.number - seatNumber
      const diff = exact ? 1 : context.state.ticketsToBuyCount
      const seatMatch = seatDiff >= 0 && seatDiff < diff
      if (rowMatch && seatMatch) {
        return true
      }
    }
    return false
  }

  const currentStatus = (): string => {
    if (seatMatch(context.state.otherTickets, true)) {
      return "purchased"
    }
    if (seatMatch(context.state.myTickets, true)) {
      return "held"
    }
```

```
    if (
      seatMatch(context.state.otherTickets) ||
      seatMatch(context.state.myTickets) ||
      seatNumber + context.state.ticketsToBuyCount - 1 >
        context.state.seatsPerRow
    ) {
      return "invalid"
    }
    return "unsold"
  }
  const onSeatChange = (): void => {
    const status = currentStatus()
    if (status === "invalid" || status === "purchased") {
      return
    }
    const actionType = status === "unsold" ? "holdTicket" : "unholdTicket"
    context.dispatch({ type: actionType, seatNumber, rowNumber })
  }
  return (
    <td>
      <ButtonSquare status={currentStatus()} onClick={onSeatChange}>
        {seatNumber}
      </ButtonSquare>
    </td>
  )
}

export default Seat
```

A lot of this is similar to the previous version of Seat. The new bits are the
currentStatus function and its attendant seatMatch function. These two functions
are the new home of the business logic for determining if the seat is available,
using many pieces of information from the context—the number of seats in
a row, the number of tickets to buy, and the list of currently held tickets.
Ultimately they return the same list of statuses as the previous version, which
are then converted to the correct background color as before.

One important change is that the onSeatChange function no longer calls handlers
back up the component tree; instead it just dispatches an action to the con-
text.dispatch method, which changes the context state and triggers redraws as
needed across the context provider. Clicking on a seat will cause the appropriate seats to be purchased; other seats to the left will become invalid, and
they will also change color.

Subtotal

Our new Subtotal component is where the deleted HTML wound up:

```
chapter_12/01/app/packs/components/subtotal.tsx
import * as React from "react"
import styled from "styled-components"
import { IsVenueContext, VenueContext } from "components/app"

const Header = styled.div`
  font-size: 1.5rem;
  font-weight: bold;
  margin-left: 15px;
  margin-right: 15px;
`

const buttonClass =
  "px-5 py-4 m-2 my-4 w-40 text-center text-white transition-colors " +
  "duration-150 bg-gray-800 rounded-lg focus:shadow-outline hover:bg-black"

const Subtotal = (): React.ReactElement => {
  const context = React.useContext<IsVenueContext>(VenueContext)

  const onClear = () => {
    context.dispatch({ type: "clearHolds" })
  }

  return (
    <>
      <Header>
        <span>Current Tickets Purchased:  </span>
        <span>{context.state.myTickets.length}</span>
      </Header>
      <Header>
        <span>Current Tickets Cost:  </span>
        <span>${context.state.myTickets.length * 15}.00</span>
      </Header>
      <div className={buttonClass} onClick={onClear}>
        Clear Tickets
      </div>
    </>
  )
}

export default Subtotal
```

We define a couple of styled components and then draw the component using the useContext hook and context.state to determine the number of purchased tickets and their cost. When the button is clicked, we invoke the onClear function, which dispatches off to the context and reducer with a new clearHolds action.

We've talked around it long enough; we need to see the venue context.

Context Reducer

The context reducer looks like this:

```
chapter_12/01/app/packs/contexts/venue_context.ts
import { AppProps } from "components/app"
import { VenueState, VenueAction } from "contexts/venue_types"

export const initialState = (props: AppProps): VenueState => {
  return {
    rowCount: props.rowCount,
    seatsPerRow: props.seatsPerRow,
    concertId: props.concertId,
    otherTickets: [],
    ticketsToBuyCount: 1,
    myTickets: [],
  }
}

export const venueReducer = (
  state: VenueState,
  action: VenueAction
): VenueState => {
  switch (action.type) {
    case "setTickets":
      return {
        ...state,
        otherTickets: action.tickets.filter(
          (ticket) => ticket.status === "purchased"
        ),
        myTickets: action.tickets.filter(
          (ticket) => ticket.status === "held"
        ),
      }
    case "setTicketsToBuy":
      return { ...state, ticketsToBuyCount: action.amount }
    case "holdTicket": {
      const newTickets = Array.from(
        Array(state.ticketsToBuyCount).keys()
      ).map((index) => {
        return {
          id: 0,
          row: action.rowNumber,
          number: action.seatNumber + index,
          status: "held",
        }
      })
      return {
        ...state,
        myTickets: [...state.myTickets, ...newTickets],
      }
    }
```

```
    case "unholdTicket": {
      const newTickets = state.myTickets.filter((ticket) => {
        const rowMatch = ticket.row == action.rowNumber
        const seatDiff = ticket.number - action.seatNumber
        const seatMatch =
          seatDiff >= 0 && seatDiff < state.ticketsToBuyCount
        return !(rowMatch && seatMatch)
      })
      return { ...state, myTickets: newTickets }
    }
    case "clearHolds": {
      return { ...state, myTickets: [] }
    }
    default:
      return state
  }
}
```

What's interesting is that basically none of this is React-specific.

We define two methods. The first, initialState, creates an initial state from the incoming props passed to the app. The return type of the state is called VenueState, and it is defined in the venue_types file.

The second method is venueReducer, which is the reducer function itself. All of our business logic has been reworked to match the reducer pattern—which is to say, the logic has been reworked to use the state coming into the reducer function and return a new state object with the changes.

There are five actions in the venueReducer, all of which return a new state object. They all heavily use the JavaScript spread operator, which makes it easy to say that an object should be copied but specific fields should be overridden. The JS { ...state, ticketsToBuy: action.amount } means create a new object with the same attributes as the existing state but override ticketsToBuy with the action.amount.

The five actions are:

- setTickets is called after we fetch the ticket data from the server, and it passes that data to myTickets, a list of tickets held by the user, and otherTickets, a list of tickets held by others.

- setTicketsToBuy is called when the number of tickets in the pull-down menu changes, updating the ticketsToBuy in the state.

- holdTicket is called when the user clicks on an available seat, which generates ticket data for multiple tickets based on the ticketsToBuy count, then adds that data to the myTickets.

- unholdTickets, the reverse of holdTicket, happens when the user clicks on an already held seat. It uses filter to create a new list of myTickets without the unheld seats, then makes that new list part of the state.

- clearHolds is called when the user clicks the new holds button and sets the myTickets list to zero.

In all of these cases, the useReducer hook causes our components to be rerendered when the state changes, so all of these changes are immediately visible in the display. Specifically, for our purposes, the calculation of the subtotal, which is based on the length of the myTickets array, changes when the state changes.

We need to define two types, (1) the VenueState type that has all the state information, and (2) the VenueAction type that the reducer uses to determine which action has been called. We've put both these types in their own file, called venue_types.ts.

Here's the state data declaration:

chapter_12/01/app/packs/contexts/venue_types.ts
```
export interface TicketData {
  id: number
  number: number
  row: number
  status: string
}
export interface VenueState {
  concertId: number
  myTickets: TicketData[]
  otherTickets: TicketData[]
  rowCount: number
  seatsPerRow: number
  ticketsToBuyCount: number
}
```

For the state, we have the same row count, seats per row, concert ID, and tickets to buy count that we've been using. We also add the list of tickets coming in from the server as otherTickets or myTickets based on whether the status is purchased or held.

Then we have a series of types for each dispatch action, which uses some new TypeScript. It looks like this:

chapter_12/01/app/packs/contexts/venue_types.ts
```
interface SetTicketToBuy {
  type: "setTicketsToBuy"
  amount: number
```

```
}

interface HoldTicket {
  type: "holdTicket"
  seatNumber: number
  rowNumber: number
}

interface UnholdTicket {
  type: "unholdTicket"
  seatNumber: number
  rowNumber: number
}

interface ClearHolds {
  type: "clearHolds"
}

interface SetTickets {
  type: "setTickets"
  tickets: TicketData[]
}

export type VenueAction =
  | ClearHolds
  | HoldTicket
  | SetTicketToBuy
  | SetTickets
  | UnholdTicket
```

The problem we need TypeScript to solve with these action types is that this reducer has multiple action objects, and each of those is going to have a type property. That's how dispatch works.

However, the other properties of each action are different. The shape of each action's data depends on exactly what kind of action the object is. A hold ticket action needs the seat and row number of a ticket, but the set tickets to buy count action only needs the new number of tickets to buy. TypeScript needs to know what data is available when we execute each action so it can say whether the code is type-safe.

We could handle this by creating a parent class that only has a type property and then having subclasses, but then we wouldn't be able to use object literal syntax to create objects, and I would like to have the convenience of { type: "AddFilter" }.

Happily, TypeScript includes a feature called a *string literal type* that allows us to declare interfaces based on literal string values.

For each individual action, we declare a TypeScript interface where the type property is set to a literal string value and the other properties are added as needed. Then we declare an VenueAction type to be a combination of all the types we've declared. VenueAction is a *union type*, which means that an object can be a VenueAction if it matches any of the types that make up the union. Now when we use these objects, TypeScript will pattern match based on the value of the type property to determine which interface the object matches.

To use these types, we declare the action argument of the reducer to be of type VenueAction, meaning it can be one of any of the component types of the Venue-Action union type.

If we just keep the object as type VenueAction, we can only access properties that are common across all of the component types, which in this case, means only type.

That's not very useful, but TypeScript is really smart about this. In our reducer function, when we switch based on action.type, TypeScript infers the interface being used. In other words, when we branch into, say, the setTicket-sToBuy branch, TypeScript knows that the action is of type SetTicketToBuy and that it has a dateFilter property, but if we branch in to ClearHolds, TypeScript knows the action is a ClearHolds and does not have a dateFilter property. This is quite nifty and makes it easy to type-check our actions.

And that gives us almost all of our functionality rewritten to use context and a reducer. What I like about this version is that the functionality is more clearly split into concerns, and each individual component is better able to define its own terms. They are all dependent on the global context, but that seems to me to be an easier dependency to manage than to manage all the interdependencies between components.

However, the page doesn't quite work yet. We haven't added in our server communication, and it turns out that if we continue to use ActionCable, the asynchronous server behavior makes everything a little more complicated.

Adding Asynchronous Events to Contexts

With all of that out of the way, we can add the ActionCable subscription back to the system, but we have a logistical problem to deal with first.

The logistical problem is that the ActionCable subscription needs to both be global and have external access to the existing VenueContext reducer. It needs to be global because multiple components may need access to the subscription data. But it also needs to be external from the VenueContext because the subscription uses the concert_id, which is now data in the state. It will also need to use the dispatch function because the subscription receives data about what tickets have been held from the ActionCable channel, and it will need to use dispatch to update global state based on that data. This means the subscription needs to know about the reducer when it's defined, so it has to be external to the reducer.

We can manage this problem in a few different ways. The solution I chose for our purposes is to create a new context to make the subscription a separate part of global data, declared like this:

chapter_12/02/app/packs/components/app.tsx
```
export const SubscriptionContext = React.createContext<Subscription>(null)

let appSubscription: Subscription = null

const initSubscription = (
  state: VenueState,
  dispatch: React.Dispatch<VenueAction>
): Subscription => {
  if (!appSubscription) {
    appSubscription = createConsumer().subscriptions.create(
      { channel: "ConcertChannel", concertId: state.concertId },
      {
        received(tickets) {
          dispatch({ type: "setTickets", tickets })
        },
      }
    )
  }
  return appSubscription
}
```

This is mostly the same initSubscription code that we used before. The only difference is that when it receives ticket data, it dispatches to the same setTickets action that we wrote for the useEffect when the page loads. We don't even have to cover the JSON; ActionCable has already done so.

And then the new context is used like this:

chapter_12/02/app/packs/components/app.tsx
```
return (
  <VenueContext.Provider value={{ state, dispatch }}>
    <SubscriptionContext.Provider
      value={initSubscription(state, dispatch)}>
      <Venue />
    </SubscriptionContext.Provider>
  </VenueContext.Provider>
)
```

Here we create a new context whose data is just an ActionCable subscription, and we nest that context inside our existing VenueContext so it is both able to use state and dispatch and is global to the rest of the components. (Note that a couple of items need to be imported at the top of the file for this to work.)

I'll be honest: this feels a little string and sealing wax, and it wasn't the first thing I tried, but it does work, and it is mostly transparent to the rest of the internals. Please note that we still need to keep a global variable around to prevent the subscription from being created multiple times—I'm not completely sure why the value prop is evaluated over and over again, but experimentation shows that it sure is.

We also need to tweak the server side (in ConcertChannel) so that it sends down the same set of tickets, Ticket.data_for_concert(data["concertId"]), that we used in the TicketController#index method.

The Seat component calls useContext a second time to get access to the subscription context:

chapter_12/02/app/packs/components/seat.tsx
```
const context = React.useContext<IsVenueContext>(VenueContext)
const subscription = React.useContext<Subscription>(SubscriptionContext)
```

Then it sends a command back to the subscription, almost exactly as before:

chapter_12/02/app/packs/components/seat.tsx
```
const onSeatChange = (): void => {
  const status = currentStatus()
  if (status === "invalid" || status === "purchased") {
    return
  }
  const actionType = status === "unsold" ? "holdTicket" : "unholdTicket"
  context.dispatch({ type: actionType, seatNumber, rowNumber })
  subscription.perform("added_to_cart", {
    concertId: context.state.concertId,
    row: rowNumber,
    seatNumber: seatNumber,
    status: actionType === "holdTicket" ? "held" : "unsold",
    ticketsToBuyCount: context.state.ticketsToBuyCount,
  })
}
```

Similarly, the Subtotal component needs to tell the server side that all the personally held tickets can be moved to the unsold state:

```
chapter_12/02/app/packs/components/subtotal.tsx
const subscription = React.useContext<Subscription>(SubscriptionContext)

const onClear = () => {
  subscription.perform("removed_from_cart", {
    concertId: context.state.concertId,
    tickets: context.state.myTickets,
  })
  context.dispatch({ type: "clearHolds" })
}
```

There's a server-side component to this command that is another method in the concert channel:

```
chapter_12/02/app/channels/concert_channel.rb
def removed_from_cart(data)
  cart = ShoppingCart.find_or_create_by(user_id: data["userId"])
  cart.clear(
    concert_id: data["concertId"],
    tickets: data["tickets"]
  )
  result = Ticket.data_for_concert(data["concertId"])
  ActionCable.server.broadcast("concert_#{data["concertId"]}", result)
end
```

And a small clear method in the shopping cart:

```
chapter_12/02/app/models/shopping_cart.rb
def clear(concert_id:, tickets:)
  tickets.each do |ticket|
    db_ticket = Ticket.find_by(
      row: ticket["row"], number: ticket["number"], concert_id: concert_id
    )
    db_ticket&.update(status: :unsold)
  end
end
```

We have one more problem with using our ActionCable subscription in React. So far, we've been using reducers in the single-threaded, synchronous Java-Script world. Specifically, this means that all the state changes that go through the reducer happen in order, and we know when we call dispatch exactly what order state changes will happen and when state changes are done.

Asynchronous changes break that assumption. We don't know when state changes are going to happen once we introduce asynchronous activities like talking to the sever or receiving data from ActionCable. This is why we had to do our asynchronous fetch data call outside the reducer.

The key here is that we need to keep asynchronous actions away from the reducer. The incoming subscription data only calls the reducer after the data has arrived—the waiting on ActionCable is not part of the reducer or its associated state. Our outgoing server calls as a result of user changes also happen in the React component and are not part of the reducer.

This gets a little more complicated if these dispatch calls that are associated with asynchronous server calls happen from multiple places. We either need to remember to pair the dispatch with the server call or create a wrapper around both the dispatch and the server call.

What's Next

Having now learned how to use the reducer pattern in React, we're going to take a look at Redux, a library that is a very commonly used implementation of the reducer pattern that is often integrated with React. Once we move our code to Redux, we'll see how an add-on to Redux will help us manage our asynchronous actions.

Using Redux to Manage State

Now that we are using a reducer to manage state in our React app, we've come up against an issue with integrating our asynchronous actions with our reducer. We've chosen to keep our asynchronous actions outside our reducer, which means we need to remember to trigger the asynchronous actions when we call the reducer.

This brings us to a tool called Redux[1] and its associated library, React-Redux.[2] Redux is a more complex version of the reducer and store pattern we've been working with. I'm not going to cover a lot of the extended complexity here, but Redux has support for more complex combinations of reducers and actions than we need, at least at the moment. It bills itself as a "Predictable State Container for JS Apps," which for our purposes is the marketing-speak version of what we've been talking about in the previous chapter. By "state container," it's referring to what we've been calling a store, and by "predictable," it's referring to the way reducers give you state objects that won't change behind your back.

The main concept of Redux is the *store*, and generally Redux assumes that there will only be one store visible to any given chunk of the React DOM tree. We can't usefully nest Redux stores the way that we were nesting React contexts, though.

In this chapter, we're going to refactor our code to use Redux and then we're going to use Redux to let us better integrate the asynchronous events into our page.

---

1. https://redux.js.org
2. https://react-redux.js.org

Installing and Using Redux

We first need to install Redux, the Redux bindings for React, and their associated type definitions:

```
$ yarn add redux react-redux @types/redux @types/react-redux
```

Then, we'll create a Redux store in our app.

Creating a Redux Store

To create a store in our app, we'll use the function provided by Redux called createStore, which takes a reducer function as its one argument. (There's a Redux Toolkit library that has support for creating more complex stores and reducers. We won't be using it in this book, but if you are building true single-page applications with Redux, you should definitely look at it.)[3]

The reducer we've been building in our page so far is almost exactly structured to work in Redux as is. The main difference is in initialization. Our existing reducer derives its initial state from the props passed to the App component. Redux, on the other hand, requires its reducers to be able to initialize themselves without any input.

Happily, we can adjust our reducer to behave the way Redux expects with just a few small changes. First, we need to change our initial state to a value rather than a function, and we also need to change the signature of the reducer function to take the initial state as a default argument (note the import { createStore } from "redux" statement at the top of the file):

```
chapter_13/01/app/packs/contexts/venue_context.ts
export const initialState = {
  rowCount: 1,
  seatsPerRow: 1,
  concertId: 0,
  otherTickets: [],
  ticketsToBuyCount: 1,
  myTickets: [],
}

export const venueReducer = (
  state: VenueState = initialState,
  action: VenueAction
): VenueState => {
  switch (action.type) {
    case "setTickets":
      return {
```

---

3.   https://redux-toolkit.js.org

```
    ...state,
    otherTickets: action.tickets.filter(
      (ticket) => ticket.status === "purchased"
    ),
    myTickets: action.tickets.filter(
      (ticket) => ticket.status === "held"
    ),
  }
case "setTicketsToBuy":
  return { ...state, ticketsToBuyCount: action.amount }
case "holdTicket": {
  const newTickets = Array.from(
    Array(state.ticketsToBuyCount).keys()
  ).map((index) => {
    return {
      id: 0,
      row: action.rowNumber,
      number: action.seatNumber + index,
      status: "held",
    }
  })
  return {
    ...state,
    myTickets: [...state.myTickets, ...newTickets],
  }
}
case "unholdTicket": {
  const newTickets = state.myTickets.filter((ticket) => {
    const rowMatch = ticket.row == action.rowNumber
    const seatDiff = ticket.number - action.seatNumber
    const seatMatch =
      seatDiff >= 0 && seatDiff < state.ticketsToBuyCount
    return !(rowMatch && seatMatch)
  })
  return { ...state, myTickets: newTickets }
}
case "clearHolds": {
  return { ...state, myTickets: [] }
}
case "initFromProps": {
  return {
    ...state,
    concertId: action.props.concertId,
    rowCount: action.props.rowCount,
    seatsPerRow: action.props.seatsPerRow,
  }
}
```

```
    default:
      return state
  }
}
```

```
export const venueStore = createStore(venueReducer)
```

We can then do our actual setup, the one that uses data that comes from the props, by dispatching an action to the reducer just like any other action, like this:

chapter_13/01/app/packs/contexts/venue_context.ts
```
case "initFromProps": {
  return {
    ...state,
    concertId: action.props.concertId,
    rowCount: action.props.rowCount,
    seatsPerRow: action.props.seatsPerRow,
  }
}
```

The venue_types file needs to add a supporting action:

chapter_13/01/app/packs/contexts/venue_types.ts
```
export interface InitFromProps {
  type: "initFromProps"
  props: AppProps
}

export type VenueAction =
  | ClearHolds
  | HoldTicket
  | InitFromProps
  | SetTicketToBuy
  | SetTickets
  | UnholdTicket
```

Next, we have our first real interaction with Redux. We call createStore to create a store and export the value to be available to other parts of the code:

chapter_13/01/app/packs/contexts/venue_context.ts
```
export const venueStore = createStore(venueReducer)
```

With this in place, our App component has to change slightly to use our new Redux store. We'll update that next.

Using a Redux Store

To use our new Redux store, we need to import the venueStore function from the venue_reducer file. The App component will then look like this:

```
chapter_13/01/app/packs/components/app.tsx
export const App = (props: AppProps): React.ReactElement => {
  venueStore.dispatch({ type: "initFromProps", props })
  React.useEffect(() => {
    const fetchData = async () => {
      const response = await fetch(
        `/tickets.json?concert_id=${props.concertId}`
      )
      const tickets = await response.json()
      venueStore.dispatch({ type: "setTickets", tickets })
    }
    fetchData()
  }, [])

  return (
    <Provider store={venueStore}>
      <Venue />
    </Provider>
  )
}
```

Before we passed our initial value to the reducer on first creation, we directly dispatch the initialization action we just wrote with the App props as the argument. We still need to have the useEffect call to do the asynchronous ticket load, but we'll fix that by the end of this chapter.

To use the Redux store in any of the child components, we need to wrap all the components in a Redux JSX component called a Provider. (You might see a certain common quality to the Redux names and the React internal names we've been using—the Redux names came first, for what it's worth.) The provider takes one prop argument, the store. Notably, the state of the store is now as it is after we dispatched our init action. The Provider is not named to differentiate it from other providers—the expectation is that Redux providers will not be nested.

To use the Redux store within those child components, we need two hooks: useDispatch and useSelector. useDispatch takes no arguments and returns a dispatch function, so the usage is typically const dispatch = useDispatch(). The returned dispatch function is used just like the other dispatch functions we've been discussing—you pass it a known action and it returns the new state.

useSelector lets us get to the state of the store directly, and the argument is maybe not quite what you'd expect. The argument to useSelector is a function. This argument function takes one argument—the state of the Redux store—and returns whatever the heck you want. So you could just get back the entire state with const state = useSelector(state => state). In practice, though, you typically limit the return value to just the parts of the state that the component needs, so const seatsInRow = useSelector<VenueState, number>(state => state.seatsInRow).

The generic types on useSelector are the type of the entire state and the type of the return value. Limiting the return values is useful because then Redux will only trigger a redraw of the component if the return value changes rather than the state as a whole. If the state is large and the component small, this can lead to performance improvements by minimizing component redraws.

For each of our components, then, we need to add the useDispatch hook, if needed, and craft a useSelector call for the values the component needs. For example, the Subtotal component hook calls look like this:

```
chapter_13/01/app/packs/components/subtotal.tsx
const myTickets = useSelector<VenueState, TicketData[]>(
  (state) => state.myTickets
)
const dispatch = useDispatch()

const onClear = () => {
  dispatch({ type: "clearHolds" })
}

return (
  <>
    <Header>
      <span>Current Tickets Purchased:  </span>
      <span>{myTickets.length}</span>
    </Header>
    <Header>
      <span>Current Tickets Cost:  </span>
      <span>${myTickets.length * 15}.00</span>
    </Header>
    <div className={buttonClass} onClick={onClear}>
      Clear Tickets
    </div>
  </>
)
```

Notice the use of useSelector to return just the myTickets and then the references across the component where we refer to data as content.state.myHeldTickets that are changed to just myHeldTickets, because that's where we've assigned the return value of the hook.

We're not going to look at all the changes to the components here, because the changes are very mechanical and similar to the one we've just seen, and also because we're going to look at the final form of most of the components in just a second once we add the ActionCable subscription back. You can see the current state of the components in the chapter_13/01 directory in the code download for this book.

Adding Asynchronous Actions to Redux

When we last looked at our asynchronous actions before we added in Redux, what we basically had was a combination of our ActionCable calls and our reducer calls. The problem with this is that the combination is somewhat awkward and requires always remembering that the two parts need to be called together. What we really want is for our store, which is now provided by Redux, to allow us to mix these asynchronous actions with our regular reducer calls.

To do this, we are going to use an add-on to Redux called Redux Thunk.[4] Redux Thunk is actually based on a pretty small idea. Up until now, the actions we've been passing to our reducer have just been data objects. What Redux Thunk asks is, "What if those arguments are something else?"

Redux Thunk allows for a different kind of argument to be passed to dispatch, namely a function that itself returns a function. Hence the name Redux Thunk, because *thunk* is a generic term for a function that returns a function.

You dispatch the function by calling it, so where we before had calls like dispatch({type: "doSomething"}), we now have dispatch(doSomething()) where the call to doSomething itself returns a function.

I pause here to note that it is super common in the React world to wrap action calls to reducers inside functions that return the action object. So rather than dispatch({type: "doSomething"}), we'd write dispatch(doSomething()) where doSomething is defined as:

```
const doSomething = () => {
  return { type: "doSomething" }
}
```

The argument for doing this is that the functions are easier to manage in complex cases. We haven't been doing that so far because it seems like a bit too much boilerplate code for our purposes, but it's very common in practice. (As Betsy Haibel, co-founder of the engineering education firm Cohere, points out, a big difference between JavaScript libraries and Ruby ones is that the JavaScript libraries often consider boilerplate to be a good thing, whereas Ruby libraries try to avoid it.)

So when using a thunk, the call might still look like dispatch(doSomething()) but would differ by returning a function as in:

```
const doSomething = () => {
```

---

4.   https://github.com/reduxjs/redux-thunk

```
    return async (dispatch) => {
      await doSomethingAsynchronous()
      dispatch({ type: "doSomethingElse" })
    }
  }
}
```

Adding Redux Thunk into the mix changes Redux slightly. Once Redux Thunk is added, when Redux receives an argument to a dispatch call that is a function rather than an action type, Redux executes the function passed to it, giving that function a dispatch argument (and, as we'll see, a getState argument). By doing this, Redux Thunk controls the execution of our action and allows us to do asynchronous stuff and coordinate it with our reducer while still using the same dispatch method to communicate with it.

For our purposes, what we need to do is install Redux Thunk, add a mechanism to put our ActionCable subscription in our state, and then convert our existing actions that deal with the subscription into Redux Thunk functions.

The installation is just another yarn package:

```
$ yarn add redux-thunk
```

The Redux Thunk package takes care of its own TypeScript types, so we don't need to install another types package.

We do need to change our createStore method to register Redux Thunk. Redux has the concept of *middleware*, which is software that hooks into Redux to change its behavior. We need to add an argument to tell Redux to apply Redux Thunk as middleware.

We have some imports to add:

chapter_13/02/app/packs/contexts/venue_context.ts
```
import { createStore, applyMiddleware } from "redux"
import thunk from "redux-thunk"
import { ThunkAction, ThunkMiddleware } from "redux-thunk"
import { createConsumer } from "@rails/actioncable"
```

And some type changes. Here we add an ActionCable subscription to the VenueState and a new action type to set the subscription:

chapter_13/02/app/packs/contexts/venue_types.ts
```
export interface InitFromProps {
  type: "initFromProps"
  props: AppProps
}

export interface VenueState {
  concertId: number
  myTickets: TicketData[]
```

```
  otherTickets: TicketData[]
  rowCount: number
  seatsPerRow: number
  ticketsToBuyCount: number
  subscription: Subscription
}

export interface SetSubscription {
  type: "setSubscription"
  subscription: Subscription
}

export type VenueAction =
  | ClearHolds
  | HoldTicket
  | InitFromProps
  | SetTicketToBuy
  | SetTickets
  | UnholdTicket
  | SetSubscription
```

And then the call to createStore at the very end of the file:

chapter_13/02/app/packs/contexts/venue_context.ts
```
export const venueStore = createStore(
  venueReducer,
  applyMiddleware(thunk as ThunkMiddleware<VenueState, VenueAction>)
)
```

The second argument to createStore uses the applyMiddleware function with thunk as an argument—the TypeScript type declaration as ThunkMiddleware<VenueState, VenueAction> is there so that TypeScript will allow our eventual dispatches to be functions. The two types in the generic type declaration is the type of the state of the store and the type of the action argument—the two types that would be passed to the inner function of Redux Thunk action functions.

With that done, we can initialize the subscription in the VenueState to nil and then we can write a thunk to initialize the subscription:

chapter_13/02/app/packs/contexts/venue_context.ts
```
export const initialState = {
  rowCount: 1,
  seatsPerRow: 1,
  concertId: 0,
  otherTickets: [],
  ticketsToBuyCount: 1,
  myTickets: [],
  subscription: null,
}

type VenueThunk = ThunkAction<void, VenueState, null, VenueAction>
```

```
export const initSubscription = (): VenueThunk => {
  return (dispatch, getState) => {
    if (getState().subscription) {
      return
    }
    const subscription = createConsumer().subscriptions.create(
      { channel: "ConcertChannel", concertId: getState().concertId },
      {
        received(tickets) {
          dispatch({ type: "setTickets", tickets })
        },
      }
    )
    dispatch({ type: "setSubscription", subscription })
  }
}
```

This initSubscription function encapsulates the same subscription behavior we've seen before. The initSubscription method is a thunk, which means it returns a function that does the real work.

That inner function takes two arguments provided by Redux Thunk: dispatch, which is the dispatch function for the reducer, and getState, which is the state function for the reducer. You need to be careful with getState here. You can use getState to read the value of the state and do things based on that, but if you are going to change the state, you need to use dispatch to call back into the reducer.

Our code here guards against re-creating the subscription if it's already there. If the subscription is not there, then we have the same creation code as before, using the dispatch function to set the venue data. At the end we reference a new action to add the subscription into the state. The new action needs a type declaration like the others, but the implementation is just one line:

```
chapter_13/02/app/packs/contexts/venue_context.ts
case "setSubscription": {
  return { ...state, subscription: action.subscription }
}
```

One other thing to mention is the typing on the return value of the outer function, VenueThunk. In the previous snippet, we use TypeScript's type command to define VenueThunk as an alias for a more complicated generic type based on Redux Thunk's existing ThunkAction type. The arguments to the generic include the following:

- The expected return type of the inner function. For us it's void, but sometimes these actions can return JavaScript promises if you want more asynchronous behavior.

- The type of the state of the reducer, which for us is VenueState.

- The type of an optional argument that you can get Redux Thunk to add to each call. We're not doing that, so the argument is null.

- A type that encapsulates all the actions that might be dispatched by the inner function. We're just using the VenueAction here, so we aren't limiting ourselves. If we were being super careful, we might want to use a specific action or union of actions.

We can also move our API-based data fetch to a thunk:

chapter_13/02/app/packs/contexts/venue_context.ts
```
export const fetchData = (): VenueThunk => {
  return async (dispatch, getState) => {
    const response = await fetch(
      `/tickets.json?concert_id=${getState().concertId}`
    )
    const tickets = await response.json()
    dispatch({ type: "setTickets", tickets })
  }
}
```

It's the exact same logic, but instead of an inner function inside the useEffect hook, it's an inner function inside the thunk. We're declaring the inner function as async and using await on the fetch call, which means the client-side state will only change after the server call is complete.

With that in place, all the asynchronous code can be moved out of the App component, leaving it much shorter:

chapter_13/02/app/packs/components/app.tsx
```
import * as React from "react"
import Venue from "components/venue"
import {
  fetchData,
  initSubscription,
  venueStore,
} from "contexts/venue_context"
import { Provider } from "react-redux"

export interface AppProps {
  concertId: number
  rowCount: number
  seatsPerRow: number
}

export const App = (props: AppProps): React.ReactElement => {
  venueStore.dispatch({ type: "initFromProps", props })
  venueStore.dispatch(initSubscription())
  venueStore.dispatch(fetchData())
```

```
    return (
      <Provider store={venueStore}>
        <Venue />
      </Provider>
    )
}
```

export default App

We're now doing three dispatches to set the initial state: one for the props, one for the subscription, and one for the data fetch. They could be combined, but it seemed clearer to separate them. The call to initialize the subscription is just venueStore.dispatch(initSubscription()), using the thunk function just as if it were an action type, and the dispatch is just venueStore.dispatch(fetchData()).

Next up, we have two actions on the page that both call the dispatcher and notify the subscription—the on-click methods for clicking a seat and the Clear All buttons. We can turn both of those into thunk actions as well:

chapter_13/02/app/packs/contexts/venue_context.ts
```
export const seatChange = (
  status: string,
  rowNumber: number,
  seatNumber: number
): VenueThunk => {
  return async (dispatch, getState) => {
    const actionType = status === "unsold" ? "holdTicket" : "unholdTicket"
    await getState().subscription.perform("added_to_cart", {
      concertId: getState().concertId,
      row: rowNumber,
      seatNumber: seatNumber,
      status: actionType === "holdTicket" ? "held" : "unsold",
      ticketsToBuyCount: getState().ticketsToBuyCount,
    })
    dispatch({ type: actionType, seatNumber, rowNumber })
  }
}

export const clearCart = (): VenueThunk => {
  return async (dispatch, getState) => {
    await getState().subscription.perform("removed_from_cart", {
      concertId: getState().concertId,
      tickets: getState().myTickets,
    })
    dispatch({ type: "clearHolds" })
  }
}
```

The pattern is similar: we have an outer function that returns a VenueThunk and an inner function that uses the dispatch and state to do the real work.

Again, we're declaring the inner function as async and using await on the subscription call.

With that in place, here's the entire Subtotal component using Redux hooks and Redux Thunk:

chapter_13/02/app/packs/components/subtotal.tsx
```
import * as React from "react"
import styled from "styled-components"
import { useSelector, useDispatch } from "react-redux"
import { clearCart } from "contexts/venue_context"
import { VenueState, TicketData } from "contexts/venue_types"

const Header = styled.div`
  font-size: 1.5rem;
  font-weight: bold;
  margin-left: 15px;
  margin-right: 15px;
`

const buttonClass =
  "px-5 py-4 m-2 my-4 w-40 text-center text-white transition-colors " +
  "duration-150 bg-gray-800 rounded-lg focus:shadow-outline hover:bg-black"

const Subtotal = (): React.ReactElement => {
  const myTickets = useSelector<VenueState, TicketData[]>(
    (state) => state.myTickets
  )
  const dispatch = useDispatch()

  const onClear = () => {
    dispatch(clearCart())
  }

  return (
    <>
      <Header>
        <span>Current Tickets Purchased:  </span>
        <span>{myTickets.length}</span>
      </Header>
      <Header>
        <span>Current Tickets Cost:  </span>
        <span>${myTickets.length * 15}.00</span>
      </Header>
      <div className={buttonClass} onClick={onClear}>
        Clear Tickets
      </div>
    </>
  )
}

export default Subtotal
```

The Redux hook useSelector takes a TypeScript generic with the type of the entire state and the type of the return value, and we're using it to limit the available data to only the data that the component needs. (Technically, we could return myHeldTickets.length here rather than calculate it later.) Also, the dispatch again uses our thunk-function rather than an action type.

The Seat component is longer, so I'm not going to rerun the whole thing again. The two interesting parts are the declarations of the React hooks:

chapter_13/02/app/packs/components/seat.tsx
```
const state = useSelector<VenueState, VenueState>((state) => state)
const dispatch = useDispatch()
```

The Seat uses a bunch of the parts of the state, so it was just easier to return the whole thing as is from useSelector.

Then the onSeatChange method calls dispatch with our thunk actions:

chapter_13/02/app/packs/components/seat.tsx
```
const onSeatChange = (): void => {
  const status = currentStatus()
  if (status === "invalid" || status === "purchased") {
    return
  }
  dispatch(seatChange(status, rowNumber, seatNumber))
}
```

And that is pretty much that. The code should now be working again.

What's Next

We've spent a lot of time using reducers and Redux to manage state. Now I'd like to talk about ways to validate that our code does what we expect. In the next part of the book we're going to take a look at using TypeScript to further validate our code's internal behavior. We'll also look at some testing and debugging tools that will help us feel confident in the code.

Part IV

Validating Your Code

Writing JavaScript is hard. The chapters in this part are about validating your code. TypeScript can be used to make invalid code states impossible to reach by adding and manipulating types. Automated testing helps verify that your code does what you want, and the rich set of debugging tools available allows you to view your code as it runs.

CHAPTER 14

Validating Code with Advanced TypeScript

Over the course of this book, we've been using TypeScript to make assertions about the structure of our code, which has made it easier to validate that our code is correct. Now we're going to focus on features of TypeScript itself that we can use to enhance the typing of our system, with the goal of making it even harder to write code that puts the system in an invalid state.

Many JavaScript programs use a lot of code to protect against invalid data being passed around, continually performing null checks or other type checks. We can use our TypeScript system to make certain kinds of invalid states impossible without using run-time checks. We can, for example, specify that a certain value can't be set to null, and then at compile-time, the compiler must be convinced that a null value can't get there. These techniques are often more verbose than plain JavaScript, but the hope is that the extra typing up front makes the run-time behavior of the code a lot easier to deal with over the long term.

In this chapter, we're going to look at a few different helpful TypeScript features: *union types,* which allow us to create new types by combining existing types; *literal types* and *enums,* which let us limit a type to a set of values; and *mapped types* and *utility types,* which allow us to apply a feature to an existing type. Then we'll explore configuring TypeScript to change the behavior of the compiler itself.

Creating Union Types

I want to start with a concept we've already seen, but which I want to talk about in more depth because it winds up being important for understanding other TypeScript techniques. The feature is called a *union type,* and we used it to create the type checking for our action types in our various reducers in

Chapter 12, Managing State in React, on page 227 and in Chapter 13, Using Redux to Manage State, on page 253.

You create a union type by combining existing types with the pipe operator (|). The existing types can be built-in or specific to your code. One of our union types, for example, looks like this:

```
chapter_14/01/app/packs/contexts/venue_types.ts
export type VenueAction =
  | ClearHolds
  | HoldTicket
  | InitFromProps
  | SetTicketToBuy
  | SetTickets
  | UnholdTicket
  | SetSubscription
```

We're using the type keyword here to assign a type to a new name, which we then use in our method signature:

```
chapter_14/01/app/packs/contexts/venue_context.ts
export const venueReducer = (
  state: VenueState = initialState,
  action: VenueAction
): VenueState => {
```

We don't have to use the type keyword, though. We could use the union type inline:

```
export const venueReducer = (
  state: VenueState = initialState,
  action: SetTicketToBuy
  | HoldTicket
  | UnholdTicket
  | SetVenueData
  | ClearHolds
  | InitFromProps
  | SetSubscription
): VenueState => {
```

We use the type keyword for the same reasons we'd name any variable: to give a complex operation a simpler, more semantically meaningful name, making the type easier to use and the code easier to read.

Now we can say that a variable is a member of a specific type, like let s: HoldTicket, or we can declare the variable to be a member of the union type, as in let u: VenueAction. These two declarations have different meanings and allow access to different attributes.

When we declare the variable as a member of the specific type, such as let s: HoldTicket, TypeScript lets the variable have access to all the attributes of HoldTicket.

When we say that a variable is a member of the union type, as in let u: VenueAction, that declaration in TypeScript only lets that variable have access to methods or attributes that are common to all the specific types that make up the union. In this case, we have seven different types in that union. All three of them have a type attribute, which means we can call u.type. As it happens, some of those types have a seatNumber attribute, but the rest don't, so if we call seatNumber, TypeScript will fail to compile.

All that said, if you look in our reducer code back in Chapter 12, Managing State in React, on page 227, you'll see that we do declare the action as the generic type Action, and then inside the case statements, we do, in fact, call attributes like action.dateString, so there must be some way to tell TypeScript that you are looking at only one of the specific types of the union type. TypeScript actually has a few different ways of differentiating between types. We'll talk about the specific one used in our reducer code in Using Enums and Literal Types, on page 277.

Union Types and Type Guards

TypeScript calls the functionality that lets TypeScript know it can use a specific type a *type guard*. A type guard is a block of code in which you narrow the definition of a union type in such a way that TypeScript can infer the narrower type and use that information to type check the code.

For example, one use of a union type is to allow your method to take in multiple different types of arguments, so you might have a method like this, admittedly a little contrived:

```
const logAThing(log: number | string | boolean | symbol) {
}
```

We want to treat the log argument differently based on its type, which likely involves calling methods that only make sense for the actual type of the argument, not the union type, so we want to be able to have a type guard based on the type. The way in which we can create a type guard depends on what kind of types we have making up our union types.

In this case, where the types are all JavaScript primitive types, you can use the keyword typeof as a type guard. Using typeof only works on the four types shown in this snippet:

```
const logAThing(log: number | string | boolean | symbol) {
  if (typeof log === string) {
    logString(log)
  } else if (typeof log === boolean) {
    logBoolean(log)
  }
  // ...and so on
}
```

Inside the first if statement, TypeScript is able to treat log as a string, and inside the second, TypeScript will treat log as a boolean. You can also do a negative check, which would look like typeof !== symbol, if there's some reason why that makes sense to do so.

Using typeof has a serious limitation, however. It only acts as a type guard with those four primitive types. Specifically, typeof does not allow you to differentiate between different classes—they are all of type object.

For differentiating between classes, TypeScript provides instanceof type guards. An instanceof type guard behaves the same way as typeof and works on any type that is created with a constructor.

So we can do something like this:

```
const area(thing: Square | Triangle | Circle): number {
  if (thing instanceof Square) {
    return thing.width * thing.height
  } else if (thing instanceof Triangle) {
    return thing.width * thing.height * 0.5
  } else if (thing instanceof Circle) {
    return PI * 2 * thing.radius
  }
}
```

The important bit here is that inside each if block, we can use attributes specific to each class, like width or radius, because TypeScript uses instanceof to infer the type.

This doesn't exactly solve our reducer issue because our reducer actions aren't created with JavaScript constructors, they are just JavaScript literals. TypeScript provides a different way to type guard generically on the existence of a particular field in the type.

We can use the in keyword to test for the existence of a particular attribute in the object, as shown here:

```
const area(thing: Square | Triangle | Circle): number {
  if ("radius" in thing) {
    return PI * 2 * thing.radius
```

```
  } else {
    return thing.width * thing.height
  }
}
```

What's happening here is subtle, and this code actually has a bug when compared to the previous code. The in operator returns true if the object on the right contains the attribute on the left. From a typing perspective, this also acts as a type guard, and inside the if block protected by the in statement, TypeScript works on a list of available attributes based on the elements of the union type that contain that attribute. If multiple component types contain the attribute—both Square and Triangle have a width attribute, for example—then inside the type guard, TypeScript will only allow you to access an attribute that is available in *all* the component types with that attribute. In our case, we now have a bug because both Square and Triangle would go down the second branch, but the formula is for square, which should give you a sense of the limitations of this mechanism.

An important extension here is that we don't need to specify that the else branch is a Circle; TypeScript will infer that the else branch is all the types in the union type not covered by the if branch.

Admittedly, the in operator can be tricky. Alternatively, you can write your own functions and have TypeScript treat them as type guards. For example:

```
function isCircle(shape: Square | Triangle | Circle): shape is Circle {
  return (shape as Square).radius !== undefined
}
```

The syntax for this is, frankly, a little verbose and weird. The function takes an argument, which would typically have the entire union type as its type (otherwise you wouldn't be able to call the function with any potential member of the union type). The return value of the function is what TypeScript calls a *type predicate* and the syntax is <variable> is <type>; the variable name has to match the name of the argument to the function.

The body of the function is whatever you want, basically, as long as the function returns true when you can show that the argument is of the type needed. The recommended way to do that is to check for the existence of an attribute that is in that class. In our case, we're checking to see if the shape is a circle by testing for the existence of a radius attribute.

We can then use this function as we've been using our other type guard:

```
const area(thing: Square | Triangle | Circle): number {
  if (isCircle(thing)) {
```

```
    return PI * 2 * thing.radius
  } else {
    return thing.width * thing.height
  }
}
```

This code is bug-for-bug compatible with the previous snippet in that all objects deemed a Circle will go down the if branch, and all not-Circle objects will go down the else branch.

There are some clear limitations in doing type guards based on whether a single attribute is present or absent. As in our example, there might be multiple types with the same attribute and therefore, the type check might not be exact enough.

TypeScript, however, is extremely flexible in how it allows you to signal types, and while the type guards we've looked at in this section can be great, especially when dealing with external code, we do have other options.

Specifying Types with Literal Types

TypeScript lets you limit the values a string or number variable can have to a set of specific literal values. This *literal type* is not exactly a pure enumeration type, but you can think of it as basically an enumeration type because the behavior is almost identical.

Why would we want to limit the values of a variable? In many cases, we actually have a specific, defined list of values that can be sent to a variable, and we'd like to have TypeScript insist on it. For example, in our concert app, tickets have one of five specific states: unsold, held, purchased, refunded, or invalid. On the Rails side, those values are protected with an ActiveRecord and Postgres enum, but we don't have anything like that on the client side.

Let's declare a literal type based on those values. We'll put it in our venue_reducer file:

```
chapter_14/01/app/packs/contexts/venue_types.ts
export type TicketStatus =
  | "unsold"
  | "held"
  | "purchased"
  | "refunded"
  | "invalid"

export interface TicketData {
  id: number
  number: number
```

```
  row: number
  status: TicketStatus
}
```

This declares a new type TicketStatus that can only have the five string values listed. Now, in places that use that value, we replace the declaration of string with TicketStatus, starting right away with the TicketData interface.

Making this change causes one type error in the venue_reducer file, having to do with the return value when we hold the ticket. We need to import the TicketData type and make one further change:

```
chapter_14/01/app/packs/contexts/venue_context.ts
case "holdTicket": {
  const newTickets = Array.from(
    Array(state.ticketsToBuyCount).keys()
  ).map(
    (index): TicketData => {
      return {
        id: 0,
        row: action.rowNumber,
        number: action.seatNumber + index,
        status: "held",
      }
    }
  )
  return {
    ...state,
    myTickets: [...state.myTickets, ...newTickets],
  }
}
```

As a reminder, what the code here is doing is that when a holdTicket action is called, it's taking the row/seat combination that triggered the call and creating a new TicketData object for that seat and however many seats to the right are needed based on the "How Many Tickets" pull-down menu.

The catch in the new code comes from hardcoding the status as "held" without further specifying the type. TypeScript will infer that "held" is a string but won't infer by itself that the expected type is TypeStatus, even if "held" is a valid value for TypeStatus. The solution is to explicitly specify that the return value is a TicketData object, which also specifies that the status value is a TypeStatus, which causes TypeScript to validate that assignment correctly. You can confirm that the validation is happening by changing that "held" value to something that isn't one of the five literal values and see that TypeScript throws a type error.

Similarly, we can specify a few cases in the Seat component file to take our new TicketStatus type rather than a string. After importing the TicketStatus type, change the type of the status argument in the stateColor function, and also in the SquareProps interface declaration and the return value of the currentStatus function.

In addition to string literal types, TypeScript also allows you to have numeric literal types:

```
type StarCount = 0 | 1 | 2 | 3 | 4
```

The meaning is the same as string literal types. TypeScript doesn't have a range type, but a numeric literal can be used if your range is finite and made of integers.

One thing worth mentioning is that, for all purposes other than type checking, the literal type behaves like a string or number. This means you can assign our TicketStatus to a string or add a StarCount to another number. But the result of say, StarCount + number is a number, not a StarCount. In other words, you can perform operations on your literal types, but the result will be typed as whatever the underlying type is, not the literal type.

Now we get to what we actually used to build the actions in our reducer, which is a TypeScript concept called a *discriminated union*. A discriminated union takes a set of interfaces that have a common property that is defined with a different string literal (the discriminator) and a union type that combines them (the union).

In our reducer, we have a bunch of action interfaces that have a type property with a string value, like these:

chapter_14/01/app/packs/contexts/venue_types.ts
```
interface HoldTicket {
  type: "holdTicket"
  seatNumber: number
  rowNumber: number
}
```

And a union type that combines all the actions:

chapter_14/01/app/packs/contexts/venue_types.ts
```
export type VenueAction =
  | ClearHolds
  | HoldTicket
  | InitFromProps
  | SetTicketToBuy
  | SetTickets
  | UnholdTicket
  | SetSubscription
```

When these two pieces are combined, TypeScript treats if or switch statements that check for the value of the discriminant as a type guard. In our actual reducer function, we have switch (action.type) and then a lot of clauses like case "setTicketsToBuy":. TypeScript treats each of those like a type guard, meaning that inside each clause, TypeScript uses the value of the literal to infer which member type of the union is being used. As we saw when we originally wrote this code, we can refer to attributes of that interface that are specific to that one particular type. (Your IDE might helpfully annotate the code to tell you where TypeScript has used a type guard to narrow the type of the action to a specific interface.)

Exhaustiveness Checking

 One thing you might like to have that is not very convenient given the way we have TypeScript set up is *exhaustiveness checking*. It'd be nice to know that if we have an if or switch statement based on a literal type or a discriminated union, our code can handle any of the possible values. Unfortunately, the way TypeScript handles null and undefined makes this challenging. By default, any TypeScript value can be null or undefined, and as a result, it's hard to get the compiler to prove that a switch statement is exhaustive.

Using Enums and Literal Types

TypeScript is nothing if not chock-full of many different ways to specify a type that is limited to a few values. We've just looked at literal types, but those are effectively just a subset of what you can do in TypeScript using an enumerated type, or enum.

Defining Enums

TypeScript enums are very flexible and allow you to do a lot of things that seem, frankly, to be rather pointless. I'll try to minimize talking about those.

At the simplest, you can define an enum in TypeScript just by providing a list of values for it. So if we wanted to convert our TicketStatus type to an enum, we could do this:

chapter_14/02/app/packs/contexts/venue_types.ts
```
export enum TicketStatus {
  Unsold,
  Held,
  Purchased,
  Refunded,
  Invalid,
}
```

We can then use these statuses as TicketStatus.Unsold, TicketStatus.Held, and so on. By convention, the individual elements of the enum are capitalized because they are also types.

However, if we make this change, we get a lot of downstream compiler errors. Every time we assign a string to a TicketStatus or compare a string to a TicketStatus, we need to replace that string with one of the enum values.

For example, in our pre-enum seat.tsx file, we currently have:

chapter_14/01/app/packs/components/seat.tsx
```
const stateColor = (status: TicketStatus): string => {
  if (status === "unsold") {
    return "white"
  } else if (status === "held") {
    return "green"
  } else if (status === "purchased") {
    return "red"
  } else {
    return "yellow"
  }
}
```

which we now need to change to use the enums:

chapter_14/02/app/packs/components/seat.tsx
```
const stateColor = (status: TicketStatus): string => {
  if (status === TicketStatus.Unsold) {
    return "white"
  } else if (status === TicketStatus.Held) {
    return "green"
  } else if (status === TicketStatus.Purchased) {
    return "red"
  } else {
    return "yellow"
  }
}
```

There are a few similar boilerplate changes in a few other places that need to be made, and the code compiles again, now using the enumerated type rather than a string.

Using the enum here instead of the literal type gives you a couple of small advantages. It's arguably easier to read in that the intent of the enum is potentially clearer than a literal string or number.

I'd also like to say you get better type checking in that you can't accidentally assign a TicketStatus to a value of another type, but that's not actually true, as you can see if you put this in one of your files:

```
const x: number = TicketStatus.Held
```

TypeScript will casually allow you to assign your TicketStatus enum to a variable declared as a number, which means we need to talk about the values Type-Script gives to enums.

Assigning Enum Values

By default, TypeScript enums are numbers, starting at 0 and autoincrementing. Behind the scenes, TypeScript basically creates a lookup table matching the enum properties to their values.

If you'd like, you can explicitly specify the value of each element in the enum:

```
enum TicketStatus {
  Unsold = 1,
  Held = 2,
  Purchased = 3,
  Refunded = 4,
  Invalid = 5
}
```

I strongly recommend that if you are specifying the value for one of the enums, that you specify it for all of them. If you don't, TypeScript will autoincrement from the closest specified enum, but it's potentially surprising and hard to debug when TypeScript implicitly specifies the numbers, so you may as well specify all of them.

You can also specify your enums to have string values, so we could do this:

chapter_14/03/app/packs/contexts/venue_types.ts
```
export enum TicketStatus {
  Unsold = "unsold",
  Held = "held",
  Purchased = "purchased",
  Refunded = "refunded",
  Invalid = "invalid",
}
```

For all intents and purposes, this is functionally identical to the string literal type we used earlier. Personally, I think I'd stick to string literals—they seem less complex to me—unless there was some clear readability reason why the enum was better (for example, if there were several groups with overlapping set names and you wanted to ensure they were explicitly made distinct).

It's worth noting that, as written currently, the ticket status values coming from the server are still strings, so this version still works with the server, but the previous version where the enums were numbers won't. It's also true that changing the values from numbers to enums doesn't affect other uses of TicketStatus; anything that is looking at values like TicketStatus.Held will still work no matter what the type of the underlying value is.

To answer your next question, yes, you can have enums where some of the values are strings and some of the values are numbers. You can also have enums where the values are computed at run time. Please don't do either of those things. You only get the full value of enums as a type guard if all the values are set at compile time.

Building Mapped Types and Utility Types

In addition to limiting variables to a set of specific literal values and defining enums, TypeScript allows you to define types that are based on other types, kind of like super-powered generics. These are called *mapped types*. TypeScript also has a bunch of predefined mapped types that it calls *utility types*.

So let's say we have our existing type TicketData:

```
interface TicketData {
  id: number
  row: number
  number: number
  status: TicketStatus
}
```

And let's say we have a data source that is unreliable and we want to make all the fields optional for data coming from that source. We could create a new type:

```
interface OptionalTicketData {
  id?: number
  row?: number
  number?: number
  status?: TicketStatus
}
```

But that's kind of verbose, and if the TicketData type changes, we also have to change the new type.

TypeScript lets us do this more generically:

```
type OptionalTicketData = [P in keyof TicketData]?: TicketData[P]
```

I don't want to get wildly hung up on the syntax here, but basically we have a variable P that iterates over each type (in keyof and then adds the optional signifier to each type ?). Essentially what we're getting here is a new type where every key in the old type is optional. This is something kind of like a type declaration and kind of like a function declaration.

Somewhat more usefully, you can create a mapped type with a generic type rather than with a specific type:

```
type Partial<T> = { [P in keyof T]?: T[P] }
type OptionalTicketData = Partial<TicketData>

# or you can skip the declaration
const x: Partial<TicketData>
```

I think that you are unlikely to be creating these in your day-to-day life, but TypeScript defines a few of them,[1] and I can see a few being useful now and again, like Readonly<T> (which makes all the properties of the type read only) or NonNullable<T> (which constructs a new type excluding null or undefined) or ReturnType<T> (which resolves to the return type of a functional type).

TypeScript Configuration Options

At this point, I think we have all the tools we need to start discussing Type-Script configuration.

Here's our tsconfig.json file, which controls the configuration of our compiler:

chapter_14/03/tsconfig.json

```json
{
  "compilerOptions": {
    "declaration": false,
    "emitDecoratorMetadata": true,
    "experimentalDecorators": true,
    "lib": ["es6", "dom"],
    "jsx": "react",
    "module": "es6",
    "moduleResolution": "node",
    "baseUrl": ".",
    "paths": {
      "*": ["node_modules/*", "app/packs/*"]
    },
    "sourceMap": true,
    "target": "es5",
    "noEmit": true
  },
  "exclude": ["**/*.spec.ts", "node_modules", "vendor", "public"],
  "compileOnSave": false
}
```

---

1. https://www.typescriptlang.org/docs/handbook/utility-types.html

The configuration file has two main purposes: (1) specify the list of files to compile, and (2) specify the behavior of the compiler itself.

You can specify the files explicitly using a files property that takes a list of files to compile. Or you can use include and exclude properties. If you don't have a files or an include—which our project doesn't—the default behavior is to compile any .ts or .tsx files that are not on the exclude list.

Both include and exclude can be made up of explicit file names or you can use patterns with ? to match a single character, * to match any characters except directory separators, and ** to match all subdirectories. Our project is currently excluding specs (**/*.spec.ts), and three other directories that might have files we don't want to deal with. A file matched by include can be blocked by exclude, but a file in the files list is compiled even if it matches an exclude pattern.

There are quite a few compiler options.[2] In general, the options either govern the behavior of the compiler in judging what code is legal, or they change the nature of the JavaScript code generated by the compiler.

Let's look at the options already specified in our project.

Handling input we have the experimentalDecorators property, which allows us to use the new decorator JavaScript syntax. We've got the lib property, which covers what versions of the standard JavaScript library will be allowed in TypeScript. We're using the es6 version, which in addition to syntax, has some implications for what methods exist on basic types like strings. We're also using the dom library, which gives us DOM-related classes like HTMLElement. There are a number of other options, including newer and more experimental ES versions.

A lot of properties govern module lookup. The module property, which we have set to es6, governs what syntax TypeScript will use to specify modules, and the moduleResolution property governs the algorithm TypeScript uses to determine which module you are pointing to with a declaration (you're unlikely to change that one, I think). The baseUrl specifies the top-level directory for module declarations that are not relative to the current directory, and paths indicates other places to look for relative module declarations.

Specifying output, we have the "declaration": false, which tells the compiler not to spit out a type declaration d.ts file, which is used to add type declarations to files that don't have them. The emitDecoratorMetadata property is related to experimentalDecorators and governs some decorator-specific output data. The target

---

2.   https://www.typescriptlang.org/docs/handbook/compiler-options.html

property specifies what level of JavaScript should be output by the compiler. We have chosen the relatively safe es5 level, but we could choose es6, es2016, es2017, or esNext if we were willing to give up some browser compatibility.

A number of other options control how strict the compiler is. In particular, the strict option turns on quite a few strict checks that are turned off by default. The strict option:

- No longer allows the implicit use of any; all types must be declared (this option can be accessed using the property noImplicitAny);

- Requires the this variable to be explicitly declared in all internal functions with noImplicitThis;

- Includes more strict type checking around metaprogramming functions like call and apply;

- No longer allows null or undefined to be assigned to any value;

- Includes stricter type checking of function type matching;

- Requires class properties that can't take null or undefined to be explicitly initialized in the constructor.

Let's see what happens if we turn on some of the strict options in this project. We're going to try and find a balance that allows us to actually compile (our dependence on third-party tools not written in TypeScript may make perfect strictness impossible). And, as I write this, I really don't know what will happen, so let's turn on some strictness by inserting the line "strictNullChecks": true, into the tsconfig.json file and go from there.

Dealing with Strictness

Compiling the file, we get a few errors.

- The venue-display file that is kicking off the call to React is not handling a potential undefined value.

- The SortController is doing a parseInt with a potentially null value.

- The debounce method in SearchController is unhappy and we may just need to restructure that.

- The CalendarController has a few cases where we use target.dataset.

- The thunk dispatches in App don't like that they may potentially have nulls.

Using other strict options would give us more errors, in particular, I think the "no explicit any" might be a big problem, but I think this should be enough for us to deal with to get the idea.

Our venue_display file has basically the same issue four times over: we have code like element.dataset["rows"], which is now technically of type string | undefined, meaning the union type of a string or undefined, and we are passing it through to arguments that expect strings.

What we need to do is allow for the possibility that the values are undefined by creating default values. This is a little slapdash, but it works fine for our purposes:

```
chapter_14/04/app/packs/entrypoints/venue_display.tsx
import * as React from "react"
import * as ReactDOM from "react-dom"
import App from "components/app"

document.addEventListener("turbo:load", () => {
  const element = document.getElementById("react-element")
  if (element) {
    ReactDOM.render(
      <App
        rowCount={parseInt(element.dataset.rowCount || "0", 10)}
        seatsPerRow={parseInt(element.dataset.seatsPerRow || "0", 10)}
        concertId={parseInt(element.dataset.concertId || "0", 10)}
      />,
      element
    )
  }
})
```

In all these cases, we're using the or operator (||) and the fact that undefined values are false to specify a value to be passed on if the lookup is undefined.

The SortController has a similar issue, also solvable with the same solution in the sortValue method. (This file as written has a couple of minor warnings that you could also fix.)

The debounce function has a few problems. One is that the first line of the code sets timeoutId = null, which, on the one hand, means TypeScript now uses inference to assume the type will always be null, and on the other hand, the later call to clearTimeout wants the default value to be undefined. Also, we want to specify the window.setTimeout function, which explicitly returns a number for the timeoutId rather than the one from NodeJS that TypeScript is going to choose by default.

We also never specified a type for the functional argument or the return value, which should have the same type, namely a function that takes arbitrary arguments and returns void.

Put it all together, and you get this:

```
chapter_14/03/app/packs/controllers/search_controller.ts
basicSubmit(): void {
  if (this.inputTarget.value === "") {
    this.reset()
  } else {
    this.formTarget.requestSubmit()
  }
}

submit(): void {
  this.debounce(this.basicSubmit.bind(this))()
}

debounce(functionToDebounce, wait = 300) {
  let timeoutId = null

  return (...args) => {
    clearTimeout(timeoutId)
    timeoutId = setTimeout(() => {
      timeoutId = null
      functionToDebounce(...args)
    }, wait)
  }
}
```

It turns out to be a little easier to manage this typing if debounce is a function rather than a method, which is fine. The timeoutId is now explicitly declared as a union type of a number and undefined, and it's set to undefined both of the places it's set.

I've declared a type called Debounceable, which is just a function that takes arguments and returns void. And then the actual debounce function declares a generic function extending Debounceable and says that both the argument function and the return function have that type, which specifies that the return value of debounce has the same signature as the argument function, which is what we want.

The issues in the CalendarController seem legit to me; it's a failure of the code to deal with the case where the target.dataset.scheduleAttribute doesn't exist. So either we need to explicitly say it could be undefined, or we need to provide a default value. I think the thing to do is allow the argument to be undefined, but then guard against it:

```
chapter_14/04/app/packs/controllers/calendar_controller.ts
scheduleElementFor(target: HTMLElement): HTMLElement | null {
  const scheduleId = target.dataset.scheduleId
  if (!scheduleId) {
    return null
  }
  return document.getElementById(scheduleId)
}

filter(): void {
  const everyDayUnselected = this.everyDayUnselected()
  this.calendarDayTargets.forEach((target: HTMLElement) => {
    const show =
      everyDayUnselected || target.dataset.cssStatusValue === "true"
    this.toggleAssociatedConcerts(target.dataset.scheduleAttribute, !show)
  })
}

showAll(): void {
  this.calendarDayTargets.forEach((target: HTMLElement) => {
    target.dataset.cssStatusValue = "false"
    this.toggleAssociatedConcerts(target.dataset.scheduleAttribute, false)
  })
}

toggleAssociatedConcerts(
  attributeName: string | undefined,
  toggleValue: boolean
): void {
  if (!attributeName) {
    return
  }
  document
    .querySelectorAll(`.concert[${attributeName}]`)
    .forEach((element) => {
      element.classList.toggle("hidden", toggleValue)
    })
}
```

We've changed the argument of toggleAssociatedConcerts to explicitly allow an undefined value, then we return out if the value is undefined, which might be technically unnecessary but does make it explicit that we're dealing with the undefined value.

Finally, the issue in App.tsx is related to the type of the VenueThunk and is fixed by changing the null argument in that type definition to undefined.

And now our code compiles again, just a little bit stricter. We've fixed one potential bug in the CalendarController and, in the other cases, mostly just made the code more consistent.

These potential errors are minor, but they allow us to change the way we have been thinking about type checking. So far, we've been looking at type checking as a form of communication between the coders and the compiler, telling the compiler about the types so that the compiler can warn you about mismatches between different parts of the code.

Now we can start looking at type checking as a way to prevent run-time errors by making it impossible for invalid states to make it past the compiler. In this case, the invalid state is the case where the selector that we are assuming is in the DOM isn't there. In other words, the compiler here is alerting us to a case that our code doesn't handle, and we need to figure out what we want to do.

Our response to this compiler error depends on how confident we are that the null condition won't happen. If we're pretty certain we know more about the code than the compiler does, we can make the compiler error go away by using a type assertion.

What's Next

In this chapter, we explored how to ensure the validity of our code by making our type system more robust. In the next chapter, we'll talk about another way to ensure validity: testing.

Testing with Cypress

Testing JavaScript code is notoriously difficult. Because JavaScript typically runs in a browser environment and interacts closely with the DOM and user behavior, it is often challenging to write tests that have value *and* are consistent and fast.

When thinking about testing JavaScript, it's helpful to think about what you want to get out of testing. In this chapter, we'll focus on two goals:

- Using tests to validate that the code is doing the things we think it is doing

- Using tests to help development by allowing us to rapidly run situations that would take a long time to recreate manually

While a wide variety of testing tools are available in JavaScript, in this chapter, our focus is on end-to-end testing with Cypress, which is a tool that will allow us to simulate interactions with our Rails server and the browser.[1]

Why focus on just one tool? Well, the various tools overlap in functionality but differ in terminology just enough that trying to talk meaningfully about more than one of them at a time is a pretty good recipe for confusion on my part, and probably also yours.

And why end-to-end testing? The Stimulus team is explicit that end-to-end server testing is the preferred way of testing Stimulus behavior. While it's theoretically possible to test Stimulus controllers or React components in isolation from a server, it's not recommended for Stimulus, and the React process is also slightly complex. If you want more information about unit testing JavaScript in a Rails environment, check out *Rails 5 Test Prescriptions* (Pragmatic Bookshelf, 2018).

---

1. https://www.cypress.io

Why Cypress?

Cypress is a testing tool that bills itself as "fast, easy, and reliable testing for anything that runs in a browser." (In case you haven't noticed yet, I'm always fascinated by how these tools describe themselves.) It is committed to making testing stable in JavaScript-land, and as a newer tool, it has taken design lessons from older tools. It can run from a command line and also has a test runner application that allows you to run tests interactively. Rails integration isn't perfect, but it's manageable.

Capybara is the traditional end-to-end testing tool in Rails.[2] And like Cypress, Capybara also allows you to interact with a simulated browser. (You can read all about testing JavaScript and Rails using Capybara in *Rails 5 Test Prescriptions*.)

Cypress has a couple of advantages over Capybara and one significant disadvantage. The disadvantage is that Cypress is not as good as Capybara in integrating with our Rails code. Capybara tests can use RSpec and be run as part of a normal Rails testing process. Although it's discouraged, Capybara tests can access ActiveRecord for setting up data or making assertions about data after the fact.

Cypress tests are written in JavaScript and run in their own process. The cypress-rails gem allows us some access to Rails for setup, but overall, it's still a more awkward setup in Cypress than in Capybara. That's the downside.

On the upside, Cypress has a different architecture than Capybara. Cypress is effectively in control of the entire run process, including the browser process. Cypress has its own testing UI that we can use to choose which tests run or use to have tests auto-run on file changes. Because Cypress controls the run process, it's more robust than Capybara when waiting for actions to complete, and it's better able to provide debugging tools and automated screenshots and videos of tests. Cypress can even simulate the server and provide fake responses if you'd like.

Installing Cypress

Setting up Cypress involves two different steps. First, we need to install Cypress itself and then install the cypress-rails gem to help us integrate Cypress into our system.

Install Cypress as a package:

```
$ yarn add --dev cypress@4.12.1
```

---

2. https://github.com/teamcapybara/capybara

On Cypress Versions

As I write this, there is some sort of compatibility issue involving the current versions of Cypress, TypeScript, and webpack 5 such that I can't quite figure out how to make them all work together. I *think* this will be fixed when Cypress officially adds support for webpack 5, but in the meantime, to get this to work, I had to stick with the version that was current when I started the book, Cypress 4.12.1.

The current version of Cypress (7.1.0 as I write this) works fine if you don't have TypeScript in your project. Despite the version number change, the code in this book should be substantially the same in current versions of Cypress. I'm sorry about this; it happened midway through writing the book. I hope that by the time you read this the version issues will be worked out.

On the Rails side, we need to add two gems: the cypress-rails gem and the dotenv gem. The gems both go in the Gemfile in the development and test groups:

```
group :development, :test do
  # <existing gems...>
  gem "cypress-rails"
  gem "dotenv-rails"
end
```

The cypress-rails gem uses environment variables to manage some settings, so to make our life a little easier, we're going to use the dotenv gem. Do a bundle install, and we're ready for the next step.

Now we need to initialize Cypress, which we do with a rake task created by the cypress-rails gem:

```
$ rails cypress:init
```

This gives us a cypress.json file with some default parameters that we're not going to worry about yet.

Now we can see what all the fuss is about by running Cypress. The cypress-rails gem gives us a shortcut to opening the Cypress UI:

```
$ rails cypress:open
```

Note that if this is your first time running a new version of Cypress, Cypress will attempt to verify that the downloaded version is legit. On my machine, this sometimes leads to the open command failing with a timeout error. Rerunning rake cypress:open causes it to work normally.

If you don't already have a cypress folder, which we don't have at this point, Cypress will create a folder and populate it with a bunch of sample tests. It's worth digging through those sample tests, as they give examples of using Cypress to do various kinds of tests. (If you are using a more recent version of Cypress, it will no longer populate with sample tests.)

Cypress will also start its own UI, as shown in the following screenshot:

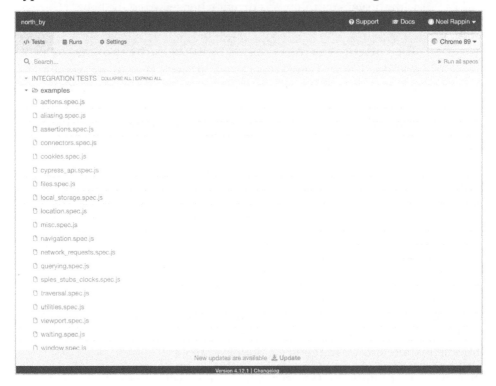

On the left side of the screen is a list of all the test files, which at the moment shows the sample tests Cypress created. On the right side are two important elements: the pull-down menu currently labeled "Chrome 89," which lets us choose which browser Cypress will use when it runs, and the "Run all specs" link. Along the top is a settings tab, which displays the configuration that Cypress was started under, and allows for you to change a few other items, such as what editor to open Cypress tests in if selected from the Cypress UI.

We can run a test by either clicking on one specific test or folder on the left or by clicking the "Run all specs" link. Doing so brings up the actual test runner, as shown in the screenshot on page 293.

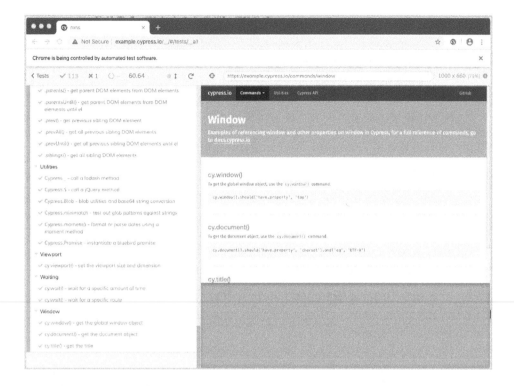

On the left side of this screen is a list of all the steps in all the tests. On the right is the running display of the browser window as the tests run. This is a normal browser window, and you can interact with and inspect it just as you would a regular window. A toolbar at the top of the screen provides an overview of the tests that are being run and allows you to set the size of the viewport in which the tests are operating. (No, I have no idea why one of their sample tests are failing.) If the viewport window is open and you change a Cypress test file, the test will rerun automatically.

Once the tests run you can revisit each step in the test and see a before and after snapshot of the step. If the step has a useful result, then clicking on the step outputs that result to the browser console.

Cypress Browser Support

I'll note up front that there's a significant limitation in Cypress's browser support: it does not support Safari. It does support Chrome, Edge, Electron, and Firefox in all their various release and developer stream configurations, but Safari support (including iOS Mobile Safari) is probably not coming in the near future, though it is on the future roadmap. I mention that now in case

---

Cypress Browser Support

it's a deal breaker. It's more or less the position of the Cypress lead developer that running the same tests in multiple browsers is not tremendously valuable, but that said, Safari has some quirks and niches where many teams would likely want it as their primary test browser.

Cypress also has a command-line version of the app:

```
$ rails cypress:run
```

This version will run all the tests without the UI and is suitable for use in a continuous integration server. By default, the command-line version of the tool will take a snapshot of failing steps and put them in tmp/cypress/snapshots. It will also take a video of all steps and place it in tmp/cypress/videos. The videos will automatically be deleted before the next run.

One more nice-to-have before we start writing our own tests is integration with the ESLint system so that our Cypress tests don't cause lint errors. Add the following NPM module:

```
$ yarn add eslint-plugin-cypress --dev
```

In the extends key in the eslintrc.js file, add "plugin:cypress/recommended" to that list. Now, ESLint will be aware of Cypress testing commands (you may need to restart your editor for it to take effect).

Configuring Cypress and Rails

We need to manage a couple of Rails-specific setup issues before we can write our first test. (Sorry about all this setup. Honestly, Cypress is easier in this respect than some of the other testing tools.) Specifically, we need to have the cypress-rails gem start its own instance of a Rails server that points to our test database rather than our development database, and we need to seed that server with data.

Because Cypress is not really part of the Rails system, it doesn't automatically start up any Rails-specific process, which is where the cypress-rails gem comes in. The cypress-rails gem automatically starts up a Rails server at a port that we determine. We'll use an environment variable to specify the number of the port, and we're going to use the dotenv gem to manage that variable.

The dotenv gem lets us specify arbitrary environment variables in a .env file and loads them as part of our environment setup. Cypress has four configuration variables, of which the only one we care about is CYPRESS_RAILS_PORT:

chapter_15/02/.env
```
CYPRESS_RAILS_PORT=5678
```

The actual value of CYPRESS_RAILS_PORT doesn't matter as long as we remember it and the port number isn't already in use. We'll also set a baseUrl using that port in the cypress.json configuration file:

chapter_15/02/cypress.json
```
{
  "baseUrl": "http://localhost:5678",
  "screenshotsFolder": "tmp/cypress_screenshots",
  "videosFolder": "tmp/cypress_videos",
  "trashAssetsBeforeRuns": false
}
```

Adding the baseUrl setting allows us to assume the common part of the server URL during our Cypress testing.

As for data, cypress-rails gives us a handful of hooks that it automatically invokes during the testing process and that we can use to load data. We can set up an initializer to configure how we want to interact with these hooks, like this:

chapter_15/02/config/initializers/cypress_rails.rb
```
return unless Rails.env.test?

Rails.application.load_tasks unless defined?(Rake::Task)

CypressRails.hooks.before_server_start do
  Rake::Task["db:seed"].invoke
end

CypressRails.hooks.after_transaction_start do
end

CypressRails.hooks.after_state_reset do
end

CypressRails.hooks.before_server_stop do
  Rake::Task["db:test:prepare"].invoke
end
```

The four hooks are:

- before_server_start—This hook is invoked by cypress-rails when we start the Cypress server. In our case, we're asking it to run our rake:db:seed task to set up test data. That's not ideal, because it's a) randomized data and b) a little slow, but we'll deal with it for the moment.

- after_transaction_start—The cypress-rails gem sets up a transactional test environment by default, meaning that it creates a database transaction when the server starts, similar to how Rails itself behaves during testing. This hook is called when the transaction is started, either at the beginning of the test run or on reset. We're not doing anything here.

- after_state_reset—The cypress-rails gem provides a special route, /cypress_rails_reset_state that rolls back the transaction, resetting the database state. This hook is called after that route is invoked and before the transaction start hook. We're not doing anything here.

- before_server_stop—This hook is called as part of the Cypress shutdown process. We're using it to reset the test database with the db:test:prepare rake task.

Cypress May Not Shut Down Properly

It's been my experience that if you don't shut the Cypress app down properly, the before_server_stop may not be called before shutdown. This may cause an error on restart because the database might not allow the seed file to rerun correctly. If that happens, you need to reconfigure the test database with the command rails db:test:prepare. I've also seen Cypress fail to return database pool connections if not shut down properly, which may require restarting Cypress or the database.

The seed data we are using for our development server is randomized, which is fun for development but not ideal for testing. For testing we want less data and data that is predictable. So…

You'll notice that the db.seeds.rb looks like this (based on a gist from Nathan Perry):[3]

```
chapter_15/02/db/seeds.rb
["all", Rails.env].each do |seed|
  seed_file = Rails.root.join("db", "seeds", "#{seed}.rb")

  if File.exist?(seed_file)
    require seed_file

  end
end
```

It allows us to run different seed scripts based on the Rails environment when we run the seed file.

---

3. https://gist.github.com/servel333/47f6cca9e51497aeefab

The seeds we've been using are in db/seeds/development.rb.

Now put this in db/seeds/test.rb:

chapter_15/02/db/seeds/test.rb

```ruby
ActiveRecord::Base.transaction do
  Gig.delete_all
  Ticket.delete_all
  Concert.delete_all
  Band.delete_all
  Venue.delete_all
  User.delete_all

  User.create!(
    full_name: "Awesome Reader",
    email: "areader@example.com",
    password: "awesome"
  )

  venue = Venue.create!(name: "Rosemont Horizon", rows: 10, seats_per_row: 10)

  brandi = Band.create(
    name: "Brandi Carlile",
    description: "Singer songwriter",
    genre_tags: "Singer/Songwriter,Country"
  )

  beatles = Band.create(
    name: "The Beatles",
    description: "The Fab Four",
    genre_tags: "Rock & Roll,Classic Rock"
  )

  billy = Band.create(
    name: "Billy Joel",
    description: "Piano Man",
    genre_tags: "Rock & Roll,Pop"
  )

  [brandi, beatles, billy].each_with_index do |band, index|
    concert = Concert.create(
      name: "#{band.name} In Concert",
      description: "#{band.name} In Concert",
      start_time: Date.parse("2021-04-10 19:00") + index + 1,
      venue: venue,
      ilk: "concert",
      access: "general",
      genre_tags: band.genre_tags,
      gigs: [Gig.create(band: band, order: 1, duration_minutes: 60)]
    )

    concert.venue.rows.times do |row_number|
      concert.venue.seats_per_row.times do |seat_number|
        concert.tickets.create!(
```

```
                    row: row_number + 1,
                    number: seat_number + 1,
                    status: "unsold"
                )
            end
        end
    end
end
```

That gives us three days and three concerts and one user, which should be enough data to write tests against.

The cypress-rails gem also recommends that you turn off caching in your Rails test environment so that changes in your Rails code are reflected in your Cypress tests without having to restart Cypress. You can do this in the environment/test.rb file:

chapter_15/02/config/environments/test.rb
```
config.cache_classes = false
config.action_view.cache_template_loading = false
```

Now that we have Cypress installed and configured, we're ready to write a test.

Writing Our First Test

Delete the cypress/integration/examples directory with all the existing Cypress tests. Then, restart Cypress with rake cypress:open. This gives us the Cypress window with a message saying we have no tests. (Or it might re-create the same sample tests, in which case just delete them again, write the next test, and then open Cypress.) Let's write the first line of a new test. Create a file named cypress/schedule/schedule_spec.js. As soon as you save it, the Cypress window changes to show that file. If you start to "Run all specs," you get the test runner with a message that no tests are found in the file.

Now let's start writing the test:

chapter_15/02/cypress/integration/schedule/schedule_spec.js
```
describe("On the schedule page", function () {
  beforeEach(function () {
    cy.request("/cypress_rails_reset_state")
  })

  it("Visits our schedule page ", function () {
    cy.visit("/")
  })
})
```

Note: This is in JavaScript, not TypeScript, because it's going to make very little difference in writing tests, and also the TypeScript setup for Cypress is a bit of a pain.

The test syntax here is similar to the Jasmine or Jest JavaScript tools. A describe method defines a series of tests, while the it method describes an individual test. Both of those methods take a string argument that is a name and a function argument that is the actual test or set of tests being defined.

Looking at the top of this test file, you'll see we've included a beforeEach block, which is evaluated before every test in the describe block. Our beforeEach makes a special call to a route defined by the cypress-rails gem called /cypress_rails_reset_state. That route does two things: if the environment variable CYPRESS_RAILS_TRANSACTIONAL_SERVER is true, it rolls back the transaction, and then it runs anything in the after_state_reset hook. This resets our Rails state to a default.

All this test does is visit our schedule page in the browser, using the command cy.visit. We're able to just write the URL as / because we've already specified the base URL of the test server in the cypress.json configuration file, so Cypress will combine the two and visit http://localhost:5678/. If you run this test in the Cypress test runner, you should see the schedule page in the viewport with the test seed data. And the test should pass—even though we haven't written any assertions yet, Cypress would fail the test if the server did not respond to the request, and the server error would show up in the console.

Like the cy.visit command in this test, all our interactions with DOM objects and the like will start as commands sent to the global Cypress cy object.

Let's write a complete test first and then we'll look at the implications of using the cy object:

chapter_15/03/cypress/integration/schedule/schedule_spec.js
```js
describe("On the schedule page", function () {
  beforeEach(function () {
    cy.request("/cypress_rails_reset_state")
  })

  it("Allows the user to create a favorite", () => {
    cy.visit("/users/sign_in")
    cy.get('[name="user[email]"]').type("areader@example.com")
    cy.get('[name="user[password]"]').type("awesome")
    cy.get('[name="commit"]').contains("Log in").click()
    cy.visit("/")
    cy.get("#favorite-concerts-list").as("favorites")
    cy.get(".concert").first().as("concert")
    cy.get("@concert").find(".button_to").find("input").first().click()
```

```
    cy.get("@favorites").find("article").should("have.lengthOf", 1)
    cy.get("@favorites").find(".name").first().should("contain", "Brandi")
  })
})
```

There's a lot going on here, some of which is behind the scenes. Let's start with a straightforward translation of what Cypress is doing.

The beforeEach function is called before each spec runs. In this case, the function is making a web request to our special cypress-rails reset route. As we saw earlier, this resets the database back to its original state.

To test favorite behavior, we need a logged-in user, so we start the test by using cy.visit("users/sign_in") to visit our login page. Then we use cy.get to retrieve our email form field and password field, and type to simulate typing in the email and password. Finally, we find the login button and use click to simulate a click. This logs our sample user in, but this process is a bit clunky to do all the time, and we'll explore alternatives later on.

Once we are logged in, we call cy.visit("/"), which also, as we saw before, makes a web request to our Rails server and takes us to the schedule page.

Our next two lines identify parts of the page that we'll be looking at in this test. First, we call cy.get("#favorite-concerts-list").as("favorites"), then cy.get(".con-cert").first().as("concert"). Let's unpack this.

We start with get, which is one of several dozen commands the Cypress object receives. (The full list can be found online.)[4] The get command takes in a CSS selector, which in this case is either .#favorite-concerts-list, meaning "the element with the DOM ID favorite-concerts-list," or .concert, meaning "elements with the DOM class concert." The get command behaves like the jQuery $ operator, if that reference is useful for you.

We can then chain more operations on the set of DOM elements that match the selector passed to get. I'm deliberately not saying that get returns a set of DOM elements, as technically it doesn't because Cypress works asynchronously. More on that in a moment.

If there are no elements matching the selector, Cypress waits for a specified amount of time (the default is four seconds), and if the element is still not there, Cypress fails the test. This gives Cypress some stability against a dynamic web page where objects might show up or vanish at any time.

---

4.   https://docs.cypress.io/api/api/table-of-contents.html

In this test, we do get DOM elements—we get the section for favorites and a list of our concerts. We continue to act on the DOM elements we found by chaining more methods. We just need to test one of the matching concerts, so we use first to limit our activity to just the first element. The final part of this chain, as("favorites") or as("concert"), gives us a handy alias to use later on to refer to this element. The asynchronous nature of the Cypress object means we can't just assign the return value to a regular synchronous variable, so this as command allows us to refer to the element later on.

In fact, all our subsequent lines start with cy.get("@concert") or cy.get("@favorite"), which uses the same get command, but instead of a selector, it has the name of an alias, which allows us to work the DOM element previously stored under that alias.

Next, we use the @concert alias to find and click the Make Favorite button: cy.get("@concert").find(".button_to").find("input").first().click(). At this point, the concert should be included in the favorites list, which we verify with cy.get("@favorites").find("article").should("have.lengthOf", 1), to test that there's exactly one article in the list, and then with cy.get("@favorites").find(".name").first().should("contain", "Brandi"), which tests that the name of the concert in the favorites list is what we expect.

The should command takes one of several assertion types as the first argument. (Cypress uses the Chai library to manage assertions.)[5] We're building up a string of assertion method calls—in this case have.lengthOf—which use the Chai library to actually make assertions. Again, Cypress will wait until the timeout to actually fail the assertion.

And that's the test. If you run it in the cypress test runner, you should see the screen shown on page 302.

As the test runs, you can see all the steps happen, including, say, typing in the email and password on the login screen. Each individual step on the left will be set in green as it passes. Even better, clicking on one of the lines on the left changes the viewport view to a snapshot of the screen as it appeared during that step with the element being acted on highlighted. These screenshots are really helpful in debugging tests to be able to see exactly what happened step by step.

---

5.   https://www.chaijs.com

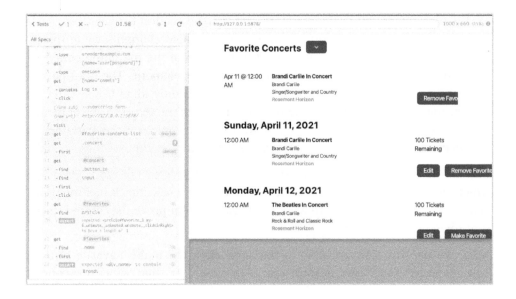

Understanding How Cypress Works

Although the Cypress test seems simple, Cypress is a tool where the apparent simplicity of the developer commands hides a fair amount of complexity behind the scenes. In order to effectively write tests in Cypress, it is important to take a step back to understand how Cypress works to avoid a lot of confusion later on. Cypress's asynchronous structure means that a lot of common JavaScript patterns either won't work or aren't recommended in Cypress. For example, using regular variable assignment is going to cause you trouble.

The most important thing to understand about Cypress is that although Cypress commands appear to be regular JavaScript function calls, in fact all Cypress commands are asynchronous. In effect, each time you use the cy command, you are creating something like a JavaScript promise, and subsequent cy commands are in the then clause of the preceding command, meaning that each successive cy command only executes after the previous one has completed.

When the Cypress command is actually run as part of the test, it queues itself a list of commands in the test and returns immediately. What we think of as the actual command—the get or click or whatever—only executes as part of this queue of promises once the entire test has loaded.

The most important implication of this behavior is that Cypress is a world unto itself. Normal JavaScript assignment or logic that is not mediated through Cypress does not see Cypress stuff at all, and conversely, everything you do in a Cypress test needs to go through the cy command. Cypress has constructs to allow you to do things like variable assignment and logic inside Cypress-land, but if you write normal variable assignments with let or const, those assignments will happen as the test loads. They will not be able to see Cypress data, and Cypress commands won't be able to see those variables.

I do need to point out here that Cypress commands are not exactly the same as JavaScript promises and you can't directly mix the two. Specifically, using async/await in a Cypress test will not put your async code in the Cypress chain of commands.

In order to use variables, make assertions, and do all the things you'd expect to do in a test, Cypress allows you to chain methods to the cy command and also allows you to use as to hold on to values for later use.

So in our test, the line

```
cy.get(".concert").first().as("concert")
```

allows us to hold on to the value returned by first() using the alias concert, such that subsequent Cypress commands can use cy.get("@concert") to access the same DOM element. Later lines of code chain the method should into the cy command so that the assertions take place inside the Cypress asynchronous commands.

Although we don't use it in this test, you can chain the method then to any Cypress command to execute arbitrary code inside Cypress, like this:

```
cy.get(".concert").first().then(element => {
    // do whatever we want in here...
}
```

From Cypress's perspective, making each command asynchronous gives Cypress full control over how each test executes. When testing JavaScript, the fact that DOM elements are often changing, appearing, or disappearing makes the tests very complicated to run, and an extremely common problem is that the test and the timing of the DOM changes don't quite line up, leaving tests that intermittently fail for no reason.

Cypress attempts to bypass those flaky timing errors by guaranteeing that each command is only executed after the previous command has fully completed. The first line (after login) of our test is cy.visit("/"). The second line, cy.get("#favorite-section").as("favorites") only begins execution after the visit command has completed. Furthermore, if the cy.get("#favorite-section") command does not initially find any matching elements in the DOM, Cypress will automatically wait—by default, up to four seconds—for the element to show up. Only once it shows up does Cypress move on to execute the as command. A side effect of this behavior is that many Cypress commands, even those that are not explicitly making assertions, are making existence checks, and a Cypress test that just uses get commands is still making implicit assertions about the structure of the page.

Before we write more Cypress tests, let's take a break to step through some of the most common commands that you can send to the cy object.

Navigation

Typically, the first thing you'll want to do in a Cypress test is load a web page. We've already seen the cy.visit command, which takes a URL argument and loads the resulting DOM. The visit command takes a lot of optional arguments that allow you to specify the HTTP method or pass data, as in:

```
cy.visit("/tickets",
  {method: 'POST',
  body: {concert_id: '3', row: '2', seat: '1'}
  })
```

The visit command places the DOM into the Cypress system. If, for some reason, you want to yield from a visit command like cy.visit.then((window) => {}), the window object is yielded.

Cypress also provides the request command, which is used to help test APIs. The request command takes a similar set of arguments but yields a response object. There are a couple of common ways to use a request:

- To seed data, especially in cases where your page would make one or more API calls to set up the page structure, as in:

```
cy.request(url).then((response) => {
  // Do something here
}
```

- To verify that an HTTP request that you make would have the desired effect, as in a case where your page might make a call to change something on the server, like this:

```
cy.request(url).should((response) => {
  expect(response).to // something
}
```

Cypress also has commands for interacting with cookies and local storage, and a go command that allows you to interact with the browser web history, cy.go("back").

Finders

Once you've visited a site and set up DOM elements, you probably want to search them for specific elements. Cypress provides a lot of find and search methods that are heavily influenced by jQuery, which is to say that the methods typically take a selector and yield a Cypress object that contains a list of DOM elements that match the selector. The selector syntax is the same as jQuery's: . indicates a DOM class, # is a DOM ID, and an [attribute=value] matches a DOM attribute. If you are concerned about selectors changing in your code due to design changes, Cypress recommends fixing elements by setting a data-cy attribute on them and then querying with something like cy.get("[data-cy=myelementidentifier]").

Only a few of these finder commands actually are callable directly on the cy object, like cy.get(".thing"). Most of them chain off the result of the get, as in cy.get(".thing").first(). Most of the time, you will start with cy.get(). Alternately, you can start with cy.contains("Text"), which searches for a DOM element containing the given text or matching a given regular expression.

Once you have a set of DOM elements via get or contains, you can traverse the DOM tree in several ways. You can continue to search with your DOM elements with find, which filters on another selector, cy.get(".thing").find(".other"), and yields elements with DOM class other that are inside elements with DOM class thing. A series of other commands allow you to traverse the tree, like children, parents, and so on, but they are less common. You can get a specific element from a list with first, last, or eq(index). The index in eq either starts with 0 to get the first element and goes up to move forward, or with -1 to get the last element and goes down to move backward.

If the result of these find commands is empty, all of these find commands will wait up to the timeout period for matching elements to be found, and will fail the test if no matching element is found at the end of the timeout period.

Cypress works asynchronously, so you can't return the results of a finder method to a variable; you typically continue to chain method calls that send actions or assertions.

That said, if you want to hold on to a DOM element or elements that you've located, you can use the as command to store those elements as an alias, as we've seen with cy.get(".concert").first().as("concert"). You can access that alias later in the test with cy.get("@concert"). Aliases are not limited to DOM elements; you can use them to store other data, and aliases that you define in a beforeEach method are accessible in the tests that use that method.

Actions

Once you've identified the DOM element or elements you want to interact with, you can then send actions to those elements. Our first test used click to interact with a DOM element on the page and send it an action. Cypress provides basically any action you'd want:

- Click actions: click, dblclick, rightclick
- Form actions: check, clear, select, submit, type, uncheck
- Focus actions: blur, focus
- Scroll actions: scrollIntoView, scrollTo
- Send a generic event: trigger

All of these are basically the names of their associated actions. The ones that might not be forthcoming are type, which places text into a text field, and clear, which clears a text field. You use all of them by chaining onto a set of commands that yields DOM elements.

Cypress Has No Hover

 The missing action here is hover. Cypress does not have a hover command. It so much doesn't have a hover command that if you try cy.hover(), you will get a run-time error and a link to a page explaining why Cypress doesn't have a hover command.[6] There isn't a hover command because it's apparently difficult or impossible to implement one in a way that would activate the css :hover pseudo-selector. The recommended workaround is to trigger a mouseover event, as in cy.get("#element").trigger("mouseover"). There are other possible workarounds in the Cypress documentation.[7]

Assertions

After you've done all the actions, you're likely going to want to make some assertions about what's on the page. Cypress assertions are kind of complicated on one level in that there are a lot of options, but at the same time, the syntax has a couple of common patterns.

You can chain an assertion at the end of a series of commands with should. However, you need to do something between cy and should. You can't just write cy.should("exist"), but you can write cy.get("selector").should("exist").

---

6. https://docs.cypress.io/api/commands/hover.html
7. https://github.com/cypress-io/cypress-example-recipes/tree/master/examples/testing-dom__hover-hidden-elements

The should command typically takes as its first argument what the Cypress docs call a *chainer*. Cypress takes its assertions from a library called Chai. Assertions in Chai are a chain of methods, as in to.be.null, or to.have.class or to.be.visible. A Cypress chainer is a string version of everything in the Chai method chain after to, so those assertions in Cypress would be should("be.null"), should("have.class", "class") or should("be.visible"). If the assertion needs an expected value, the way have.class does, then that value is the second argument. In a few cases, there are two arguments, so you'd add both arguments, like so: should("have.attr", "href", "/tickets").

In the argument case, you can also use the its command to coax the variable from the selected object. The its command applies a property getter to the currently yielded elements, so you could do cy.get(".thing").its("class").should("include", "thing") as a synonym of cy.get(".thing").should("have.class", "thing").

You can chain multiple should commands after each other, and if you want, you can use and as a synonym of should, as in should("have.class", "foo").and("be.visible").

The should command can also take a function. Within the function you can do assertions using regular Chai syntax, involving expect—the yielded argument is the set of elements:

```
cy.get(".tickets").should(($tickets) => {
  expect($tickets).to.have.length(10)
  expect($tickets.find("is-visible")).to.have.length(3)
}
```

You can also use expect syntax inside any then function in a Cypress command.

Stubs

Cypress uses the Sinon library for mock and stub behavior.[8] I'm not going to get into all the details of Sinon here, but it does provide the ability to define stub methods cy.stub(foo, 'bar').returns('baz') or cy.stub(obj, 'method').resolves('foo') and then assertions like expect(foo.bar).to.be.calledOnce.

You can also control the clock with cy.clock(). Once you've called cy.clock(), you can move the clock forward with cy.tick(milliseconds).

Maybe more usefully, you can also simulate a server and request data. To start this process you call cy.server(). After turning on a cy.server(), you can direct that server to produce canned responses to routes with the cy.route() command:

```
cy.server()
cy.route("/tickets", {id: 1, concert_id: 3, row: 2, seat: 3})
```

---

8.   https://sinonjs.org

In this case, the first argument to route is a string or regular expression. Or it's two arguments where the first one is an HTTP method, and the second is the string or regex. The last argument is a string, array, object, or function.

Once a route is set, then HTTP requests that match the string or regex argument are not routed to the server but instead return the last argument. Requests that don't match a Cypress-defined route just go to the underlying server as expected.

This gets a little more interesting in conjunction with the cy.fixture() command. Cypress lets you keep fixture data, typically JSON or a string in files, in the cypress/fixtures directory. You can then use cy.fixture() to access the file and then use the data as the result of a routes.

So if we've got a file cypress/fixtures/tickets.json, we could then do this:

```
cy.server()
cy.fixture("tickets.json").as("tickets")
cy.route('POST', '**/tickets', '@tickets')
```

Then any post request to tickets in your page will return the fixture file, making that data available for testing.

Troubleshooting

Cypress has a few ways to let you see what's going on during testing. First off, each step in a test produces a snapshot that you can look at in the test runner and also inspect via the browser console that you are using. You can also trigger a screenshot to the cypress/screenshots directory by using the screenshot command.

You can send an arbitrary message to the browser console log with cy.log("message"), and you can have Cypress log the result of any chain of message by placing debug() at the end of the chain. In the next chapter, we go into the specifics of using the Cypress test runner to debug Cypress tests.

What's Next

In this chapter, we installed Cypress, wrote our first test, and toured the Cypress commands. Next, we'll write more complex Cypress tests to cover the rest of our application functionality and talk more about general troubleshooting of our application.

More Testing and Troubleshooting

In the last chapter, we focused on end-to-end testing with Cypress. We installed Cypress, wrote our first test with Cypress, and became familiar with the commands. In this chapter, we'll apply Cypress testing to the rest of our Hotwire and React pages and look at some ways to get more information in Cypress and in a browser. We're also going to talk about some ways to troubleshoot tests and code in the browser.

Writing More Cypress Tests

Let's pick up our Cypress tests. In the last chapter, we wrote a test that shows that our add favorite functionality works. Now we want to show that our remove favorite functionality also works.

We could just add more lines to the existing test to continue that scenario with a removal of favorite functionality. That's a reasonable thing to do in some circumstances. However, longer tests like that tend to be more brittle, and a failing test gives you less information because the failure might be anywhere along the sequence of the test.

But in order to get a test to a state where we can remove a favorite, we kind of have to go through all those same steps: log in a user and add a favorite. Ideally, we'd be able to start the test in that state. However, the cypress-rails gem is deliberately structured without a built-in mechanism to trigger test-specific Rails data setup from within a Cypress test.

Instead, what cypress-rails expects us to do is write test-specific Rails controller code and invoke it from our tests using cy.request. Loading data from a controller has a couple of advantages. It clearly places the responsibility for setting up data in a regular Rails process that does regular Rails things and is therefore easier to understand. Also, it separates the test and the data in a way that if we were ever to need to either move Cypress to its own code repository or change the server from Rails, we could do so with minimal change to the test itself.

Here's what that looks like in code. We just need a controller that will provide a home for test setup:

chapter_16/01/app/controllers/test_setup_controller.rb

```ruby
class TestSetupController < ApplicationController
  before_action :require_test_environment

  def log_in_user
    sign_in(:user, User.find_by(email: "areader@example.com"))
  end

  def add_favorite
    concert = Concert.find_by(name: "Brandi Carlile In Concert")
    Favorite.create!(user: current_user, concert: concert)
  end

  private def require_test_environment
    redirect_to(root_path) unless Rails.env.test?
  end
end
```

This is mostly a Rails controller. I've added a before_action that blocks the action from being run if you aren't in a test environment, for security purposes. I think in a production environment I'd consider setting up my deploy such that this file doesn't deploy to production at all. There are two short controller actions, one that uses Devise helpers to log in a test user, and another that gives the test user a favorite concert.

We also need to add these controller actions to the routing table, which now looks like this:

chapter_16/01/config/routes.rb

```ruby
Rails.application.routes.draw do
  resources(:favorites)
  resource(:schedule)
  resources(:shopping_carts)
  resources(:ticket_orders)
  resources(:tickets)
  resources(:gigs)
  resources(:concerts)
  resources(:bands)
  resources(:venues)
  resource(:sold_out_concerts, only: :show)
  devise_for(:users)
  root(to: "schedules#show")
```

```
  post("test/log_in_user", to: "test_setup#log_in_user")
  post("test/add_favorite", to: "test_setup#add_favorite")
end
```

And here's the test:

chapter_16/01/cypress/integration/schedule/schedule_spec.js
```
it("Allows the user to remove a favorite", () => {
  cy.request("POST", "/test/log_in_user")
  cy.request("POST", "test/add_favorite")
  cy.visit("/")
  cy.get("#favorite-concerts-list").as("favorites")
  cy.get(".concert").first().as("concert")
  cy.get("@favorites").contains("Remove Favorite").first().click()
  cy.get("@favorites").find("article").should("have.lengthOf", 0)
  cy.get("@concert").contains("Make Favorite")
})
```

We use cy.request twice to call each of our controller actions, then basically do the previous test in reverse: we find the first instance of a Remove Favorite button, click it, then validate that the favorites section no longer has any elements in it and that the button in the existing concert is back to being labeled "Make Favorite."

This test passes, and you'll also note that it's way, way faster to get through the setup than the previous test that manually logs in via the actual form. It's a good idea to have at least one test that walks through the form, but other than that, you're better off doing the setup remotely.

Testing the Schedule Filter

Let's write more examples in Cypress that at least partially cover the rest of the features we've written in Stimulus and React. Here's a longer series of tests that deals with the calendar filter at the top of the schedule page. The behavior we're checking here is to confirm that clicking on a calendar item makes only concerts with that date visible and that clicking back to a state of no clicks makes everything visible again. Here's the code:

chapter_16/02/cypress/integration/schedule/schedule_spec.js
```
describe("calendar filters", () => {
  beforeEach(() => {
    cy.visit("/")
    cy.get("#calendar-day-2021-04-11").first().as("dayOne")
    cy.get("#calendar-day-2021-04-12").first().as("dayTwo")
    cy.get("#calendar-day-2021-04-13").first().as("dayThree")
    cy.get("[data-2021-04-11=true]").as("dayOneConcerts")
    cy.get("[data-2021-04-12=true]").as("dayTwoConcerts")
    cy.get("[data-2021-04-13=true]").as("dayThreeConcerts")
```

```
    })
    it("makes everybody visible with no clicks", () => {
      cy.get("@dayOneConcerts").each((item) => {
        cy.wrap(item).should("be.visible")
      })
      cy.get("@dayTwoConcerts").each((item) => {
        cy.wrap(item).should("be.visible")
      })
      cy.get("@dayThreeConcerts").each((item) => {
        cy.wrap(item).should("be.visible")
      })
    })
    it("shows only that day on calendar click", () => {
      cy.get("@dayOne").click()
      cy.get("@dayOne").should("have.class", "border-red-700")
      cy.get("@dayOneConcerts").each((item) => {
        cy.wrap(item).should("be.visible")
      })
      cy.get("@dayTwoConcerts").each((item) => {
        cy.wrap(item).should("not.be.visible")
      })
      cy.get("@dayThreeConcerts").each((item) => {
        cy.wrap(item).should("not.be.visible")
      })
    })
    it("shows all on show all", () => {
      cy.get("@dayOne").click()
      cy.get("@dayTwo").click()
      cy.contains("Show All").click()
      cy.get("@dayOne").should("not.have.class", "border-red-700")
      cy.get("@dayTwo").should("not.have.class", "border-red-700")
      cy.get("@dayOneConcerts").each((item) => {
        cy.wrap(item).should("be.visible")
      })
      cy.get("@dayTwoConcerts").each((item) => {
        cy.wrap(item).should("be.visible")
      })
      cy.get("@dayThreeConcerts").each((item) => {
        cy.wrap(item).should("be.visible")
      })
    })
  })
})
```

Because we changed the concert listing to have the day headers managed in
CSS, we don't have easy div elements for each day, so we need to get a little
fancier.

The test section here starts with a beforeEach, which starts by using visit to get to the schedule page. We then need to do a little selector manipulation to get the DOM IDs for each of the three days that are in the seeded data—the seeded data hard codes the dates so that we can do this very thing. Similarly, we use the same data attributes we use in the dynamic CSS to build up a list of the actual concerts associated with each day. (Because we don't use first in these lines, Cypress is still going to treat the results as a list of elements.)

The first test kind of gives the pattern of how we can use Cypress to check the visibility status. We use cy.get to grab each alias and then call .each to iterate over each element in the group. Inside the function, we call cy.wrap, which allows us to treat each individual element as a Cypress object for the purposes of chaining and asynchronous behavior, then we use should to test whether each element should be visible. In the first test, where no calendar filters have been clicked, everything is visible.

In the second test, we get the first calendar item and click on it, then test that the item has gained its border. Then we do the same visibility check, except that only the concerts associated with the day that was clicked should be visible. The others should, and I quote, not.be.visible.

The test for the Show All button uses a similar set of assertions but a different click pattern: We click on two of the calendars, then click the Show All button to verify the page changes back.

The search test uses the type action:

```
chapter_16/02/cypress/integration/schedule/schedule_spec.js
describe("search", () => {
  beforeEach(() => {
    cy.visit("/")
  })

  it("updates on search typing", function () {
    cy.get("#search_query").type("billy")
    cy.get("#search-results").as("searchResults")
    cy.get("@searchResults").find("article").should("have.lengthOf", 1)
    cy.get("@searchResults")
      .find(".name")
      .first()
      .should("contain", "Billy")
  })
})
```

Here we're grabbing the #search_query element to find the box and type to put text in it. For the rest of it, we're checking that the contents of the search results contain the element that we expect.

Cypress-Rails, Databases, and You

 One thing I noticed while using the cypress-rails gem is that the hook that is supposed to clear the database on exit doesn't always get executed, especially if you force-quit out of the program somehow. In that case, you might get a database error on reload, when the cypress-rails gem tries to reapply the database seeds. When that happened to me, running $ rails db:test:prepare fixed the problem. I also found that I occasionally had to restart Postgres because force-quit Cypress might not return database connections correctly.

Cypress and React

We don't need to do anything in general to test React since the Cypress tests don't care about the underlying framework. (Okay, Cypress has recently added an alpha framework for testing React components in isolation. That's interesting, but it's still a little too early to include here.)

We do, however, have a specific problem relating to the React tools in our code. That problem is named *styled components*.

Styled components, which we added to our React code in Chapter 5, Cascading Style Sheets, on page 91, are lovely, but they also work by adding a dynamic, random class name to the component. Dynamic, random class names are not easy to find in a test and make assertions about. There doesn't seem to be a way to manage this on the styled-components side—you could imagine a test setting for styled components where the class names were discoverable, but it doesn't look like anybody has done that.

The easiest way to get attributes that our tests can find is to add them ourselves, so we add a couple of new attributes to the ButtonSquare component inside the Seat component—if you are concerned about performance, you can make the use of these attributes conditional with not being in production, but I don't think it's going to be a noticeable issue in this case:

chapter_16/02/app/packs/components/seat.tsx
```
return (
  <td>
    <ButtonSquare
      status={currentStatus()}
      onClick={onSeatChange}
```

```
      data-cy={`${rowNumber}x${seatNumber}`}
      data-color={stateColor(currentStatus())}>
      {seatNumber}
    </ButtonSquare>
  </td>
)
```

Here we're adding a data-cy that will be of the form 1x5 and will allow us to identify the row and seat number of an element in one attribute. We're also adding a data-color, which is the color that the styled component will also be using as the background color of the class. This is not ideal, and I think that if I were starting over, I'd probably find something other than styled components, but it's workable and we can write tests against it, like so:

chapter_16/02/cypress/integration/concert/concert_spec.js
```
describe("On a concert page", () => {
  beforeEach(function () {
    cy.request("/cypress_rails_reset_state")
    cy.request("POST", "/test/log_in_user")
    cy.visit("/concerts/1")
  })

  it("blocks tickets on edge when ticket list changes", () => {
    cy.get("[data-cy=1x10]").should("have.attr", "data-color", "white")
    cy.get("[data-cy=ticketsToBuy]").select("3")
    cy.get("[data-cy=1x10]").should("have.attr", "data-color", "yellow")
    cy.get("[data-cy=1x9]").should("have.attr", "data-color", "yellow")
    cy.get("[data-cy=1x8]").should("have.attr", "data-color", "white")
  })

  it("marks a ticket as sold on click", () => {
    cy.get("[data-cy=1x10]").click()
    cy.get("[data-cy=1x10]").should("have.attr", "data-color", "green")
    cy.get("[data-cy=1x9]").should("have.attr", "data-color", "white")
    cy.get("[data-cy=ticketsPurchased]").should("have.text", "1")
    cy.get("[data-cy=ticketCost]").should("have.text", "$15.00")
  })

  it("marks a group of tickets sold on click", () => {
    cy.get("[data-cy=ticketsToBuy]").select("2")
    cy.get("[data-cy=1x9]").click()
    cy.get("[data-cy=1x9]").should("have.attr", "data-color", "green")
    cy.get("[data-cy=1x10]").should("have.attr", "data-color", "green")
    cy.get("[data-cy=1x8]").should("have.attr", "data-color", "yellow")
    cy.get("[data-cy=ticketsPurchased]").should("have.text", "2")
    cy.get("[data-cy=ticketCost]").should("have.text", "$30.00")
  })

  it("undoes a sale on second click", () => {
    cy.get("[data-cy=1x10]").click()
    cy.get("[data-cy=1x10]").should("have.attr", "data-color", "green")
    cy.get("[data-cy=1x10]").click()
```

```
      cy.get("[data-cy=1x10]").should("have.attr", "data-color", "white")
      cy.get("[data-cy=ticketsPurchased]").should("have.text", "0")
      cy.get("[data-cy=ticketCost]").should("have.text", "$0.00")
    })
    it("clears from the clear ticket button", () => {
      cy.get("[data-cy=1x10]").click()
      cy.get("[data-cy=1x4]").click()
      cy.get("[data-cy=1x3]").click()
      cy.get("[data-cy=clearButton]").click()
      cy.get("[data-cy=1x10]").should("have.attr", "data-color", "white")
      cy.get("[data-cy=ticketsPurchased]").should("have.text", "0")
      cy.get("[data-cy=ticketCost]").should("have.text", "$0.00")
    })
})
```

Our beforeEach function starts each test by resetting, then visiting a specific concert page. The first test checks that seats become invalid after the number of tickets to buy at a time changes. To make this work, I added a data-cy attribute to the tickets to buy pull-down menu and a few other elements in the subtotal and header.

Then we check that individual tickets, group tickets, and the Clear All button work, using a combination of select and click events: the have.attr and have.text assertions.

We're not testing the return back to the server; however, we could, by refreshing the page and showing that sales persist. We're also not testing the ActionCable activity of what happens if another browser causes an ActionCable message to be sent. Cypress doesn't let you test multiple browsers at once, so I think the ActionCable would have to be tested by forcing the seat change action to happen from a spec.

Cypress Utilities and API

Cypress also has a command-line tool that allows you to run Cypress from a terminal or from a command line in a continuous integration tool. In our environment, we start that tool with rake cypress:run. Doing so will run the tests against the Electron JS run time by default. If you run this command, you'll get output directly in your terminal. You'll get a line for each individual test with a time amount (for example, ✓ marks a group of tickets sold on click (487ms)), you'll get a summary table for each file, and you'll get a final summary table that gives the time and test count for each file.

You will also get files in tmp/cypress_videos, one for each test file, that show a video capture of the browser for each test in the file. A failing test adds a screenshot of the failure into the folder tmp/cypress_screenshots.

This command is usually going to be run on a continuous integration server. In actual development, you may want the interactive test runner and access to the browser tools.

Troubleshooting

Sometimes things just don't work the way you expect, either when testing your code in Cypress or when just running it in the browser. Browsers have a lot of different tools to allow you to explore what is happening. We'll take a look at those tools first, then look at debugging Cypress tests in the Cypress test runner. We'll end by taking a quick peek at a browser extension to troubleshoot React components.

Using the Console Log

If you are me, logging has always been a big part of your debugging flow. Visual debuggers are nice, but being able to send "yep, the code got here" and "the username is Fred" messages to the console are pretty powerful ways to understand what's going on in your code. The console in your browser has a lot of helpful tools to make your logs more valuable. Here's a survey.

The big one, of course, is console.log, which takes an arbitrary number of arguments and prints them to the console. If the argument is an object or an array, usually the browser provides triangle show-hide buttons for the structure of the object. Multiple arguments are printed to the console side by side. Log also allows you to use string substitution as a replacement for a template string, so you can do either ' console.log(User: ${user}\ ) ' or console.log("User: %o", user), where %o is a placeholder for an object—you also have %s for strings and %i or %f for numbers. The template strings are usually shorter, but some browsers display objects better using the string substitution method.

The log method has a bunch of friends: debug, error, info, and warn. These methods all behave the exact same way; however, the browser might choose to use a slightly different style when displaying them. For example, Chrome color-codes error and warn, and also automatically adds a stack trace to the console when those are used. Browsers typically also allow you to filter based on which method is used to send the message to the console.

You can get more structured output with console.table, which takes your arrays, objects, arrays of objects, or objects of arrays and tries to put them in a convenient tabular format in the console. (I need to remember to use this one more—it's quite useful.)

If you'd like a different way to call attention to your message, you can actually embed CSS into the call using string substation and a %c, as in console.log("%c user: %o", "font-size: 24pt; color: green", user). Most text-based CSS will work here; again, browsers will vary.

Sometimes all you want to know is whether a particular line is called and you don't really have a message. The console.count method just prints out a count, incrementing by one every time it is called. If you give count an argument, that argument is displayed with the count as tag, and count maintains a separate value for each tag. The method countReset resets the count back to zero and may or may not display a 0 message depending on the browser.

Often you only want a message to appear in the console conditionally. The method, console.assert takes two arguments: a boolean expression and a string. The method only displays the string if the assertion is false. Again, different browsers will display the assertion failure differently.

Accessing objects in the Webpacker namespace of your code is a little tricky. I recommend explicitly (and temporarily) assigning an object that you are concerned about to the global object with something like window.object_under_debug = user, and then you can access it in the console as object_under_debug. If you want to do some DOM manipulation, $0 provides the object that is currently selected in the DOM element selector part of the browser, and you can also do $("selector") as a shortcut for document.querySelector.

Using the Cypress Test Runner

Debugging Cypress tests in the Cypress test runner gives you a few additional features than browser tools.

Just in the test runner itself, which we saw earlier in the screenshot on page 293, clicking on any of the command steps in the left-hand column displays the result of that step in the console where you can examine it more closely. Similarly, clicking on error messages on the left side will put the error stack trace in the console.

The cy.log command takes a string message and an arbitrary object. When invoked, it prints the message and the object to the left-side command rundown of the test runner, and clicking on that message puts the arbitrary object into the console. This can be a helpful way to log messages in tests and have them be displayed in the context of the code that displays the message.

Also, right above the actual browser display is a text bit that starts with cy.get or something similar. This is a little UI for interacting with the browser on display. You can enter a Cypress finder method at the top, see the result of that selector highlighted in the document, and print it to the console.

Using the React DevTools Extension

A few React-specific troubleshooting tools are worth becoming familiar with too. The most important is a browser extension called React DevTools. You can download this extension from the extension store of your favorite browser, and it looks something like the screen show here (this is the Chrome version):

On the left side of the screen is a tree of the React app on the page ordered by React component, not DOM element. Notice in the image that our component names like VenueHeader, VenueBody, Row, and Seat are used. Selecting a particular component shows details of that component on the right, most notably, the current values of the props for that component, and then you also get a look at hooks used for that component and the entire tree of components that contain the selected component.

In the top-right corner of the screen are some icons. The watch icon pauses that particular component from rerendering. The eye opens the DOM inspector to the selected element, the bug logs information to the browser console, and the brackets take you to the source code for that component.

What's Next

Over the course of this book, you've seen how to use TypeScript, Webpacker, Stimulus, and React to add rich client interactions to your Rails application. You've seen how to use CSS to add styling and animations, you've used more complex features of these tools to give them more functionality, and you've seen how to use Cypress to write tests to validate the behavior of our app.

What's next? Go out and build something great!

Framework Swap

You may look at the examples in the book and wonder if I deliberately or accidentally tuned the examples to show off Hotwire or React in a better light. Both examples have features that are there because they are particularly well-suited to the tool being shown. The schedule page has the inline edits, for example, while the React page has the way that the entire page redraws available seats when the pull-down menu is changed.

I thought it'd be interesting to close out the book by showing what the React page looks like in Hotwire and vice versa. This lets you see each tool in a slightly different light and also exposes the fact that somehow the schedule page got significantly more complex than the concert ticket page.

My ground rules:

- I tried to mimic the functionality of the page as best I could in the other tool. With one exception—I did skip the inline edit in the React schedule page. More on that in a bit.

- I did not add any other new libraries that might have helped, though I was tempted to add an animation library to the React version of the schedule page.

- There are absolutely other ways of building these pages in the tools.

The clearest thing that you see when doing this exercise is that the React version of both pages is significantly more verbose than the Hotwire version.

It's a little hard to compare lines of code between TypeScript, Ruby, JSX, and ERB. But the React versions of both pages are about just way more lines of code. The Hotwire version of the venue page was about 300 lines of code, replacing about 500 lines of React/JSX. When you consider that a large chunk of that 300 is just the same markup translated, that's a very big reduction in code logic. (Probably also worth mentioning that my previous Stimulus-without-Hotwire take on this page was about 400 lines of code.) If anything, the difference on the schedule page is even larger; there's a lot of React code needed on that page to cover the things that Hotwire did in a couple of lines.

When looking at the difference in code, we see it comes from a few different sources:

- *TypeScript boilerplate.* React encourages the creation of more domain objects, and in conjunction with TypeScript, that means more code devoted to defining types. This is especially true given the way we wrote interfaces for each individual action object in the reducers.

- *React boilerplate.* Component definitions, calling hooks, managing the reducers, a little extra server-side code to shape the data. It's a general feature of JavaScript style that there is more typed boilerplate than in Rails style. Rails tends to avoid boilerplate code where possible; most JavaScript frameworks tend to have more of it. Also, React encourages smaller components, which means more boilerplate in terms of declarations, headers, and the like.

- *Extra state.* The React code requires us to keep a whole bunch of system state client side, nearly all of which is arguably duplicative of either the server state, or the state of the DOM itself. Another way of saying that last part is that in React, the DOM reflects the state of the client, whereas in Hotwire, the DOM is itself the state of the client.

All that said, I don't think there is a dramatic difference in how long one version or the other version took. I've been working with these samples for a long time, and they aren't *that* big, and the underlying logic mostly transferred. The Hotwire translation probably took less time but not, like, an order of magnitude or anything like that.

The two systems do have a different model of how they work. In Hotwire, the more you can think of things as basically regular HTTP requests with special processing of an HTML response, the easier things get. In React, you're more likely to think in terms of changing internal client-side data with the HTTP requests and even think of the HTML markup as kind of a side effect of changing state.

React encourages a separation of presentation and domain logic, which means you can do a lot of work within the domain logic and the presentation will just automatically change. So the last step of making things work in React is very satisfying. It also means that basically Hotwire is letting you take a shortcut for simple interactions that don't require a lot of domain logic. As the Hotwire logic becomes more complex, you might wind up building in the domain logic and reactivity that React gives you. Still, there's a long way to go before the Hotwire bit becomes as verbose as a simple React app.

Here's a tour of both apps. I'm going to show each one fully formed rather than walking through the individual steps. I'm also not going to show all the code changes, just the important or interesting ones. You can see the full apps in the sample code directory as appendix_hotwire/01 or appendix_react/01.

The All-Hotwire App

The list of features in the venue page that I wanted to replicate in Hotwire were:

- Unroll the markup from the React components and go back to an ERB template.

- Add the interaction for changing the number of tickets to buy, which also changes the status of seats from valid to invalid and vice versa. This includes talking to the server.

- Add the interaction for clicking on a seat, which updates the status of that seat, the seats to its left and right (which might be purchased or become invalid), and the subtotal. This also includes talking to the server.

- Add the interaction for the Clear All button.

- Add ActionCable functionality for communicating between multiple browsers.

I had a couple of design decisions to make. My goal here was to make this app as Hotwire-forward as I could, meaning state and logic on the server to the extent possible. (*Note:* If you had an earlier beta of this book, this is a significantly different design for the Stimulus version of the app.) It seemed to me as I started that both the ticket to buy and the seat button press could be modeled as HTTP form requests with Turbo Stream responses.

The piece that looks tricky is the last one where browsers are communicating ticket purchases. The reason I think this might be complicated is that it's the one place where the client-side state actually matters. As currently written, the server can't correctly send the new state of the client as pure HTML to all browsers because the other browsers might have a different "Tickets to Buy" set, and therefore would send different HTML based on a client-side value that the server doesn't know about.

Converting JSX to ERB

I think the place to start here is to show the ERB files converted from the React. The structure is actually quite similar.

Here's part of the concert show page itself:

```
appendix_hotwire/01/app/views/concerts/show.html.erb
<div class="concert">
  <%= render(@concert.venue, concert: @concert, user: current_user) %>
</div>
```

We're rendering the venue as its own object, meaning the partial is in app/views/venue/_venue.html.erb:

```
appendix_hotwire/01/app/views/venues/_venue.html.erb
<%= turbo_frame_tag(dom_id(venue)) do %>
  <section>
    <%= render("venues/subtotal", concert: concert, user: user) %>
    <%= render("venues/venue_header", concert: concert, venue: venue) %>
    <%= render(
          "venues/venue_body",
          venue: venue,
          user: user,
          concert: concert,
          tickets_to_buy_count: 1
        ) %>
  </section>
<% end %>
```

This venue is just splitting off into different partials, with basically the same breakdown as the React components had.

The subtotal partial has some Hotwire markup surrounding the "Clear Tickets" button:

```
appendix_hotwire/01/app/views/venues/_subtotal.html.erb
<%= turbo_frame_tag("subtotal_frame") do %>
  <section class="subtotal" id="subtotal">
    <div class="text-2xl font-bold mx-4">
      <span>Current Tickets Purchased:  </span>
      <span data-cy="ticketsPurchased">
        <%= Ticket.user_for_concert(concert.id, user&.id).count %>
      </span>
    </div>
    <div class="text-2xl font-bold mx-4">
      <span>Current Tickets Cost:  </span>
      <span data-cy="ticketCost">
        <%= Ticket.user_for_concert(concert.id, user&.id).count * 15 %>.00
      </span>
    </div>
```

```erb
    <div class="<%= SimpleForm.button_class %> w-36 font-bold"
        data-cy="clearButton"
        data-controller="clear-all"
        data-clear-all-hidden-id-value="tickets_to_buy_count"
        data-action="click->clear-all#submit">
      <%= form_with(
            url: clear_all_tickets_url,
            method: "delete",
            data: {"clear-all-target": "form"}
          ) do |f| %>
        <%= hidden_field_tag(:concert_id, concert.id) %>
        <%= hidden_field_tag(
              "tickets_to_buy_count",
              "",
              id: "clear_all_tickets_count",
              data: {"clear-all-target": "hiddenField"}
            ) %>
        Clear Tickets
      <% end %>
    </div>
  </section>
<% end %>
```

The venue header is a little more interesting, as we define two Stimulus controllers, both of which take the form as a target:

```erb
appendix_hotwire/01/app/views/venues/_venue_header.html.erb
<section class="venue-header">
  <div>
    <div class="flex text-2xl font-bold mx-4">
      <span>How many tickets would you like?</span>
      <span class="select ml-4"
            data-controller="form cable-receiver"
            data-cable-reciever-channel-name-value="ConcertChannel"
            data-cable-reciever-concert-id-value="<%= concert.id %>">
        <%= form_with(
              url: tickets_to_buy_count_path,
              method: "patch",
              data: {
                "form-target": "form",
                "cable-receiver-target": "form"
              }
            ) do |f| %>
          <%= hidden_field_tag(:concert_id, concert.id) %>
          <%= hidden_field_tag(:venue_id, venue.id) %>
          <%= select_tag(
                :tickets_to_buy_count,
                options_for_select(1..venue.seats_per_row),
                "data-cy": "ticketsToBuy",
                "data-action": "change->form#submit"
              ) %>
```

```
        <% end %>
      </span>
    </div>
  </div>
</section>
```

The select box also triggers a Stimulus action when it changes, and we'll see what that action does in a moment.

The venue body loops over rows in much the same way the React code did:

```
appendix_hotwire/01/app/views/venues/_venue_body.html.erb
<section class="venue-body">
  <%= turbo_frame_tag("venue-body") do %>
    <table className="table">
      <tbody>
        <% concert.rows(tickets_to_buy_count: tickets_to_buy_count)
              .each do |row| %>
          <%= render(row, user: user, concert: concert) %>
        <% end %>
      </tbody>
    </table>
  <% end %>
</section>
```

I've made Row and Seat both Rails ActiveModels, which means even though they don't specifically map to the database, we can use Rails naming conventions on them. For our purposes right now, that means rendering a row object invokes a file at app/views/rows/_row.html.erb:

```
appendix_hotwire/01/app/views/rows/_row.html.erb
<tr class="h-20" id="<%= dom_id(row) %>">
  <% row.seats.each do |seat| %>
    <%= render(seat, user: user, row: row, concert: concert) %>
  <% end %>
</tr>
```

Which, in turn, loops over seats that have partials at app/views/seats/_seat.html.erb:

```
appendix_hotwire/01/app/views/seats/_seat.html.erb
<td>
  <span class="p-4 m-2 my-10 text-lg
              transition-all duration-1000 ease-in-out
              hover:<%= seat.hover_color_for(user) %>
              border-black border-4 <%= seat.color_for(user) %>"
        data-cy="<%= seat.row_seat %>"
        data-color="<%= seat.color_for(user) %>"
        data-status="<%= seat.status(user) %>">
    <% if seat.status(user) == "unsold" || seat.status(user) == "held" %>
      <%= button_to(
            seat.number,
```

```
        seat_path(
          id: seat.id,
          user_id: user.id,
          row_number: row.number,
          seat_number: seat.number,
          tickets_to_buy_count: row.tickets_to_buy_count,
          concert_id: concert.id
        ),
        method: seat.status(user) == "unsold" ? "put" : "delete",
        form: {class: "inline"},
        class: "bg-white"
      ) %>
  <% else %>
    <%= seat.number %>
  <% end %>
  </span>
</td>
```

The seat file is worth a little unpacking. We've got a span with the same CSS to draw the border plus a couple of special data attributes, two of which are there to manage the Cypress tests, and the other of which, we'll see, is used by the ActionCable handler. Inside the span, if the seat is available to be purchased, we use the Rails button_to helper to make it a button that submits a form. We use the existing status of the seat to determine whether the form submit is a PUT for a purchase or a DELETE for an unpurchase.

To get the data set up properly, the controller doesn't change, but I did add some methods to the Concert class so that it would create the new Row models:

appendix_hotwire/01/app/models/concert.rb
```ruby
def row_at(tickets:, number:, tickets_to_buy_count: 1)
  Row.new(
    tickets: tickets,
    number: number,
    tickets_to_buy_count: tickets_to_buy_count
  )
end

def tickets_in_row(row)
  tickets.select { |ticket| ticket.row == row }.sort_by(&:number)
end
```

This creates Row objects for each row of tickets in the concert, giving each row the proper set of tickets and allowing it to know what the ticket to buy number is so that it can pass that along to determine the status of each seat.

The Row and Seat classes basically implemented the status logic that the React row and seat components did, with the Row building a list of Seat objects when created:

appendix_hotwire/01/app/models/row.rb
```ruby
class Row
  include ActiveModel::Model
  include ActiveModel::Conversion
  attr_accessor :tickets, :number, :seats, :tickets_to_buy_count

  def initialize(tickets:, number:, tickets_to_buy_count: 1)
    @tickets = tickets
    @number = number
    @tickets_to_buy_count = tickets_to_buy_count
    @seats = tickets.map { |ticket| Seat.new(ticket: ticket, row: self) }
  end

  def id
    number
  end

  def seats_in_row
    seats.count
  end

  def seat_available?(seat)
    return false if close_to_edge?(seat)
    return false if close_to_purchased_ticket?(seat)
    true
  end

  def close_to_edge?(seat)
    seat.number + tickets_to_buy_count - 1 > seats_in_row
  end

  def close_to_purchased_ticket?(seat)
    seats.filter do |s|
      s.number.in?(seat.number...(seat.number + tickets_to_buy_count))
    end.any?(&:unavailable?)
  end
end
```

and then the Seat taking care of status and background color and relating them to the underlying ticket object, though it does make the target for the button smaller—as currently written, you have to actually click on the number itself:

appendix_hotwire/01/app/models/seat.rb
```ruby
class Seat
  include ActiveModel::Model
  include ActiveModel::Conversion
  attr_accessor :ticket, :row

  STATUSES = %w[unsold unavailable held purchase refunded invalid]

  delegate :number, :unavailable?, to: :ticket
```

```
def status(user)
  return "invalid" if !row.seat_available?(self) && !unavailable?
  return "other" if ticket.user && ticket.user != user
  ticket.status
end

def clickable?(user)
  status(user) == "unsold"
end

def id
  "#{row.number}_#{number}"
end

def row_seat
  "#{row.number}x#{ticket.number}"
end

def hover_color_for(user)
  return "bg-blue-100" if status(user) == "unsold"
  color_for(user)
end

def color_for(user)
  case status(user)
  when "unsold" then "bg-white"
  when "invalid" then "bg-yellow-500"
  when "other" then "bg-red-600"
  when "purchased" then "bg-green-600"
  when "held" then "bg-green-600"
  end
end
end
```

Using Stimulus to Take Action

All that code gets us the display and the data state in our initial HTML rendered on the server. Now we need to implement the interactivity.

The first interactive bit is that changing the pull-down menu for the number of tickets being purchased changes the state of tickets in the display and requires the entire display to be redrawn. We're going to do this as a regular form submission that uses a Turbo Stream to update the page.

If you look up at the earlier _venue_header partial view file, the form is already declared inside a Stimulus controller named form and is the form target of that controller. The form itself sets a URL of tickets_to_buy_path and the select box sets a Stimulus action of "change->form#submit", meaning that when the select box changes it will call a submit method on the Stimulus controller.

The controller itself is very generic:

```
appendix_hotwire/01/app/packs/controllers/form_controller.ts
import { Controller } from "stimulus"
import "form-request-submit-polyfill"

export default class SearchController extends Controller {
  static targets = ["form"]
  formTarget: HTMLFormElement

  submit(): void {
    this.formTarget.requestSubmit()
  }
}
```

All it does is allow Stimulus to submit a form (it's a simplification of the controller you saw in Chapter 9, Talking to the Server, on page 161).

The form submission goes to a new controller with a new resource called tickets_to_buy, which we need to declare in the Rails routes file:

```
appendix_hotwire/01/config/routes.rb
resource(:tickets_to_buy_count, only: :update)
resource(:clear_all_tickets, only: :destroy)
resources(:seats, only: %i[update destroy])
```

This gives us tickets_to_buy as a Rails singular resource, meaning we can call the update route without needing an ID for a resource being updated. Perfect for us because this resource is effectively common for this page.

We're not actually saving the ticket to buy number server side; we're just using it to trigger a redraw. Here's the controller:

```
appendix_hotwire/01/app/controllers/tickets_to_buy_counts_controller.rb
class TicketsToBuyCountsController < ApplicationController
  def update
    @venue = Venue.find(params[:venue_id])
    @concert = Concert.find(params[:concert_id])
    @user = current_user
  end
end
```

The controller just does the default action of finding a turbo_stream view:

```
appendix_hotwire/01/app/views/tickets_to_buy_counts/update.turbo_stream.erb
<%= turbo_stream.replace(
    "venue-body",
    partial: "venues/venue_body",
    locals: {
      concert: @concert,
      user: @user,
      tickets_to_buy_count: params[:tickets_to_buy_count].to_i
    }
  ) %>
```

```erb
<%= turbo_stream.replace(
    "subtotal",
    partial: "venues/subtotal",
    locals: {concert: @concert, user: @user}
) %>
```

The view does two Turbo Stream replace actions. One of them is to the venue_body redrawing the partial for the entire grid with the new value for tickets to buy. This causes a new grid of seats to be set server side with new validation calculations and replaces the existing grid of seats. The other Turbo Stream replace updates the subtotal display. We don't actually need it here, but it's going to be helpful for the ActionCable updates.

The other user interaction here comes from clicking on a seat—we've used button_to to make those buttons into individual form submissions, going to a Seat controller. The controller is more complicated than the ticket to buy one because it needs to manage saving the new ticket holds and also broadcast those changes via ActionCable. Essentially, it has the exact logic that the last React version was doing via ActionCable uploads in the ConcertChannel:

appendix_hotwire/01/app/controllers/seats_controller.rb
```ruby
class SeatsController < ApplicationController
  before_action :load_data, only: [:update, :destroy]

  def update
    @cart.add_tickets(
      concert_id: params[:concert_id].to_i,
      row: params[:row_number].to_i,
      seat_number: params[:seat_number].to_i,
      tickets_to_buy_count: params[:tickets_to_buy_count].to_i,
      status: "held"
    )
    load_row
    @concert.broadcast_schedule_change
  end

  def destroy
    @cart.clear(
      concert_id: params[:concert_id],
      row: params[:row_number].to_i,
      seat_number: params[:seat_number].to_i,
      tickets_to_buy_count: params[:tickets_to_buy_count].to_i,
      status: "unsold"
    )
    load_row
    @concert.broadcast_schedule_change
  end

  private def load_data
    @user = current_user
```

```
    @cart = ShoppingCart.find_or_create_by(user_id: params[:user_id])
    @concert = Concert.find(params[:concert_id])
  end

  private def load_row
    @row = @concert.row_at(
      tickets: @concert.tickets_in_row(params[:row_number].to_i),
      number: params[:row_number].to_i,
      tickets_to_buy_count: params[:tickets_to_buy_count].to_i
    )
  end
end
```

Both of these actions have the same structure: they grab their data and update
the shopping cart, which uses previously written code to update Ticket records
in the database to their new purchased or unpurchased state.

They make two ActionCable broadcasts: one to any page open to the schedule
that the number of tickets available has changed (I've offloaded that one to
Concert):

```
appendix_hotwire/01/app/models/concert.rb
def broadcast_schedule_change
  ActionCable.server.broadcast(
    "schedule",
    {concerts: [{concertId: id, ticketsRemaining: tickets.unsold.count}]}
  )
end
```

and one to any other page opened to the same concert that the ticket status
has changed. I've offloaded that one to Ticket, using an ActiveRecord callback,
so that the change happens any time a ticket is updated:

```
appendix_hotwire/01/app/models/ticket.rb
after_update_commit -> do
  Turbo::StreamsChannel.broadcast_stream_to(
    concert,
    content: {seat: id, status: status}.to_json
  )
end
```

They then both render default Turbo Stream views. Both views are the same;
I'll only show one:

```
appendix_hotwire/01/app/views/seats/update.turbo_stream.erb
<%= turbo_stream.replace(
    dom_id(@row),
    partial: "rows/row",
    locals: {row: @row, concert: @concert, user: @user}
  ) %>
<%= turbo_stream.replace(
```

```
    "subtotal",
    partial: "venues/subtotal",
    locals: {concert: @concert, user: @user}
  ) %>
```

This triggers two Turbo Stream replace actions. The second is the same update of the subtotal that we did before, though this time we would expect the total to change. The first we take advantage of having used ActiveModel, and we just replace the row that the seats are in—given our application logic, no other part of the venue grid outside that row will change.

Finally, the Clear Tickets button requires a little bit of Stimulus because it needs to pass the tickets to buy count to the server so the server can hand down a cleared venue with the right invalid tickets. I've got it set up as a form submit that reaches to the existing pull-down menu to get its value before submitting:

```
appendix_hotwire/01/app/packs/controllers/clear_all_controller.ts
import { Controller } from "stimulus"
import "form-request-submit-polyfill"

export default class FormController extends Controller {
  static targets = ["form", "hiddenField"]
  formTarget: HTMLFormElement
  hiddenFieldTarget: HTMLFormElement

  static values = { hiddenId: String }
  hiddenIdValue: string

  submit(): void {
    const hiddenValueElement = document.getElementById(
      this.hiddenIdValue
    ) as HTMLFormElement
    if (hiddenValueElement) {
      this.hiddenFieldTarget.value = hiddenValueElement.value
    }
    this.formTarget.requestSubmit()
  }
}
```

There's probably a more generic version of this if I needed it again.

The form submits to a controller that is very similar to the Seat controller, but we'll give it its own REST action:

```
appendix_hotwire/01/app/controllers/clear_all_tickets_controller.rb
class ClearAllTicketsController < ApplicationController
  def destroy
    @cart = ShoppingCart.find_or_create_by(user_id: params[:user_id])
    @concert = Concert.find(params[:concert_id])
    @user = current_user
```

```
    @cart.clear_all(concert_id: @concert.id, user_id: @user.id)
    @concert.broadcast_schedule_change
  end
end
```

And a Turbo Stream view that redraws the venue:

appendix_hotwire/01/app/views/clear_all_tickets/destroy.turbo_stream.erb
```
<%= turbo_stream.replace(
    "venue-body",
    partial: "venues/venue_body",
    locals: {
      concert: @concert,
      user: @user,
      tickets_to_buy_count: params[:tickets_to_buy_count].to_i
    }
  ) %>
<%= turbo_stream.replace(
    "subtotal",
    partial: "venues/subtotal",
    locals: {concert: @concert, user: @user}
  ) %>
```

Receiving Commands via ActionCable

The interactions work now, but we still need to be able to catch the ActionCable broadcast if another browser on the same page holds a ticket. The tricky part here is that the display depends on a piece of client-side state—the "tickets to buy count" number—that the server won't know when it makes the broadcast.

I thought of three ways that this might work:

- We could make the "tickets to buy count" number server-side state by having the server store it in a session or something and also broadcast that information to other browsers via ActionCable when it changes. I decided this would be confusing for our mythical users.

- We could have the ActionCable broadcast send versions of the seat grid with all possible ticket to buy numbers and have the receiver pick the correct one for display. I considered this one pretty seriously, and I think it might be a good choice in another context, but in this case I thought the possible amount of extra data being sent was too high.

- What I eventually chose was to have the ActionCable broadcast be received as a signal for the client to call the server and request the seat grid with the correct ticket to buy number. There's an extra server call here, but overall I think this is the easiest solution to manage.

One reason why I think the last version works for us is that the request the client would make—please give us the new seat grid and subtotal—is exactly the same request we're already making when the pull-down menu changes. So we can leverage that. (This is why we added the subtotal call to the form response.)

We've already set this up in the markup: the pull-down form declares a Stimulus controller called cable-receiver, which also declares the form element as a target. Here's the code for that Stimulus controller:

appendix_hotwire/01/app/packs/controllers/cable_receiver_controller.ts

```typescript
import { Controller } from "stimulus"
import { createConsumer, Channel } from "@rails/actioncable"

interface SeatChangedData {
  seat: string
  status: string
}

export default class CableReceiverController extends Controller {
  static values = { channelName: String, concertId: Number }
  channelNameValue: string
  concertIdValue: number

  static targets = ["form"]
  formTarget: HTMLFormElement

  channel: Channel

  connect(): void {
    if (this.channel) {
      return
    }
    this.channel = this.createChannel(this)
  }

  createChannel(source: CableReceiverController): Channel {
    return createConsumer().subscriptions.create(
      { channel: "ConcertChannel", concertId: this.concertIdValue },
      {
        received(data: SeatChangedData) {
          source.seatUpdated(data)
        },
      }
    )
  }

  seatUpdated(data: SeatChangedData): void {
    const seatElement = document.getElementById(data.seat)
    if (!seatElement || seatElement.dataset.status !== data.status) {
      this.formTarget.requestSubmit()
    }
  }
}
```

It declares two Stimulus values that are also in the markup: the name of the ActionCable channel server side, `ConcertChannel`, and the concert ID we're dealing with. Similar to the other Stimulus controller we wrote that talks to ActionCable, it creates an ActionCable subscription, this time on `connect`, when the controller becomes part of the DOM. When the ActionCable subscription receives data, the data is in the form of key/value where the key is the ID of the seat and the value is the new status of the seat. The controller checks to see if the seat as displayed has the same status, and if not triggers the form to submit itself and force a redraw of the venue.

At this point, the Hotwire version of the page has pretty nearly the same functionality as the React version did at a fraction of the lines of code. The performance is somewhat worse for the pull-down menu, but some of that is the logging that's happening on the development side. I think it'd be fixable in practice.

The All-React App

Now the React page. Here are the features I created:

- The initial data for the page comes from an API call to the server that returns JSON.

- Clicking a date in the calendar filter at the top of the page makes that date visible and other dates invisible, with the same logic and the same "Show All" button as we had before.

- The search bar calls the server for search results and displays them in a modal window.

- Clicking the Make Favorites button adds a concert to the list of favorites, clicking Remove Favorites takes it out of the list, and favorites animate in and out of that list.

- The schedule page can receive ActionCable broadcasts when the user changes favorites in a different browser or with updates to the number of tickets remaining in a concert.

That's a lot, and I have to admit I didn't quite realize how much more complex the schedule page had gotten relative to the concert display page.

In creating the React page, I made a few starting decisions:

- I didn't need styled components because the CSS already existed.

- I did not try to make a React route bridge between the two React pages. Instead, the schedule page still uses the Rails server to route between the two pages.

- There's some minor date parsing and formatting on this page. Rather than introduce a new JavaScript library to manage this, I did it on the server side and had the formatted and parsed data made part of the data sent to React.

- I decided to keep the show/hide behavior via CSS classes, even though React makes it relatively easy to just remove and reinsert the DOM elements. This was to keep from also having to rewrite the tests, and also to avoid more complicated conditional logic in the React components.

We have to roll the markup up into React components and then make those components talk to and receive data from the reducers. Let's start on the Rails side.

The controller changes slightly to allow for a JSON call:

```
appendix_react/01/app/controllers/schedules_controller.rb
class SchedulesController < ApplicationController
  def show
    @concerts = Concert.includes(:venue, gigs: :band).all
    @schedule = Schedule.from_concerts(@concerts)
    @schedule.hide(params[:hidden]&.split(",") || [])
    @schedule.schedule_day_at(params[:toggle])&.toggle!
    favorites = current_user&.favorites || []
    respond_to do |format|
      format.html
      format.json do
        render(
          json: {
            scheduleDays: @schedule.days_hash,
            favorites: favorites.map { |f| f.concert.to_h },
            userId: current_user.id
          }
        )
      end
    end
  end
end
```

The JSON calls some mostly boilerplate methods on Schedule, ScheduleDay, and Concert that I'm not going to show. For right now it's enough to say they prepare the data into a useful hash that the React page can consume.

The actual view page then pretty much vanishes:

```
appendix_react/01/app/views/schedules/show.html.erb
<div id="schedule-react-element"
     data-favorite-channel-name="<%= Turbo::StreamsChannel.signed_stream_name(
                                     [current_user, :favorites]
                                   ) %>">

</div>
```

Similar to the other React app, we're creating a div element with a known ID that we'll use to attach the React app. We've put one value in the data list for the element—the encrypted name of the ActionCable channel that will manage the user favorites. More on that in a bit.

To invoke the element, we add a call into the parent pack:

```
appendix_react/01/app/packs/entrypoints/venue_display.tsx
const schedule_element = document.getElementById("schedule-react-element")
if (schedule_element) {
  ReactDOM.render(
    <ScheduleApp
      favoriteChannelName={schedule_element.dataset.favoriteChannelName}
    />,
    schedule_element
  )
}
```

It looks for the correct DOM element, and if that element exists, it attaches the React app to the element.

You can assume, by the way, that all the elements need to be included into their various files, and that all types need to be declared (I won't necessarily be showing all the boilerplate).

Fetching React Data

Let's first start by looking at how the data comes in. Here's the top-level schedule app, again with some setup elided:

```
appendix_react/01/app/packs/components/schedule_app.tsx
export const ScheduleApp = ({
  favoriteChannelName,
}: ScheduleAppProps): React.ReactElement => {
  const store = scheduleStore
  store.dispatch({ type: "initEmpty" })
  store.dispatch(initScheduleChannel())
  store.dispatch(initFavoritesChannel(favoriteChannelName))
  store.dispatch(fetchData())
  return (
    <Provider store={store}>
```

```
      <section>
        <ScheduleFilter />
        <ScheduleFavorites />
        <ScheduleDisplay />
      </section>
    </Provider>
  )
}
```

We grab the scheduleStore, which is created in our context file:

appendix_react/01/app/packs/contexts/schedule_context.ts
```
export const scheduleStore = createStore(
  scheduleReducer,
  applyMiddleware(thunk as ThunkMiddleware<ScheduleState, ScheduleAction>)
)
```

The schedule store has an initial state, and again, there's some boilerplate in setting up the reducer that I'm not showing right here as it's very similar to the last reducer.

Here's the initial state:

appendix_react/01/app/packs/contexts/schedule_context.ts
```
export const initialState = {
  scheduleDays: {},
  favorites: [],
  userId: null,
  scheduleChannel: null,
  favoritesChannel: null,
  textFilter: "",
  searchResults: [],
  favoritesVisible: true,
  mostRecentFavoriteId: null,
  removedFavoriteIds: [],
}
```

That's three elements that come from the server in the initial fetch (scheduleDays, favorites, and userId), two ActiveCable channels, and five elements that we'll be using to store client-side state as we move along. The scheduleDays object also keeps local track of the state of the calendar filters, which isn't shared with the server.

We dispatch a command to the reducer to fetch data. This is an asynchronous command, so we need to do it with a Redux thunk that grabs the data then dispatches to the actual reducer:

```
appendix_react/01/app/packs/contexts/schedule_context.ts
export const fetchData = (): ScheduleThunk => {
  return async (dispatch) => {
    const response = await fetch("/schedule.json")
    const data = await response.json()
    dispatch({ type: "initFromData", data: data as IncomingScheduleData })
  }
}
```

All that does is make a call to the Rails app, convert the resulting JSON, and dispatch it to the actual reducer, which inserts the data into the state:

```
appendix_react/01/app/packs/contexts/schedule_context.ts
case "initEmpty": {
  return initialState
}
case "initFromData": {
  return {
    ...state,
    scheduleDays: propsToMap(action.data.scheduleDays),
    favorites: action.data.favorites,
    userId: action.data.userId,
  }
}
```

Responding to Filters

The first filter we want to deal with is the calendar filter that controls whether entire days on the schedule display or not. Here's the React component for one of those calendar days—there's a parent component that I'm not showing that generates the entire list of these and passes each the appropriate ScheduleDay object:

```
appendix_react/01/app/packs/components/schedule/single_day_filter.tsx
import * as React from "react"
import { useDispatch } from "react-redux"
import { ScheduleDay } from "contexts/schedule_context"

export interface SingleDayProps {
  day: ScheduleDay
}

export const SingleDayFilter = ({
  day,
}: SingleDayProps): React.ReactElement => {
  const dispatch = useDispatch()

  const calendarClick = (): void => {
    dispatch({ type: "calendarToggle", day: day.id })
  }
```

```
  const cssClasses = (): string => {
    return `text-center border-b-2 border-transparent ${
      day.filtered === "yes" ? "border-red-700" : ""
    }`
  }
  return (
    <div className={cssClasses()} onClick={calendarClick}>
      {day.day.month} {day.day.date}
    </div>
  )
}

export default SingleDayFilter
```

Note: I created a subdirectory for the schedule components and also created one for the existing venue components, so all the imports of all those files updated, but I'm not showing that.

The only dynamic elements here are whether the calendar's filter is active, in which case it gets the extra border-red-700 CSS class, and the click handler, which dispatches a calendarToggle event back to the reducer:

```
appendix_react/01/app/packs/contexts/schedule_context.ts
case "calendarToggle": {
  const dayInQuestion = state.scheduleDays[action.day]
  const scheduleDays = {
    ...state.scheduleDays,
    [action.day]: {
      ...dayInQuestion,
      filtered: reverseFiltered(dayInQuestion.filtered),
    },
  }
  return {
    ...state,
    scheduleDays: scheduleDays,
  }
}
```

This branch of the reducer does the bookkeeping to maintain that the schedule day object in question has its filtered element flipped.

Elsewhere in the reducer file, we have a function that takes the schedule state and returns a list of visible schedule days:

appendix_react/01/app/packs/contexts/schedule_context.ts
```
export const visibleDays = (state: ScheduleState): ScheduleDay[] => {
  const anyFiltered = Object.values(state.scheduleDays).some(
    (day) => day.filtered === "yes"
  )
  if (anyFiltered) {
    return Object.values(state.scheduleDays).filter(
      (day) => day.filtered === "yes"
    )
  } else {
    return Object.values(state.scheduleDays)
  }
}
```

If any days are filtered, it returns the days with active filters, but as the logic was previously, if no days are filtered, it displays all the days.

This list is used to limit which days get drawn by a later React component on the page:

appendix_react/01/app/packs/components/schedule/schedule_display.tsx
```
import * as React from "react"
import { useSelector } from "react-redux"
import {
  ScheduleDay,
  ScheduleState,
  visibleDays,
} from "contexts/schedule_context"
import SingleDayDisplay from "components/schedule/single_day_display"

export const ScheduleDisplay = (): React.ReactElement => {
  const scheduleDays = useSelector<ScheduleState, ScheduleDay[]>((state) =>
    visibleDays(state)
  )
  return (
    <section>
      {scheduleDays.map((day, index) => (
        <SingleDayDisplay key={index} day={day} />
      ))}
    </section>
  )
}

export default ScheduleDisplay
```

This component uses the useSelector hook to return a list of visible schedule days and loops over that list, and only that list, to call the SingleDayDisplay component, which I'm not showing here because it's mostly HTML.

The Show All button is a simple component:

```
appendix_react/01/app/packs/components/schedule/clear_all_filter.tsx
import * as React from "react"
import { useDispatch } from "react-redux"

export const ClearAllFilter = (): React.ReactElement => {
  const dispatch = useDispatch()

  const clearAllClick = (): void => {
    dispatch({ type: "clearFilters" })
  }

  return <div onClick={clearAllClick}>Show All</div>
}

export default ClearAllFilter
```

which calls a clearFilters action on the reducer:

```
appendix_react/01/app/packs/contexts/schedule_context.ts
case "clearFilters": {
  const newDays = {}
  Object.values(state.scheduleDays).forEach(
    (day) => (newDays[day.id] = { ...day, filtered: "no" })
  )
  return {
    ...state,
    scheduleDays: newDays,
  }
}
```

Now the search filter. The structure here is a text element, where the typing event triggers a Redux thunk that retrieves the search data from the server.

Here's the text element again, which is inside a small parent element that I'm not showing:

```
appendix_react/01/app/packs/components/schedule/search_form.tsx
import * as React from "react"
import { useSelector, useDispatch } from "react-redux"
import { ScheduleState, search } from "contexts/schedule_context"

export const SearchForm = (): React.ReactElement => {
  const dispatch = useDispatch()
  const textFilter = useSelector<ScheduleState, string>(
    (state) => state.textFilter
  )

  const handleChange = (event: React.SyntheticEvent): void => {
    const textArea = event.target as HTMLInputElement
    dispatch(search(textArea.value))
  }

  return (
    <div className="flex justify-center">
      <div className="w-4/5">
```

```
      <input
        type="search"
        name="query"
        id="search_query"
        value={textFilter}
        placeholder="Search concerts"
        className="w-full px-3 py-2 border border-gray-400 rounded-lg"
        onChange={handleChange}
      />
    </div>
  </div>
  )
}

export default SearchForm
```

It pulls the value of the form from the global state via the useSelector call that pulls the textFilter value, then calls a Redux thunk called search when the value changes:

```
appendix_react/01/app/packs/contexts/schedule_context.ts
export const search = (searchTerm: string): ScheduleThunk => {
  return async (dispatch) => {
    let concerts: Concert[] = []
    if (searchTerm !== "") {
      const response = await fetch(`/concerts.json?query=${searchTerm}`)
      const data = await response.json()
      concerts = data.concerts
    }
    dispatch({
      type: "updateTextFilter",
      results: concerts as Concert[],
      text: searchTerm,
    })
  }
}
```

The pattern here is similar to the thunk that fetches the initial data. It makes a fetch call to the same React API (again, we've added a json path that returns the set of found concerts as JSON data, then passes that data along to the reducer to update the state):

```
appendix_react/01/app/packs/contexts/schedule_context.ts
case "updateTextFilter": {
  return {
    ...state,
    textFilter: action.text,
    searchResults: action.results,
  }
}
```

The searchResults is then used in SearchResults components. A parent element checks whether there are search results to determine whether to hide the modal:

```
appendix_react/01/app/packs/components/schedule/search_results.tsx
import * as React from "react"
import { useSelector } from "react-redux"
import { ScheduleState, Concert } from "contexts/schedule_context"
import { SearchResult } from "components/schedule/search_result"

export const SearchResults = (): React.ReactElement => {
  const results = useSelector<ScheduleState, Concert[]>(
    (state) => state.searchResults
  )

  const displayResults = (): boolean => {
    return (results?.length || 0) > 0
  }

  return (
    displayResults() && (
      <section
        className={`fixed bg-gray-300 z-10
                    rounded-3xl ring-4 ring-gray-800
                    max-w-screen-lg halfway w-full
                    mr-20 ml-32 px-6 py-2 mt-2
                    overflow-y-auto overscroll-contain`}>
        <div className="text-3xl font-bold text-center">Search Results</div>
        {results.map((result, index) => (
          <SearchResult key={index} result={result} />
        ))}
      </section>
    )
  )
}

export default SearchResults
```

This version uses useSelector to get a list of results, and if that list has a length greater than zero, it loops over the results (that is mostly just markup; I won't list that component). If there are no results, the displayResults method returns false, the return value short-circuits, and no element is displayed.

Animating Elements

The favorite elements start with a familiar pattern. We maintain a list of favorite concerts in the global state, and clicking the Make Favorite button adds that concert to the state, while clicking Remove Favorite takes it out.

There are three complications:

- Both make and remove need to make an async call to the server to register the change in the server-side database, which means they need to be Redux thunks and they need to pass through Rails authentication.

- We want only newly added favorites to animate in, which means we need to track which ones are new so that we can add the Animate.css to them.

- We want removed favorites to animate out, which means we can't just throw them out of the DOM; we need to make sure we animate and then hide them, so we need to track which elements have been removed client side.

Thanks goes to Michal Czaplinski for this blog post https://czaplinski.io/blog/super-easy-animation-with-react-hooks/ that I adapted to manage the animate-out effects.

The Make Favorite button is part of the ConcertDisplay component, which is mostly markup that I'm not showing here, but it does call a thunk for its dispatch.

Here are the make and remove favorite thunks, which are similar in structure, probably enough so to extract common code:

```
appendix_react/01/app/packs/contexts/schedule_context.ts
const csrfToken = (document.querySelector(
  "[name='csrf-token']"
) as HTMLElement).getAttribute("content")

export const makeFavorite = (concert: Concert): ScheduleThunk => {
  return async (dispatch) => {
    const formData = new FormData()
    formData.append("concert_id", String(concert.id))
    await fetch("/favorites.js", {
      method: "POST",
      body: formData,
      headers: {
        "X-Requested-With": "XMLHttpRequest",
        "X-CSRF-Token": csrfToken,
        credentials: "same-origin",
      },
    })
    dispatch({ type: "addFavorite", concert })
  }
}

export const removeFavorite = (concert: Concert): ScheduleThunk => {
  return async (dispatch) => {
    const formData = new FormData()
    await fetch(`/favorites/${concert.id}.js`, {
      method: "DELETE",
      body: formData,
```

```
      headers: {
        "X-Requested-With": "XMLHttpRequest",
        "X-CSRF-Token": csrfToken,
        credentials: "same-origin",
      },
    })
    dispatch({ type: "removeFavorite", concert })
  }
}
```

The pattern here is to simulate a DOM FormData object with the concert ID of
the new favorite and trigger an API call to Rails. We don't need the user ID
because Rails is still managing a session, but we do need the Rails csrf-token,
which is in the header and used by Rails to prevent cross-site scripting
attacks.

Once the form is submitted, both thunks dispatch to their respective actions:

appendix_react/01/app/packs/contexts/schedule_context.ts
```
case "addFavorite": {
  return {
    ...state,
    mostRecentFavoriteId: action.concert.id,
    favorites: [...state.favorites, action.concert].sort(
      (a, b) => a.sortDate - b.sortDate
    ),
    removedFavoriteIds: state.removedFavoriteIds.filter((id) => {
      return id !== action.concert.id
    }),
  }
}
case "removeFavorite": {
  return {
    ...state,
    removedFavoriteIds: [
      ...state.removedFavoriteIds,
      action.concert.id,
    ],
  }
}
```

The removeFavorite is simpler—all it's doing is adding the newly removed concert
to the list of removed favorite IDs. The addFavorite is making the new ID the
mostRecentFavoriteId, adding the new concert to the list of favorites in the state,
and removing it from the list of removedFavoriteIds if it is already there. This last
action allows us to add a favorite, remove it, and then re-add it; otherwise,
its position on the removed favorites list would prevent it from being displayed.

Here's how those values are used.

The parent component for all the favorites is called ScheduleFavorites. Here it is:

```
appendix_react/01/app/packs/components/schedule/favorites.tsx
import * as React from "react"
import { useDispatch, useSelector } from "react-redux"
import { ScheduleState, buttonClass } from "contexts/schedule_context"
import ScheduleFavorite from "components/schedule/favorite"
import ChevronRight from "images/chevron-right.svg"

export const Favorites = (): React.ReactElement => {
  const dispatch = useDispatch()
  const {
    favoritesVisible,
    favorites,
    mostRecentFavoriteId,
    removedFavoriteIds,
  } = useSelector<ScheduleState, ScheduleState>((state) => state)

  const toggleFavoriteClick = () => {
    dispatch({ type: "favoritesToggle" })
  }

  return (
    <section className="my-4" id="favorite-section">
      <div className="text-3xl font-bold">
        Favorite Concerts
        <span
          className={`${buttonClass} blue-hover bg-black ml-4`}
          onClick={toggleFavoriteClick}>
          <img
            src={ChevronRight}
            width={25}
            height={25}
            className={`inline ${
              favoritesVisible ? "is-open" : "is-closed"
            }`}
          />
        </span>
      </div>
      <div
        className={`${favoritesVisible ? "" : "hidden"}`}
        id="favorite-concerts-list">
        {favorites.map((result, index) => {
          return (
            <ScheduleFavorite
              key={index}
              favorite={result}
              animateIn={result.id === mostRecentFavoriteId}
              shouldBeVisible={!removedFavoriteIds.includes(result.id)}
            />
          )
        })}
```

```
      </div>
    </section>
  )
}
```

export default Favorites

A couple of things to note here. One is that I forgot that we also have a Show/Hide toggle button on the favorites list itself, which is managed here via a button that toggles a value in the reducer. It's also worth mentioning that we can import the image directly as if it were an ordinary module (import ChevronRight from "images/chevron-right.svg") and then use it in the image source (src={ChevronRight}). (To make this work, you need to tell TypeScript that svg is a legitimate kind of module; see the custom.d.ts file for how that works.)

The thing I really want to point out is how the individual ScheduleFavorite components are called. They have an animateIn property that is true if the concert is the mostRecentFavoriteId and a shouldBeVisible property that is true if the concert is not on the list of removed favorite IDs. Here's how those properties are used:

```
appendix_react/01/app/packs/components/schedule/favorite.tsx
import * as React from "react"
import { useDispatch } from "react-redux"
import {
  Concert,
  buttonClass,
  removeFavorite,
} from "contexts/schedule_context"

interface SearchResultProps {
  favorite: Concert
  animateIn: boolean
  shouldBeVisible: boolean
}

export const Favorite = ({
  favorite,
  animateIn,
  shouldBeVisible,
}: SearchResultProps): React.ReactElement => {
  const dispatch = useDispatch()
  const [animateOut, setAnimateOut] = React.useState(false)
  const [display, setDisplay] = React.useState(shouldBeVisible)

  React.useEffect(() => {
    if (!shouldBeVisible) {
      setAnimateOut(true)
    }
  })

  const removeFavoriteOnClick = (): void => {
```

```
      dispatch(removeFavorite(favorite))
  }

  const onAnimationEnd = () => {
    if (!shouldBeVisible) {
      setDisplay(false)
    }
  }

  return (
    display && (
      <section>
        <article
          className={`my-6
            ${animateIn ? "animate__animated animate__slideInRight" : ""}
            ${animateOut ? "animate__animated animate__slideOutRight" : ""}
          `}
          onAnimationEnd={onAnimationEnd}>
          <div className="grid gap-4 grid-cols-5">
            <div className="col-span-1 text-xl">{favorite.startTime}</div>
            <div className="col-span-3">
              <div className="name">
                <div className="text-lg font-bold">
                  <a href={`/concert/${favorite.id}`}>{favorite.name}</a>
                </div>
              </div>
              <div className="bands">{favorite.bandNames}</div>
              <div className="genres">{favorite.genreTags}</div>
              <div className="text-gray-500 font-bold">
                {favorite.venueName}
              </div>
            </div>
            <div className="col-span-1 text-xl">
              <span data-concert-target="tickets"></span>
              <br />
              <br />
              <div className="flex">
                <button
                  className={buttonClass}
                  onClick={removeFavoriteOnClick}>
                  Remove Favorite
                </button>
              </div>
            </div>
          </div>
        </article>
      </section>
    )
  )
}

export default Favorite
```

Right up front we set up two useState hook to manage a display property and an animateOut property, and we set animateOut to false and the display to the value of the shouldBeVisible property.

We then also define a useEffect hook that fires when the component renders and turns on the animateOut property if the component is not supposed to be visible. The actual markup places the Animate.css classes if needed, and also specifies a function to run using the onAnimationEnd event.

This gives us the following paths through the code:

- If a favorite is drawn because it already exists when the page is loaded, shouldBeVisible is true, and animateIn is false. The display state is true. The useEffect does nothing because shouldBeVisible is already true. Neither animation is set, so the onAnimationEnd event never fires.

- If a favorite is added via the Make Favorite button, shouldBeVisible and animateIn are both true. The useEffect does nothing, but the animate in CSS is added so the slide-in from the right animation happens. The onAnimationEnd handler does nothing because shouldBeVisible is true.

- If a favorite is removed, then shouldBeVisible and animateIn are both false. The key thing to note here is that the component has already been rendered, so the display state is still true from the previous render, the useState hook doesn't reinitialize. The useEffect does set animateOut, so the out-animation CSS is added, causing the element to slide out to the right. The onAnimationEnd event then fires, setting the display to false and causing the component not to display. On future renders, display is already false and shouldBeVisible will also be false, so the element won't display at all and it won't matter that the animation CSS is there.

This gives us the behavior we want: new favorites animate in, removed ones animate out.

ActionCable and React

This page needs two ActionCable subscriptions. The one that registers a ticket hold on a different page and updates the tickets remaining, and the one that registers the user changing their favorites in a different browser.

The ticket update subscription is more straightforward. It's already being broadcast by the concert display page and already sending JSON data, all we need to do is catch it. Here's the Redux thunk we called way back when the ScheduleApp component was created:

```
appendix_react/01/app/packs/contexts/schedule_context.ts
export const initScheduleChannel = (): ScheduleThunk => {
  return (dispatch, getState) => {
    if (getState().scheduleChannel) {
      return
    }
    const subscription = createConsumer().subscriptions.create(
      "ScheduleChannel",
      {
        async received(data) {
          const parsedData = (await data.json()) as ScheduleChannelData
          parsedData.concerts.forEach((concertData) => {
            dispatch({
              type: "updateConcertRemaining",
              concertId: concertData.concertId,
              ticketsRemaining: concertData.ticketsRemaining,
            })
          })
        },
      }
    )
    dispatch({ type: "setScheduleChannel", subscription })
  }
}
```

The pattern is similar to the React ActionCable we did in Chapter 10, Immediate Communication with ActionCable, on page 187. If the channel doesn't exist, we create it. When the channel receives data, we parse it, and for each concert that comes in, we send an updateConcertRemaining action that finds the relevant concert buried in whatever ScheduleDay holds it and updates it:

```
appendix_react/01/app/packs/contexts/schedule_context.ts
case "updateConcertRemaining": {
  const allDays = Object.values(state.scheduleDays).map((day) => {
    const matchingConcert = day.concerts.find(
      (concert) => (concert.id = action.concertId)
    )
    if (!matchingConcert) {
      return day
    }
    const newConcert = {
      ...matchingConcert,
      ticketsRemaining: action.ticketsRemaining,
    }
    const newConcerts = day.concerts.map((dayConcert) => {
      if (dayConcert.id === matchingConcert.id) {
        return newConcert
      } else {
        return dayConcert
      }
```

```
    })
    return {
      ...day,
      concerts: newConcerts,
    }
  })
  const newDays = propsToMap(allDays)
  return {
    ...state,
    scheduleDays: newDays,
  }
}
```

The other ActionCable subscription is managed by the turbo-rails helpers when Favorites are saved or destroyed. We can keep doing that; we just need to do a few things.

First, we need to make sure we are subscribing under the right name because turbo-rails encrypts the name. Way back when we instantiated the DOM element in the Rails view, we used the same internal call turbo-rails uses to generate the name, so the names should match.

Second, we need to change the helpers so that they render JSON rather than HTML:

appendix_react/01/app/models/favorite.rb
```
after_create_commit -> do
  Turbo::StreamsChannel.broadcast_stream_to(
    user, :favorites,
    content: ApplicationController.render(
      json: {type: "addFavorite", concertId: concert.id}
    )
  )
end

after_destroy_commit -> do
  Turbo::StreamsChannel.broadcast_stream_to(
    user, :favorites,
    content: ApplicationController.render(
      json: {type: "removeFavorite", concertId: concert.id}
    )
  )
end
```

The render parts of these helpers now list the JSON to send.

Then we need to create the subscription and do something when the broadcast is received:

```
appendix_react/01/app/packs/contexts/schedule_context.ts
interface FavoritesControllerData {
  type: "addFavorite" | "removeFavorite"
  concertId: number
}

const getConcerts = (state: ScheduleState): Concert[] => {
  return Object.values(state.scheduleDays).flatMap(
    (scheduleDay) => scheduleDay.concerts
  )
}

const getConcert = (state: ScheduleState, concertId: number): Concert => {
  return getConcerts(state).find((concert) => concert.id === concertId)
}

export const initFavoritesChannel = (name: string): ScheduleThunk => {
  return (dispatch, getState) => {
    if (getState().scheduleChannel) {
      return
    }
    const subscription = createConsumer().subscriptions.create(
      { channel: "Turbo::StreamsChannel", "signed-stream-name": name },
      {
        async received(data) {
          const parsedData = (await data.json()) as FavoritesControllerData
          dispatch({
            type: parsedData.type,
            concert: getConcert(getState(), parsedData.concertId),
          })
        },
      }
    )
    dispatch({ type: "setFavoritesChannel", subscription })
  }
}
```

What this does is create the channel using the signed name, and then when data is received, the data tell us what type it is, and we just dispatch that action to the reducer with the correct ID.

Comparison

I honestly wasn't quite sure what to expect when I started this exercise. Here's what I think I can say for sure:

React has more setup and boilerplate code. Because both of these pages are relatively simple, that means that there's more React code for both of them. In the case of the schedule page, there's a lot more code. Having done the concert page now three times— React, Stimulus-only (for the first drafts of this book), and Hotwire—I was still surprised how little client-side code the Hotwire version required.

There's one place where React has less code, which is in actually tying value changes to update DOM elements. This happens automatically in React when the state changes, but Hotwire requires you to explicitly trigger them (except in the somewhat specialized case of Stimulus value-changed methods). There are probably cases where that update code gets too complicated to handle. This was certainly the case in my pre–Hotwire Stimulus project, though I think that the Hotwire helpers would have improved things somewhat.

Another concern that is likely not an issue in this example—but would be in a real-world example—is performance. React is designed to make its update loop efficient, whereas doing a lot of client-side updating in Hotwire might be less so. My inclination would be not to worry about this because I think it's a theoretical issue for most projects, but who knows?

Congratulations for making it all the way through this appendix *and* this book. Now all that is left is for you to go out and build something great.

Index

Thank you!

How did you enjoy this book? Please let us know. Take a moment and email us at support@pragprog.com with your feedback. Tell us your story and you could win free ebooks. Please use the subject line "Book Feedback."

Ready for your next great Pragmatic Bookshelf book? Come on over to https://pragprog.com and use the coupon code BUYANOTHER2021 to save 30% on your next ebook.

Void where prohibited, restricted, or otherwise unwelcome. Do not use ebooks near water. If rash persists, see a doctor. Doesn't apply to *The Pragmatic Programmer* ebook because it's older than the Pragmatic Bookshelf itself. Side effects may include increased knowledge and skill, increased marketability, and deep satisfaction. Increase dosage regularly.

And thank you for your continued support,

The Pragmatic Bookshelf

Intuitive Python

Developers power their projects with Python because it emphasizes readability, ease of use, and access to a meticulously maintained set of packages and tools. The language itself continues to improve with every release: writing in Python is full of possibility. But to maintain a successful Python project, you need to know more than just the language. You need tooling and instincts to help you make the most out of what's available to you. Use this book as your guide to help you hone your skills and sculpt a Python project that can stand the test of time.

David Muller
(140 pages) ISBN: 9781680508239. $26.95
https://pragprog.com/book/dmpython

Modern CSS with Tailwind

Tailwind CSS is an exciting new CSS framework that allows you to design your site by composing simple utility classes to create complex effects. With Tailwind, you can style your text, move your items on the page, design complex page layouts, and adapt your design for devices from a phone to a wide-screen monitor. With this book, you'll learn how to use the Tailwind for its flexibility and its consistency, from the smallest detail of your typography to the entire design of your site.

Noel Rappin
(90 pages) ISBN: 9781680508185. $26.95
https://pragprog.com/book/tailwind

Essential 555 IC

Learn how to create functional gadgets using simple
but clever circuits based on the venerable "555." These
projects will give you hands-on experience with useful,
basic circuits that will aid you across other projects.
These inspiring designs might even lead you to develop
the next big thing. The 555 Timer Oscillator Integrated
Circuit chip is one of the most popular chips in the
world. Through clever projects, you will gain permanent
knowledge of how to use the 555 timer will carry with
you for life.

Cabe Force Satalic Atwell
(104 pages) ISBN: 9781680507836. $19.95
https://pragprog.com/book/catimers

Resourceful Code Reuse

Reusing well-written, well-debugged, and well-tested
code improves productivity, code quality, and software
configurability and relieves pressure on software developers. When you organize your code into self-contained
modular units, you can use them as building blocks
for your future projects and share them with other
programmers, if needed. Understand the benefits and
downsides of seven code reuse models so you can
confidently reuse code at any development stage. Create static and dynamic libraries in C and Python, two
of the most popular modern programming languages.
Adapt your code for the real world: deploy shared
functions remotely and build software that accesses
them using remote procedure calls.

Dmitry Zinoviev
(64 pages) ISBN: 9781680508208. $14.99
https://pragprog.com/book/dzreuse

Apple Game Frameworks and Technologies

Design and develop sophisticated 2D games that are as much fun to make as they are to play. From particle effects and pathfinding to social integration and monetization, this complete tour of Apple's powerful suite of game technologies covers it all. Familiar with Swift but new to game development? No problem. Start with the basics and then layer in the complexity as you work your way through three exciting—and fully playable—games. In the end, you'll know everything you need to go off and create your own video game masterpiece for any Apple platform.

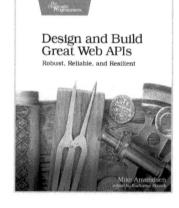

Tammy Coron
(504 pages) ISBN: 9781680507843. $51.95
https://pragprog.com/book/tcswift

Design and Build Great Web APIs

APIs are transforming the business world at an increasing pace. Gain the essential skills needed to quickly design, build, and deploy quality web APIs that are robust, reliable, and resilient. Go from initial design through prototyping and implementation to deployment of mission-critical APIs for your organization. Test, secure, and deploy your API with confidence and avoid the "release into production" panic. Tackle just about any API challenge with more than a dozen open-source utilities and common programming patterns you can apply right away.

Mike Amundsen
(330 pages) ISBN: 9781680506808. $45.95
https://pragprog.com/book/maapis

Distributed Services with Go

This is the book for Gophers who want to learn how to build distributed systems. You know the basics of Go and are eager to put your knowledge to work. Build distributed services that are highly available, resilient, and scalable. This book is just what you need to apply Go to real-world situations. Level up your engineering skills today.

Travis Jeffery
(258 pages) ISBN: 9781680507607. $45.95
https://pragprog.com/book/tjgo

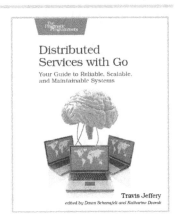

Genetic Algorithms in Elixir

From finance to artificial intelligence, genetic algorithms are a powerful tool with a wide array of applications. But you don't need an exotic new language or framework to get started; you can learn about genetic algorithms in a language you're already familiar with. Join us for an in-depth look at the algorithms, techniques, and methods that go into writing a genetic algorithm. From introductory problems to real-world applications, you'll learn the underlying principles of problem solving using genetic algorithms.

Sean Moriarity
(242 pages) ISBN: 9781680507942. $39.95
https://pragprog.com/book/smgaelixir

The Pragmatic Bookshelf

The Pragmatic Bookshelf features books written by professional developers for professional developers. The titles continue the well-known Pragmatic Programmer style and continue to garner awards and rave reviews. As development gets more and more difficult, the Pragmatic Programmers will be there with more titles and products to help you stay on top of your game.

Visit Us Online

This Book's Home Page
https://pragprog.com/book/nrclient
Source code from this book, errata, and other resources. Come give us feedback, too!

Keep Up to Date
https://pragprog.com
Join our announcement mailing list (low volume) or follow us on twitter @pragprog for new titles, sales, coupons, hot tips, and more.

New and Noteworthy
https://pragprog.com/news
Check out the latest pragmatic developments, new titles and other offerings.

Save on the ebook

Save on the ebook versions of this title. Owning the paper version of this book entitles you to purchase the electronic versions at a terrific discount.

PDFs are great for carrying around on your laptop—they are hyperlinked, have color, and are fully searchable. Most titles are also available for the iPhone and iPod touch, Amazon Kindle, and other popular e-book readers.

Send a copy of your receipt to support@pragprog.com and we'll provide you with a discount coupon.

Contact Us

Online Orders: *https://pragprog.com/catalog*
Customer Service: *support@pragprog.com*
International Rights: *translations@pragprog.com*
Academic Use: *academic@pragprog.com*
Write for Us: *http://write-for-us.pragprog.com*
Or Call: +1 800-699-7764

Lightning Source UK Ltd.
Milton Keynes UK
UKHW031524120821
388724UK00003B/9

9 781680 507218